The First

Three Years

of

LIFE

The First
Three Years
of
LIFE

by

Burton L. White

PRENTICE-HALL, INC.

Englewood Cliffs, N.J.

The First Three Years of Life
by Burton L. White

Copyright © 1975 by Burton L. White
All rights reserved. No part of this book may
be reproduced in any form or by any means,
except for the inclusion of brief quotations in
a review, without permission in writing from
the publisher.
Printed in the United States of America
Prentice-Hall International, Inc., London
Prentice-Hall of Australia, Pty. Ltd., Sydney
Prentice-Hall of Canada, Ltd., Toronto
Prentice-Hall of India Private Ltd., New
    Delhi
Prentice-Hall of Japan, Inc., Tokyo

10 9 8 7 6 5 4 3 2 1

Library of Congress Cataloging in
Publication Data

White, Burton L
    The first three years of life.

    Bibliography: p.
    Includes index.
1. Infant psychology. I. Title.
BF723.I6W46   155.4'22   75-22159
ISBN 0-13-319178-8

TO JOE HUNT *(J. McVicker Hunt)*
for an inspirational example

ACKNOWLEDGMENTS

Since this book covers virtually my entire career as a child development research worker, the number of people who have contributed to this work is very great. Perhaps a chronological organization is the only way to cope with the task.

Initial inspiration came from my father more than anyone else. Academically, Abraham Maslow's studies of "self-actualized" people, Lois Murphy's studies of healthy children, Piaget's work on the growth of the mind, and J. McVicker Hunt's analyses of the effects of experience on development were probably most influential on my thinking.

Over the years, funding agencies and particular officials were of vital assistance. The list of agencies is long: the Foundations' Fund for Research in Psychiatry, the National Institute of Mental Health, the Federal Office of Education, the Carnegie Corporation of New York, the Federal Office of Economic Opportunity, the Federal Office of Child Development, and the Robert Wood Johnson Foundation. Dean Theodore Sizer and my close colleague Gerald Lesser provided administrative support at Harvard University, along with John Herzog. Edith Grotberg, then at OEO, has been a strong supporter of the research.

My greatest debt in the area of research support, and much more, is to Barbara Finberg of the Carnegie Corporation.

In the early years of my research, Peter Wolff provided valuable guidance and arranged for me to work at several hospitals including the State Hospital at Tewksbury, Massachusetts. There, the following personnel (among many) were unfailingly kind and cooperative: Helen Efstathiou and Frances Craig.

In those early days, faithful and highly competent research assistance came from Peter Castle, Kitty Clark, Melvin Zolot, and Harold Haynes.

From 1965 on, at least thirty people worked with me at Harvard on the Preschool Project and another fifty in the early stages of the Brookline Early

Education Project. Of the former, I must single out Barbara Kaban, Mary Comita, and Bernice Shapiro, who have worked closely with me for many years.

The Preschool Project research is the major source of ideas for this book. That project was made possible not only by research personnel, the University and the granting agencies, but also by the cooperation of many public and private schools and especially by several hundred families.

It should by now be abundantly clear that anything of value in this book rests upon the efforts of a large number of people.

Finally, I am proud to thank my four children and loving wife for making my life so rich.

Burton L. White
Cambridge, Massachusetts

CONTENTS

PREFACE

After 17 years of research on how human beings acquire their abilities, I have become convinced that it is to the first three years of life that we should now turn most of our attention. My own studies, as well as the work of many others, have clearly indicated that the experiences of those first years are far more important than we had previously thought. In their simple everyday activities, infants and toddlers form the foundations of *all* later development.

I now believe that not more than one child in ten gets off to as good a start as he could. From close observations of children developing both well and poorly, I am convinced that most families, given a little help, are potentially capable of doing a good job of raising their children. Unfortunately, adequate preparation and assistance for parenthood is not currently available for most families. This book is intended to offer up-to-date information about how you can help your child acquire a solid foundation for full development. I will try to explain what you can do during those very important first thirty-six months to ensure that your child will develop the full range of social and intellectual skills that now appear to be necessary for good subsequent development.

Although this book should prove useful to anyone responsible for the care of the very young child, it is meant primarily for parents. I am well aware that rearing children is far from being an easy task. Although it can be one of life's most exciting, pleasurable, and rewarding activities, for too many parents child-rearing can also be accompanied by much stress and unhappiness. In most of the young families I have known, the very quality of everyday life seems to depend to a remarkable degree on how well the child-rearing process is proceeding. I am confident that if young couples were better informed about child-rearing, they would find more pleasure in family life as a whole.

Thus I have several reasons for writing this book. In spite of the ready availability of such excellent books as Dr. Spock's *Baby and Child Care*, government publications such as *Infant Care*, literally hundreds of magazine

xi

articles that appear each year and thousands of newspaper reports, people seem to feel they do not have as much reliable and useful information as they would like to have about certain important aspects of child-rearing. I hope that my book may help to fill that information gap.

A note of caution. I believe the information in this book is the best currently available on how to educate a child during the first three years of life. On the other hand, it is surely neither perfectly accurate nor 100 percent complete. Sadly, detailed dependable knowledge about how to rear a young child is very difficult to acquire. Furthermore, for many reasons, far from enough has been acquired to date. I am confident that over the next several decades, that deficit will be substantially overcome. For now, my claim is that this book contains my best judgments about the topic in the light of studies of child-rearing to date. With the information presented here, and a measure of good luck, I am confident that most families can do an excellent job of helping their new children make the most of their potential. I should like to think also that this book will not only help children to get a better start in life, but will help assure that childhood will be as rich and pleasurable an experience for both children and parents as it can and should be.

THE SPECIFIC ORIENTATION OF THIS BOOK

The First Three Years of Life, as the title implies, is restricted in focus. It will deal with the period from birth to three years of age. It will deal with the *education* of children during that time, and the educational goals dealt with are meant to be comprehensive. Although sensorimotor developments, such as eye-hand coordination and walking and climbing, will be discussed because they are prominent in every young child's behavior, they will not be treated as primary educational goals. Most children manage to achieve the sensorimotor abilities of the preschool years without difficulty; such is not the case, for example, for several social skills.

Also, this book will concentrate on the normal, near normal, and well-developing child. It will have little to say about seriously handicapped or underdeveloped children.

When people look for advice on rearing young children, they are usually looking for either physical or mental health information, management assistance, or guidance in helping a child develop his abilities as fully as possible. For physical health issues, I recommend Dr. Spock and/or your family physician or pediatrician. For mental health issues, I cannot recommend anyone. As to the development of a baby's abilities, I honestly believe that anyone who wants to provide a good *educational* beginning for a baby during the first three years of life will find that topic fairly covered in this volume. And, if this book provides any assistance to you in helping a child make the most of those formative years, I shall be delighted, and so, I hope, will you.

The Author

Since 1958, supported by several large private foundations and federal agencies, and assisted by several dozen talented people, I have studied the problem of how to educate babies. To my knowledge, no other individual researcher has studied the problem of influencing the development of abilities in the first three years of human life so extensively. That, in itself, is no guarantee that what I will tell you is either totally true or even more true than what you will read elsewhere. Only time will provide that answer. But what follows does come from a unique source: the most sustained (and expensive) scientific study of the role of experience in the development of human abilities in the first years of life conducted to date.

The research that has led to this book was carried out under the administration and with the support of Brandeis and Tufts Universities, the Massachusetts Institute of Technology and Harvard University. It was also carried out at home. As my final credential, I submit the fact (the meaning of which is ambiguous) that I am the father of four children, two boys and two girls, aged seven to thirteen years. I am happy to report that these children seem to be developing rather well. But I must also confess that when my wife and I were guiding them through their first years, we knew as little about the subject as most average young parents.

INTRODUCTION

For almost twenty years I have been trying to learn how it is that some people grow up to be more fully developed, more able, more complete than others. By "able" or "fully developed" I mean capable of coping with life's many aspects in a truly effective manner. This involves having the adaptability or flexibility to function well in a variety of living conditions.

When I arrived at Brandeis University in 1958 as a graduate student in psychology, I was distressed to find that so little about human behavior was understood. There seemed to be very little agreement about how a healthy, vital person got to be that way; yet it was clear that to predict how a person would behave in a test situation, at leisure, or in a social situation, one invariably needed to know about that person's previous experience. Although Freud's ideas were losing ground, most students of human behavior acknowledged in one way or another a basic shaping function in the experiences of the early years of life.

Some believed that a person was largely "born to be" what he would become, and that experience in general was of little importance. Others, however, while acknowledging limits determined by inheritance, believed that life's experiences were generally of prime importance. This latter group focused on the identification of types of important experience and the times in life likely to be of particular significance in terms of overall development.

With the help of Peter Wolff, a research psychiatrist, I began to become acquainted with babies. With the help of Richard Held, a research psychologist, I began to become acquainted with issues in the development of eye-hand behavior (*e.g.,* reaching for seen objects).

1

And guided by the writings of Piaget on the origins of intelligence and Konrad Lorenz on ethology, I began to study the details of day-to-day growth of ability in babies.

In 1958 few psychologists were actively pursuing research with children less than three years of age. Nor was the public, although interested in a general way in infant care, generally aware of any special educational significance of the early years. It was not until the late 1960s that the idea that the first few years of life might have a very special importance began really to take hold. Once it did, large grants of government and private money produced a great deal of interest in and research on the first years. That trend, thank heaven, continues.

EXPERIENCE AND THE INFANT

From 1958 to 1965 I spent many, many hours watching infants in their cribs. I learned a good deal about what they could and could not do as they developed from near helplessness at birth to the comparatively rich talent of the average six-month-old. In a series of experiments I began to see how infants would respond with enthusiasm or, at times, annoyance to alterations in their ordinary routines and physical surroundings. Over a period of years we* produced research that seemed to show that even during the first months of life, babies responded with enthusiasm to circumstances that were specifically designed to meet their rapidly changing interests and abilities. In addition, we found that how alert an infant was, how soon he began looking at his hands, and when he mastered the skill of reaching for objects were dependent in part on the design of his world.

I might have continued my work with very young infants indefinitely but for the previously mentioned general surge of interest in early development in the 1960s, signaled by the creation of Project Head Start in 1965.

Under pressure from civil-rights groups, and with support from new research findings, President Lyndon Johnson in 1965 announced that

---

* My principal colleagues in this work were Kitty Riley Clark, Peter Castle, Harold Haynes, and Richard Held.

the federal government was going to do something about early educational failure. The purpose of Head Start was to see to it that no child
entered the first grade seriously unprepared. Along with unprecedented
expenditures of money and effort on preschoolers from low-income
families, came dramatically increased support for all manner of research
and service programs for children less than six years of age. Educational
research, in particular, began to flourish.

One of several new educational research programs was established at
Harvard. Because of the increased interest in the early years, Harvard
had promised to include the study of early educational development in
the work of their new center. Since Harvard, like many graduate schools
of education, had concentrated on studies of school-aged children, they
found themselves without personnel for preschool studies; and research
on compensatory education for three- and four-year-olds headed for
educational difficulty was still favored by the majority. I objected to that
direction for two reasons: First, I did not believe that we had enough
basic knowledge about preschool children to design programs well; and
second, I believed that the more fundamental need was for research on
how to help *every* child, not just the so-called "disadvantaged" child,
get the most from his early experiences. Harvard, with its power and
rich resources, was one of a handful of institutions capable of acting on
such a long-range outlook.

I was offered a chance to implement such a study. In September 1965
the Preschool Project was launched. I hired four young Ph.D.s and
over a dozen research assistants, and we began to face the question of
how to structure experiences during the first six years of life so as to help
each child make the most of his potential. In the nine years since then, an
average of about ten people working under my supervision, with a
typical budget of about $150,000 to $200,000 per year, have been
studying development during the first years of life. As our ideas have
evolved, so too has there been a parallel evolution in thinking about
early human development on the part of educational policy makers,
federal research planners, and the public.

In 1965 the federal view of how to deal with educational underachievement focused on preventative programs for four-year-olds. A
year or two later, preventative programs were extended down to three-
year-olds and enrichment programs were added as supplements to the
elementary school. By then our research was teaching us that by the time
a child reached three years of age, he had already undergone a great deal

of "education." We had found that in any group of 20 or 30 three-year-olds, there was likely to be at least one remarkably able child. In their everyday behavior these children showed the same pattern of special abilities we found in outstanding six-year-olds. By 1968 we were quite convinced that a long-term approach to understanding good development had to start with a focus on the first three years of life.

In our studies we were not only impressed by what some children could achieve during the first years, but also by the fact that the child's own family seemed so obviously central to the outcome. Indeed, we came to believe that the informal education that families provide for their children *makes more of an impact on a child's total educational development than the formal educational system*. If a family does its job well, the professional can then provide effective training.* If not, there may be little the professional can do to save the child from mediocrity. This grim assessment is a direct conclusion from the findings of thousands of programs in remedial education, such as Head Start and Follow Through projects.

Since I endorse the view of the family as the first and most fundamental educational delivery system, I must offer parents the following words of warning. From all that I have learned about the education and development of young children, I have come to the conclusion that most American families get their children through the first six to eight months of life reasonably well in terms of education and development; but I believe that perhaps no more than ten percent at most manage to get their children through the eight- to thirty-six-month age period as well educated and developed as they could and should be. Yet our studies show that the period that starts at eight months and ends at three years is a period of primary importance in the development of a human being. *To begin to look at a child's educational development when he is two years of age is already much too late,* particularly in the area of social skills and attitudes.

Given the importance of the parental role in early childhood development, it is ironic that so few parents are properly prepared for parenthood. Not only is there little information available, but even if we *did* have sufficient reliable, research-based knowledge about effective

---

* As an aside I might comment that if a family provides a solid initial educational experience in the first year, a child will probably make the most out of any formal educational experience. In such cases, a few years with a mediocre educational system probably will not seriously hinder the child.

child-rearing practices, it would not be routinely transmitted to parents. Our society does not educate its citizens to assume the parental role.

I tried over the years to accumulate dependable knowledge about what babies are like, what their interests are, and how to provide useful and beneficial experiences for them. In the course of my research, my strategy has been to single out—at all income levels—families that seem to be doing an outstanding job with their young children without the benefit of any special training. What I have learned is the subject of this book.

The following phase-by-phase study of the child from birth to three years of age contains the distillation into practical terms of the findings of nineteen years of research. I hope that it will provide parents with some of the guidance they need to help their children develop the full range of human abilities.

Section I

THE DETAILS
of
DEVELOPMENT

CHAPTER 1

BIRTH to CRAWLING:
GUIDELINES for
PHASES I to IV

GENERAL REMARKS

The first eight months of a baby's life (what I shall later describe as Phases I to IV) have a special quality that sets them apart from all subsequent periods. During these early months the baby's general progress in development is largely assured by nature. In terms of having to make choices, it is probably the easiest of all times for parents: If they provide the baby with a normal amount of love, attention, and physical care, nature will pretty much take care of the rest.

I do not mean to imply that it is impossible to do a bad job of child-rearing during this period; it is always possible through stupidity or callousness to do lasting harm to a child of any age. Nor do I mean to say that the "normal" pattern of development during the first eight months cannot be improved upon. But the fact remains that nature, almost as if it had anticipated the uncertainties that beset new parents, has done its best to make the first six to eight months as problem-free as possible.

ESTABLISHING GOALS

No discussion of how to educate babies can make much sense unless one starts with the issue of goals. In a general sense, what most parents want out of the early years is a well-developed child, along with a good deal of simple pleasure for both the child and themselves. Also on every parent's mind is the avoidance of unhappiness, anxiety, and, of course,

9

danger to the child. If what it took to educate an infant was incompatible with his or your enjoyment, it would be unfortunate. Happily, as far as I can tell, such is not the case. Nearly every child rearing activity I can recommend, especially in the first months of life, leads to both an involved and pleased baby and a generally contented parent. And when it comes to the later stages of infancy and toddlerhood, I have found that the well-developing child is by far the most pleasant to live with.

General goals are not enough. After you have decided you want a well-developed child, then what? How do you achieve that goal? Indeed, what does that goal mean? In our studies we have concluded that rearing a child well becomes much more difficult once he begins to crawl. In thousands of situations around the world, rich or poor, most children do quite well educationally during the first six to eight months of life. It is my judgment that *the requirements for adequate development are much simpler during that first phase of life*. I do not mean to say that a baby is not vulnerable during those first months, nor that he cannot be given educationally valuable experiences. What I do mean is that in our present society neither a child who will achieve superbly, nor one who will be seriously behind when he enters the first grade, seems to show any special qualities during the first year of life.*

The goals that parents will want to work toward during the first seven months can be grouped under three headings:
1. Giving the infant a feeling of being loved and cared for.
2. Helping him develop specific skills.
3. Encouraging his interest in the outside world by stimulating his curiosity.

As we follow the developing child from Phase I through Phase IV, we will refer repeatedly to these basic aims. Let us examine them more closely.

A FEELING OF BEING LOVED AND CARED FOR

During the first two years of life, all children appear to have a special need to establish a strong attachment to one or more older humans. In the process they begin to become social animals. By two years of age we

---

* There are exceptions to this statement. Somewhat under five percent of all children are either born with a significant handicap or acquire one during the first year of life. Such exceptional cases are beyond the scope of this book.

have found that all children have acquired a personal social style. By now a child can become spoiled. I have never seen a spoiled one-year-old, but I have seen many a spoiled two-year-old.

As concerns the first seven months of life, I believe the story is much simpler. Erik Erikson, the famous personality theorist, called the primary social goal of this period a sense of "trust." I believe this term is an appropriate one. The frequency and degree of discomfort a baby feels depends largely on the kind of treatment he receives. Some discomfort is inevitable. There is no way to prevent a fair amount of unhappiness from such factors as hunger, indigestion, teething, or a wet diaper. On the other hand, you can easily see how such unhappiness can be prolonged and allowed to escalate if the avoidable discomfort is not dealt with promptly.

Fortunately for most babies, especially those reared at home by their parents, loving care and attention is the rule. However, I have found some people quite confused about the issue of spoiling an infant. There are those who believe there is a benefit to be derived by letting a baby "cry it out." Personally, *I do not believe you can spoil a baby in the first seven months of life*. I strongly suggest you respond to your baby's crying in a natural way.

There may be times when nothing you can do will comfort the baby. Such moments will be difficult to endure, but you must expect them from time to time. One of the best things you can do in such a situation is to seek out the advice of an experienced and sensible mother. Age-old practices, such as holding and rocking an infant, work remarkably well regardless of the cause of the discomfort. Many parents, as a last resort, put an inconsolable child into a car bed and take him for a long ride. A recent rediscovery which seems to be a lifesaver is the pacifier.* Although some infants have a bit of initial trouble mastering the art of holding it in the mouth, it works well for most; and dentists advise that there are no harmful later effects on the teeth. I believe you should feel free to make use of a pacifier as soon as your baby will accept it.

No requirement of good child-rearing is more natural or more

---

* In this respect I should like to add that if you can and want to breast-feed your child, I urge you to do so, both to give the child a sense of being cared for and because most mothers who breast-feed successfully find it a marvelous experience. This is of course a highly personal decision. But from an educational point of view, it is a useful way in which to assure a good deal of closeness of mother with infant and, for the baby, gives a fairly strong positive feeling of being cared for.

rewarding than the tending of your baby in a loving and attentive way.
Although there is little reason to think that an infant under seven months
of age has more than a simple awareness of his mother, most students of
human development agree that the basic foundation of a child's personality is being formed in his earliest interchanges with the nurturing
adults.

HELPING THE INFANT DEVELOP SPECIFIC SKILLS

Few living creatures are as helpless as a newborn babe. At birth, an
infant cannot think, use language, socialize with another human, run,
walk, or even deliberately move around. When on his back he cannot lift
his head; on his stomach he can barely lift his nose off the surface he is
lying on. The list of things that he cannot do is almost as long as the
complete list of adult human abilities. What *can* he do?

An infant has a small number of reflexlike sensorimotor abilities.
When placed prone, he can usually lift his head high enough to avoid
suffocation if left with his nose in the mattress. His hands and feet will
grasp objects with some strength, but only, as a rule, if someone elicits
the behavior in the correct manner. If a target is large enough (more than
a few inches) but not too large (less than eighteen to twenty-four inches),
contrasts well with the background, is no closer than six to eight inches
but no farther away than approximately twenty-four inches, and is
moving through his line of sight at or near the speed of one foot per
second, he may glance at it and even follow it with his eyes for a few
seconds. As soon as the target stops moving, he will lose interest in it.
Moreover, he will perform such a visual act only when awake, alert, and
inactive, a condition he is likely to be in for about two or three minutes
an hour during the day. Otherwise, he is not yet much interested in
looking at the world around him.

Newborns are also generally capable of finding with their mouths a
small object touching them near the lips (rooting behavior), and then
sucking on the object. They cry when uncomfortable; they also possess
a variety of simple motor reflexes like blinking the eye when the eyelid
is touched or receives a puff of air, and the knee jerk (the patellar
response) when given the proper stimulus. Of particular interest is the
startle reflex, which can be a source of needless concern to parents. A
newborn will startle if he is lowered through space rapidly, hears a sharp

loud sound, or even if a light is turned on in a dim room. More unusual than this form of sensitivity to abrupt changes (which lasts for about two months) is the spontaneous startle. During deep sleep, particularly when movement is infrequent, babies will startle in the absence of any external stimulation as frequently as every two minutes. During states when the infant is slightly more active, spontaneous startles occur, but less regularly and less frequently. In general, the more activity, the less frequent the startles.

From about six weeks of age a baby begins to acquire increasing facility in dealing with the world. By the age of seven months he has a good deal of control over his body, can hold his head erect for lengthy periods, can turn over easily, can sit unaided, and may even be able to crawl a bit. He cannot, as yet, ordinarily pull himself to a standing posture, walk, or climb, but he is quite skillful at using his hands to reach for objects. His sensorimotor abilities are extensive. He apparently sees as well as a young adult (and better than his father if his father is over forty). He locates sounds with admirable accuracy. Socially, he recognizes his family, and may even begin to be choosy about who picks him up and holds him close. As for intelligence, while still some distance from most abstract thinking capacities, he begins to solve his first simple problems, such as pushing one object aside in order to reach another.

This vigorous semiskilled creature has, in other words, begun to accumulate a fair number of specific skills. *Good child-rearing in the initial stages of a baby's life* includes knowing what the normal pattern of emerging skills is and facilitating their emergence. It should be pointed out, however, that most of these skills will evolve unaided under average circumstances. The more important reason for facilitating their development is tied up with goal number three.

ENCOURAGING INTEREST IN THE OUTSIDE WORLD

Whether a child learns to reach for objects at three or four months rather than five or six is probably of no consequence. It has been my experience, however, that *the kinds of circumstances that facilitate the acquisition of the specific skills of the early months simultaneously seem to result in a more interested, cheerful, and alert child.* In other words, if a young infant's world meshes with his developing skills, he not only moves along a bit faster, but he seems to enjoy himself more and to develop a fuller taste for exploration, learning, and enjoyment. *Therefore, good early child rearing includes seeing that your baby (especially after the first six to eight weeks) is regularly involved in activities that interest him.* After the first ten to twelve weeks he should be actively enjoying himself at least some of the time. This goal is relatively easy to achieve, as we will see in later chapters.

In summary, a baby should be reared in such a manner that he comes to feel he is cared for, that he acquires all the specific skills within his capacity, and that his inborn tendency to learn more about and to enjoy the world around him is deepened and broadened. We will be referring back to these three goals throughout the text.

CHAPTER 2

Phase I _____

BIRTH to
SIX WEEKS

GENERAL REMARKS

"Helpless as a kitten" is a popular way of describing a newborn baby, but a kitten is considerably more able at birth than a human infant. If the human newborn, like a kitten, had to depend extensively on his own abilities to find nourishment, he would not last long. The human newborn seems to be only partially prepared for life outside of the womb and the first four to six weeks of life seem more like a transitional period between two grossly different modes of existence than a time of growth.

To begin with, life out of the womb is dependent on the action of the lungs and several other systems that were not previously in use. In addition, for many infants the birth process itself is a physically difficult experience. It is, of course, not known how exhausting or stressful the typical vaginal delivery is for a baby. A conservative view, however, would be that especially when labor is prolonged or complicated, the process of birth is likely to be at least as tiring for the infant as it is for his mother. The extensive sleeping by the newborn in the first postnatal weeks lends additional support to this view.

GENERAL BEHAVIOR DURING THIS PERIOD

SLEEPINESS AND IRRITABILITY

Perhaps the most obvious quality babies show in the first weeks of life, aside from total dependence, is sleepiness. In the first days you can expect a baby to average about three minutes an hour of alertness during the day, and less at night. Such periods of wakefulness will lengthen rather slowly over the next month to an average of six or seven minutes an hour.

When he is not asleep, do not be surprised to find a newborn easily irritated.* On the other hand a newborn, unlike an adult, can shift from what seems to be great distress to a state of apparent comfort very abruptly. These quick changes of mood persist for many months and are often dramatic reminders that infants very probably experience life quite differently from adults at times.

FRAGMENTED NATURE OF INFANT BEHAVIOR

Another rather unusual aspect of a newborn's behavior is its fragmented nature. Offer a six-month-old a small rattle he has never seen before, and more often than not he will look at it, reach for it, and take it. He will then concentrate on examining it by staring at it, gumming it, or feeling it with his other hand.

Repeat the offer to a newborn and he will hardly look at the rattle. If you try to put it into his hand you will have some difficulty because his fists are usually clenched. However, once you have unfolded his fingers, the infant will grasp any small object placed high in the palm. Once he has the rattle, he may quickly drop it, or he may retain it for as long as several minutes. In either case, especially in the first weeks of life, that is all he is likely to do with it. If he has dropped the rattle, he will neither try to retrieve it nor show any awareness of its existence. If he retains it, he will neither look at it, gum it, nor intentionally explore it with his other hand.

From an adult point of view, such behavior is unexpected. It is convincingly explained, however, in Jean Piaget's brilliant *Origins of Intelligence*. According to Piaget, a baby's behavior at birth consists of a rather small number of somewhat clumsy, unfinished, and isolated

---

* Here and elsewhere it must be remembered that my remarks will not be perfectly accurate for all babies. Although in general infants behave remarkably alike in many situations and respects, one of the best-established principles of human development is the fact of individual differences. Especially in the area of irritability, there is great variability among babies. Often several children in the same family will differ remarkably in their characteristic moods from the first days of life.

reflexes. These simple bits of behavior (rooting and sucking, grasping, occasional glances at nearby objects) are the foundation elements of all later intelligence. In a stunning analysis, documented by detailed reports of the development of his own three children, Piaget has described and explained the emergence of problem-solving and thinking ability in the first two years of life. But effective action is far beyond the capacity of the baby in Phase I. His reflexes are triggered by external circumstances of which he has no awareness. They operate briefly and mechanically and, as far as anyone can tell, are in no way deliberately controlled by him.

During Phase I an infant's reflexes become more reliable and efficient through repeated triggering. In addition, the first signs of coordination begin as the baby's fist is increasingly brought to his mouth and gummed or sucked. In this manner, an object grasped is occasionally brought to the mouth and then sucked. But let that object be dropped and there will be no further sign that the baby knows it still exists. Out of hand (or mouth) is out of mind.

The tonic neck reflex ("fencer's pose")

LACK OF MOBILITY

When on his back, a baby in Phase I cannot turn his torso so that he is lying on his side, or otherwise move his body about except under one condition. Some babies, when angry, manage to propel their bodies the entire length of a crib by repeatedly digging their heels into the mattress surface and thrusting out with their legs. A soft bumper placed around the interior walls of the entire crib or bassinet is therefore advisable.

By four weeks of age the characteristic posture of a baby, when on his back, is the tonic neck reflex or "fencer's pose" with both hands fisted. About eighty-five percent of the time the head is turned to the right, although all babies exhibit both right- and left-facing postures. At birth this posture is not yet predominant, and the baby may be in a more symmetrical pose.

Ordinarily, when a Phase I baby is on his stomach, he is only capable of barely clearing the mattress surface with his nose for a moment or two. Again, however, when angry he may do considerably better. In general, it will be several months before a baby can cope well with his disproportionately large head. Propped into a sitting position, his head will slump alarmingly. It is best *always to provide head support* for a Phase I baby, especially when lifting or holding him.

HYPERSENSITIVITY

Along with his sleepiness, frailty, and irritability, the Phase I infant is in general unusually sensitive. This sensitivity can make a jumpy parent even more apprehensive. Remember that it is perfectly normal for an infant to startle and cry at any abrupt change in stimulation during his first weeks of life. Such reactions are common as a response to sharp noises, or to jolts to the crib or bassinet, or to any rather sudden change in position, particularly when the baby is inactive. A second, less dramatic indication of special sensitivity present at this age is the infant's avoidance of bright lights.

A Phase I infant will keep his eyes tightly shut in a brightly lit room or when outside in the sun. In fact, he is much more likely to open his eyes and keep them open in a dimly lit room than in one at an ordinary level of illumination. Another curiosity of his behavior is that his eyes will often open when he is lifted and held upright. This is called the doll's-eye effect. This special sensitivity to bright light is markedly reduced by the end of Phase I.

"SMILING"

The smiling behavior of the Phase I infant is also worthy of note. It is quite common for new parents to report that their infant smiles at them frequently during the first six weeks of life. I feel somewhat guilty in insisting that smiling is actually quite rare in this period. Furthermore, on the rare occasion that the infant seems to be wearing a smile, he is not likely to be looking at another person. All of us would like to think that our children feel an immediate and deep love for us, but I do not believe this is so. Toward the end of the infant's first months, however, you may begin to notice him looking at your face with increasing interest. The region between the hairline and the eyes seems to be particularly attractive. This new interest is a preliminary to true social smiling.

THE VISUAL DISCOVERY OF THE HAND

The six-week-old baby, when placed on his back, continues typically to lie in the tonic-neck-reflex position. He is able to turn his cheek off the surface of the mattress with increasing ease, but still rarely looks directly overhead. His hands, although still usually held fisted, are now frequently held aloft. The hand on the side to which his head is turned is, from time to time, directly in front of the baby's eyes; but whether the hand is still or moving through his line of sight, *the child does not seem to notice it*. The effect on an adult can be somewhat disconcerting because the baby appears to be blind. Such is very rarely the case. The Phase I baby is simply not yet able to see small nearby objects very well. One reason for this is that since his eyes do not yet converge or focus accurately on such objects, he is not yet ready for three-dimensional vision.

Sometime after five or six weeks, if you observe your infant closely you will notice him give an occasional brief glance at his hand as it moves through the line of sight. Each day the frequency and length of this activity will increase, ending in sustained hand regard. *This pattern of staring at the hand is universal, and is a signal that the infant has entered into Phase II* (see page 31). Hand regard may begin as early as one month of age (in rare cases), but is normally first seen between two and three months. In the months that follow it will lead to the gradual mastery of the use of the hand in deliberate reaching for objects. It is also a first step in the development of problem-solving or intelligent behavior. Further, it seems to be a first step in the evolution of curiosity, for during the hours spent examining his hands an infant appears extremely involved and studious.

THE APPARENT INTERESTS OF THIS AGE

Perhaps the toy most often bought for newborns is the rattle. Unfortunately, young infants have no interest at all in this toy. Even when they are four to six weeks old, babies show negligible enjoyment or even awareness of rattles. In referring back to earlier sections of this chapter, the major reasons for this lack of interest become clear. First of all, for the first few weeks of life the baby is not very interested in *any* aspect of the external environment. As we have seen, if a rattle is wedged into his clenched fist, he neither looks at it nor feels it with his other hand. Since he is not yet teething, even if he *were* to hold a sterling silver rattle to his mouth, he would not be rewarded by the relief from pain the coolness effect of the metal could bring. If a rattle is not a smart buy, what then *does* interest a newborn?

SIMPLE COMFORT

Any extensive study of newborns leads to the feeling that their major "concern" is comfort—or the absence of discomfort. The newborn infant is easily and regularly discomforted. He is very likely to be restless and in distress just before feeding. He may very well cry a good deal immediately after and between feedings. He will most likely cry if his diaper is not changed fairly promptly. A sharp loud noise or abrupt change in his position will often produce a startle and a series of piercing, "all-stops-out" squalls. It would appear that any of the several ways in which he can be disturbed from his predominant sleep state creates in the infant *an urge for relief, for peace*. In this respect, the newborn infant is unique, for beginning with Phase II, and increasingly from then on, the normal infant seeks out stimulation throughout the day, except for nap time.

BEING HANDLED AND MOVED GENTLY THROUGH SPACE

People have known for years that one way to soothe the easily disgruntled newborn baby is to pick him up, hold him close, and rock him or walk with him. As mentioned above, an automobile ride can do miracles for an infant when he seems inconsolable. The above experiences seem somehow to be so comforting or pleasurable to the Phase I infant that they can at least temporarily dispel all kinds of discomfort.

SUCKING

As the Phase I child develops, his capacity to get his fist to his mouth and keep it there increases. Whenever the fist or any part of it, or any other similar object is at the mouth, if he is awake, the baby is likely to suck. If you are patient you can get your baby to suck on a pacifier, especially in times of moderate distress. (A raging baby seems less interested in and less able to suck a pacifier.) Since sucking his hand is a very common activity in an infant of this age, we must assume the activity is very satisfying.

EDUCATIONAL DEVELOPMENTS DURING PHASE I

During the first weeks of life, educational development consists primarily of a stabilization of the unsteady, somewhat fragile pieces of behavior present at birth. These pieces of behavior were cited earlier in this chapter. For example, you will find that during the first weeks of life the baby becomes more skillful at finding and sucking the nipple, bringing his fist to the mouth and holding it there, and locating and tracking a slowly moving nearby object. In essence, what seems to happen is that the modest collection of simple reflexlike acts present at birth undergoes a gradual finishing process during the next six weeks.

Though Phase I is not characterized by dramatic educational development, some discussion of the major areas of development may be useful, partly to indicate what a baby should *not* be expected to do.

INTELLIGENCE

Students of human development are in general agreement that babies neither begin life with any extensive intelligence, nor do they acquire any for several months at least. Definitions of intelligence vary widely, and judgments about when babies first reveal any such capacity will depend on the particular definition one chooses to use. One common definition of the earliest kind of intelligent behavior focuses on simple problem solving. According to this view, expressed by J. McVicker Hunt of the University of Illinois, the first signs of intelligence in babies are evidenced when they deliberately push aside obstacles in order to get at desired objects. Such behavior is not often seen before a baby is six months old.

Most adults think of intelligence as involving ideas in the mind. As far as anyone can tell, such forms of intelligence do not make their appearance in any substantial form until late in the second year of life. There is little reason to think that Phase I babies do very much thinking, in the ordinary sense of the term. Throughout the first year and a half of life, most of whatever intelligence a baby possesses is reflected in his behavior.

The initial collection of reflexlike behavior that newborns show is not, however, irrelevant to intelligence. According to Piaget, it is from these simple isolated acts like grasping and glancing that mature intelligence develops.

There is a fascinating tie between the pieces of behavior found in human newborns, and corresponding activities in the young of other mammals. The baby kangaroo is born in a much less mature state than a human, and yet in a sense is far more capable than a human baby. Like the human, the kangaroo is born with reflexlike behaviors that include hand and foot grasp, rooting and sucking upon stimulation near the mouth, and coordinated arm and leg movements. In man, each of these behaviors operates separately. In kangaroos, these behaviors are coordinated in such a way that the newborn, who is less than an inch in length and blind, manages to find his way from the genital region up to the lip of his mother's pouch, crawl inside, and locate a nipple to which to fasten himself in order to survive. This remarkable performance is not within the ability of a newborn human, but is, of course, unnecessary since the human mother provides what instinct does not for her baby. This comparison helps students of human development understand why human babies are equipped at birth with behaviors that do not seem to serve any necessary function (*e.g.*, the grasp reflexes of the hands and feet).

EMOTIONALITY

The Phase I infant has few mood states. His favorite condition, day and night, is sleep. When awake, he is either groggy, sober, inactive, and quiet; or alert, sober, inactive, and quiet; or alert, sober, and active, with an occasional noise or two; or alert, active, and in mild distress, with occasional squalls; or obviously very unhappy (active and raging).

Throughout the first year of life, babies shift moods with surprising speed. As noted above, many kinds of distress can be relieved by gentle handling and rocking. A particularly useful item during this stage is a rocking chair and/or a rocking cradle. This old standby will not only sooth a cranky newborn, but can offer you many pleasant moments as well. In like manner, a very unhappy newborn can find comfort from sucking, even when that sucking is not followed by swallowing of milk or juice. It is as if the satisfaction from rocking or sucking is so all-satisfying that it simply shuts off any other sensations. This is seldom the case later in life. *When a toddler is badgering you for attention, do not expect him to be satisfied with a pacifier.*

MOTOR AND SENSORIMOTOR SKILLS

During Phase I an infant's motor abilities increase noticeably. By four months of age he will be routinely holding his head in an upright position for many minutes at a time, and even at six weeks of age his head control will be noticeably better than at birth. He should now be able to hold his head just clear of the surface he is on for a few seconds at a time.

Similarly, the newborn's initial tendencies to turn his head and grasp with his mouth an object that is touching his face at or near his lips will be more regular and efficient by six weeks. Some progress too will be made in tracking slowly moving objects with his eyes. By six weeks of age, reasonably smooth, reliable tracking is often seen. To test for this ability, hold a large (more than five inches) brightly colored object about a foot over the baby's eyes, shake it to get his attention, and move it rather slowly to the side. You may have to recapture his attention after a few moments. The difference in average performance between the newborn and the six-week-old is usually substantial.

Another easily observed improvement in motor ability is the increase in facility at getting the fist to the mouth and keeping it there. The newborn seems to be only partly in control of the movements of his arms and hands. By six weeks of age he much more often manages to hold his fist at his mouth. His purpose, of course, is to have something suitable to suck. This ability, by the way, may help his mother in that it provides for occasional self-pacification.

The surprising strength of grasp of the newborn is well known. Especially when alert, the newborn usually has about two pounds of pulling power in each hand. This automatic "holding-on" persists throughout the first six weeks, and gradually disappears shortly thereafter. Perhaps the earlier description of the usefulness of this behavior in baby kangaroos helps explain its presence. An accompaniment to the active holding-on by the newborn is the typical fisted position of the fingers. It appears that the Phase I infant has no control over this situation, which prevents him from extensive tactile exploration during the first weeks of life. By three months of age this restriction disappears, as does the tendency to grasp with the toes as well as the fingers.

SOCIABILITY

Newborns are not sociable in any ordinary sense of the term. However, two simple signs of sociability do emerge routinely during the first six weeks of life. The first is a tendency which may begin as early as the first week for the baby to look toward the eyes of the person holding him. The second is the aforementioned appearance of the first modest "smiles" while doing so. These behaviors have a mechanical, almost impersonal quality to them. You can often elicit similar behavior by

Phase I babies will smile at this kind of pattern.

presenting a young infant with a view of a pen-and-ink sketch of that section of a human head between the tip of the nose, the ears, and the top of the head. It seems that one of the universally inherited human behaviors is the tendency to smile at human faces (or things that look like them), especially when such a face is between six and twelve inches away.

LANGUAGE

The Phase I infant is far too young to understand words. Such a capacity will not be his for at least six months. However, he is not deaf; although his hearing is probably not quite as acute as that of a normal young adult, he can discriminate an impressive range of sounds, even during the first weeks of life. As noted, loud noises of all kinds—particularly when he is resting in light sleep—are likely to cause him to startle. This special sensitivity is most pronounced in the weeks after birth, and the startle may be followed by a good deal of crying. A baby who does not startle readily under those conditions may have a hearing loss, and is more likely to be a cause for concern than one who does.

Phase I infants do make noises. They not only cry and shriek, but may produce simple sounds when not in distress. Although they show little interest in listening to these sounds in the first weeks of life, by three to four months of age infantile babbling during play will become common.

RECOMMENDED CHILD-REARING PRACTICES AT THIS STAGE

Child-rearing practices at this stage should reinforce the general goals laid down in Chapter I for the period from birth to the crawling period of infancy (Phases I to IV), keeping in mind the infant's specific skills and interests. It is also important in this regard to remember what an infant *cannot* do and *is not* interested in.

GIVING THE INFANT A FEELING OF BEING LOVED AND CARED FOR

As noted earlier, I recommend that you handle your new infant frequently, and that you respond promptly to his cries as often as you can. You should also get into the habit of checking to see whether there is any obvious reason for the distress, but do not be surprised if you cannot always find one. Take care to look for underlying causes of distress routinely and to check with a professional if the symptoms are persistent or very severe.

HELPING THE INFANT DEVELOP SPECIFIC SKILLS

I do not believe there is much point in an extensive attempt at encouraging the development of abilities for the first few weeks of a baby's life. Placing a baby on his stomach several times each day (unless he does not tolerate the position) does however have the benefit of inducing head rearing. If the infant is always on his back, he cannot practice this skill. Since the baby is mostly a sleepy individual, his visual powers are limited and his field of visual interest covers a narrow part of space (from about eight to twenty-four inches from his eyes);

therefore, providing interesting things to look at is probably of limited use at this time. When he is being held, various bodily responses to his changed positions are presumably being exercised; but beyond these simple fragmentary notions, there is not much point in being concerned with specific skill development in the first few weeks of life. Gradually, toward the end of the first month of life, babies begin to show more interest in the world around them. I have found that many three- and four-week-old babies will look at suitably designed mobiles. Since very few properly conceived mobiles are commercially available, you may prefer to make your own (see below).

How to make a mobile for a three- to eight-week-old infant

A mobile should be placed where the infant tends to look. As mentioned earlier, a baby of this age, lying on his back, will generally look to his far right eighty to ninety percent of the time, and to the far left for the remainder. (Whether or not this early preference is predictive of later handedness is not yet known.) A mobile for a child this age should, therefore, *not* be placed directly over the baby's midline, but rather off to his far right or far left, or preferably to both sides.

A mobile should be placed at a distance the infant prefers. In the age in question most babies avoid looking at objects closer than five inches or farther than eighteen inches from their eyes. I would recommend a distance of about twelve inches.

A mobile should be designed with a view toward what the baby sees while lying on his back in the crib.

Most commercially available mobiles are designed to look attractive to a customer looking for a gift rather than considering the view the baby will have of the plaything. Since babies are especially interested in looking at that area of a human face that lies between the tip of the nose and the top of the head the mobile should feature bold, contrasting colors, and crude features that contain configurations similar to those in the upper front portion of a human face.

Some years ago I designed just such a mobile as a part of the Playtential* toy line. In home tests and extensive private use, this mobile was dramatically successful. With a little effort, good mobiles like this can be made at home, particularly since the Phase I infant for

---

* Trademark registered by Kenner Products Co., a division of General Mills, Inc. This toy line is no longer being manufactured.

whom they are designed will only *look* at them. Therefore you need not worry about a strong support for a mobile. Any method by which you can suspend several facelike patterns into the proper locations will do fine. You can even use simple sheet cardboard as the basic material on which to paint or paste patterns. By the way, though an infant of this age cannot really perceive fine detail, it will not do any harm to incorporate some in your design. So feel free to let your artistic impulses be expressed.

Although I recommend the use of mobiles, I cannot say that any striking gains in specific skill development will result from the use of such devices. Nevertheless, the earliest interest in the outside world features visual examination of parts of the near environment, to the extent that those features are easily viewed by the baby. Very few things meet those requirements except the face of whoever feeds the baby, and a suitably designed mobile.

Beyond the activities of trying to hold his head up off the surface he is lying on, and staring at face patterns, I cannot think of any other specific skills to be encouraged in Phase I. I am sure some people will advocate other ideas, but I know of no substantial basis for any.

ENCOURAGING INTEREST IN THE OUTSIDE WORLD

Except for providing a good mobile and perhaps an occasional change of scenery (by changing the baby's location several times a day), I see no point in working at encouraging curiosity until the next phase of development, when the baby's interest in exploration really blossoms.

A particularly useful physical asset during this stage is a rocking chair and/or a rocking cradle. Babies of this age have always been comforted by being rocked, and you can count on this age-old activity for help with a cranky newborn and for many pleasant moments for you as well as the baby. Also, as mentioned earlier, I believe you should feel free to make use of a pacifier as soon as your baby will accept it. Although the Phase I infant will not be very skillful at retaining the pacifier in his mouth, and certainly will not retrieve it when it pops out of his mouth, it may nevertheless come in very handy at times. Indeed, this simple, inexpensive item may save you all sorts of discomfort at times throughout the first months of life.

SOME CHILD-REARING PRACTICES
I DO NOT RECOMMEND

In addition to recommended child-rearing practices, I believe some comment on inadvisable practices is necessary to counteract existing *mis*information about child-rearing.

PROVIDING AN INFANT WITH AN
ELABORATELY "ENRICHED" ENVIRONMENT

If someone urges you to stimulate all your newborn infant's senses by purchasing and using a set of "educational" materials, be skeptical. The concept of an enriched environment (which has come into vogue in the last few years) has merit, but only if used with discrimination. Some commercial firms and some child-development personnel have misused the concept.

The Phase I infant is not much of a candidate for useful exposure to an enriched environment, especially during the first half of the period (the first three weeks of life), when he is rarely wide awake. It is not very likely that enrichment benefits a sleeping infant. When he is alert, his limited sensory capacities, combined with his primitive intellectual status, severely restrict his learning capacities. In short, *it is too soon* to be seriously concerned with extensive environment enrichment.

LETTING A BABY "CRY IT OUT"

Infants brought up in institutions cry less and less as their first year of life proceeds. They seem to learn (at some primitive level) that crying usually produces nothing but fatigue. Home-reared infants whose cries are ordinarily responded to quickly do continue to cry more than institutionally reared infants, but not as much as home-reared babies whose cries are responded to inconsistently. According to recent research by M. Ainsworth at Johns Hopkins University, regular, prompt response to an infant's crying leads to a better quality of attachment between caretaker and baby, and is to be preferred to either deliberate or inadvertent ignoring of crying.

NEGLECTING TO HANDLE YOUR INFANT
FOR FEAR OF HARMING OR OVERSTIMULATING HIM

There is a great deal of evidence indicating that newborns are beautifully designed to be handled. The parts of the nervous system that are activated by handling are much better developed than those involving the mind, the eyes, or the ears. In addition, handling a baby is clearly one of the few reliable ways of changing a baby's state from distress to apparent comfort.

As for overstimulation, as far as I can tell there need be little concern at this age that this can occur. If for some strange reason someone should insist on trying to keep a groggy infant from falling into deep sleep, overstimulation might be an appropriate label, but such behavior seems unlikely.

BEHAVIORS THAT SIGNAL THE ONSET
OF PHASE II

There are several rather dramatic changes to look for as an infant passes from Phase I to Phase II. Keep in mind, however, that these will not occur overnight. Development is a gradual process, and babies vary tremendously.

THE TRUE SOCIAL SMILE

There is no single age when true social smiling can be expected. Nevertheless, most home-reared babies do begin to smile regularly during their third month, and you may begin to see signs of such behavior as early as six or seven weeks of age.

HAND REGARD

Up through the second month of life you can expect an infant to stare right through his hand as it moves through his line of sight. He is not blind; he is just not yet very skillful at looking at nearby objects. By the third month of life, however, his visual abilities will have developed to the point where he can see a fairly clear single image of his own hand, particularly if it is at least five or six inches away from his eyes. At that time he will begin to spend long periods of time studying his hand and its movements. Signs of this activity may be present as early as seven or eight weeks of age, but often not until a month or so later. The first instances of hand regard may be in the form of brief double takes. After the hand has passed by where he is looking, the baby may abruptly look after it. Gradually, in the weeks that follow, the looking will become more sustained.

A SUBSTANTIAL INCREASE IN WAKEFULNESS

Soon after the sixth week, and especially as hand regard becomes a common activity, you are likely to observe a rather sharp increase in the number of hours each day a baby spends awake and alert. From about five minutes an hour at one month of age, the average infant of two months of age will move to about fifteen or twenty minutes of wakefulness an hour during the daylight hours. Again I must remind the reader that babies vary greatly in the pace of their development. Suffice it to say that most two- to three-month-old infants seem to be visually alert very often during the day, whereas Phase I infants are characteristically sleepy beings.

CHAPTER 3

Phase II_____

SIX WEEKS to
THREE-and-ONE-HALF
MONTHS

GENERAL REMARKS

Unlike the newborn infant whose behavior seems to convey the impression that all he wants out of life is to be left alone in peace, the Phase II infant appears to have a genuine interest in what is going on around him. This interest is most strikingly apparent in longer and longer periods of wakefulness. One of the most dramatic landmarks of this second phase is the appearance of genuine, frequent, social smiling. Another highlight of Phase II is the infant's visual discovery of his own hand, which will be followed by many hours of staring at that hand and at the fingers as they move. These two dramatic events, social smiling and hand regard, appear against the background of increased wakefulness, and seem together to represent the beginnings of true learning. Learning during Phase II, however, will be modest in total amount and type because we are still dealing with a baby of extremely limited skills, who by his sheer helplessness has to cope with all sorts of limitations upon his activities. After all, this baby still cannot move about in any real way, and for the most part has little control over his head, which is still disproportionately large. Indeed, even his visual capacities, which are so important for all kinds of learning, are only partly developed throughout the major part of this particular phase. Nevertheless, the learning processes have begun.

GENERAL BEHAVIOR DURING THIS PERIOD

BODY AND HEAD CONTROL

Although the Phase II baby is still a very limited being in many ways, this particular period of life is the scene for perhaps the most rapid rate of development that can ever be observed in a young child. The Phase II baby cannot yet turn over, reach for objects, or indeed, even turn his torso very much from side to side, yet his behavior is much more coordinated than it was in Phase I, and very different in many ways. To start with, at about six weeks of age you will still expect to see the baby, when on his back, lying in the standard tonic-neck-reflex position. But by the end of Phase II, the baby will have acquired freedom from the influence of that reflex. If you look at a three-and-one-half-month-old

Midline position of a Phase II baby

baby you will very often find him lying with his head in the midline with both arms and both legs flexed and his legs held up off the crib surface.

Interestingly, between six weeks and three and one-half months of age, the child's favorite resting posture shifts gradually from the asymmetrical side orientation (with his head resting on his cheek), through a position where his cheek may be well off the crib surface; first just a few degrees, then gradually more, and finally to the point where he is capable of holding his head at the midline for long periods of time. Unlike the child of six weeks of age, when the child of three and one-half months of age comes to favor the midline symmetrical orientation, he is not restricted predominantly to this preferred position. Whereas the six-week-old has very little fine control over his head movements, the three-and-one-half-month-old can move his head freely throughout the full 180-degree range when lying on his back. Most Phase I babies spend eighty to ninety percent of the time with their heads turned far right. When such a baby does turn his head it turns rapidly to the far left and on to the left cheek. The three-and-one-half-month-old, on the other hand, has complete control of his head (when lying on his back).

In the six-week-old, the positions of the arms are restricted by head position. In the three and one-half-month-old, however, the head position no longer seems to determine the arm position. Furthermore, each arm and hand seems to be able to act more or less independently of the other.

SOCIABILITY

Another rather dramatic change occurs in the area of sociability. The six-week-old baby, as we have seen, is a pretty sober individual. Not so the three-and-one-half-month-old—these babies seem to be happier than at any other time in life. Again, there will be exceptions to these general statements, and you need not be alarmed if your child is not regularly euphoric. By and large, however, this is a time when children seem to be chronically high. Easy and frequent social smiling seems to arrive along with a very strong interest in looking at the human face, particularly, as we have noted, between the tip of the nose and the hairline. You can expect your baby to be smiling pretty regularly sometime during the third month of life.

MOTOR BEHAVIOR

A more subtle but important change that the baby shows as he moves through Phase II is in the area of the quality of motor behavior. The six-week-old baby is in many ways like a little machine. If you touch his lip lightly with your finger, particularly when he is alert, you will find he swings his head pretty reliably over toward the stimulating finger to grasp and suck it. This rooting behavior is as mechanical as the knee jerk elicited by your pediatrician. By three and one-half months of age, however, a touch of the baby's lip will not be followed by an automatic rooting response, but instead will be followed by a pause and then perhaps a cautious searching for the stimulus. The machinelike, automatic quality is gone.

The rooting response is not the only mechanical behavior Phase I babies show. Earlier I remarked that certain kinds of objects (particularly if they are large and colored in bright, contrasting hues), when held over a resting baby could be effective in getting the child to look and to follow. Although getting a child to look at and follow a target in Phase I is usually a fairly difficult chore, babies in the six-to-ten-weeks-of-age group follow that same kind of target with great skill and rather high reliability. Again, the performance has a machinelike quality. I have seen early Phase II babies follow a seven-inch bright red circle overhead back and forth two, three, and even four dozen times in a row. It is as if they really do not have any control over their own behavior. At six weeks of age, a large target held anywhere from twelve to eighteen inches from the child, particularly slightly off to the side of his line of sight, then shaken lightly, will elicit his attention. If the target is then moved slowly, the child will often track it. By the time he gets to be three and one-half months of age, the baby will be perfectly capable of—and interested in—tracking small, irregularly shaped, and multicolored objects, as well as large objects. At this age you will notice that his tracking behavior no longer seems as *obligatory,* or automatic, as it was earlier. Now, particularly if the target is a relatively plain one, after staring at it for the first time he probably will be less inclined to spend further time looking at it or tracking it.

Another area in which machinelike, automatic responding can be seen has been studied in research laboratories. A three-inch black felt disc, started at thirty-six inches from the eyes and then slowly brought closer, will attract a six-week-old baby's attention (under ideal conditions) as it reaches about eighteen inches from his eyes. The baby seems to be obliged to watch this target until it comes as close as eight to ten inches, at which point he stops looking. Gradually, over the next few weeks, the range over which a baby will hold focus on the same target extends to its maximum, which may be from twenty-four or thirty inches all the way down to four inches. As the baby approaches three or three and one-half months of age his behavior changes—instead of what looked like compulsory staring, now you will usually see a brief glance at the target when it is about two feet away, and then a total loss of interest. These and other behaviors convince students of early human development that the two-month-old baby does not actively seek contact with the environment, but rather seems to be forced to respond to stimulation. In contrast, the baby of three and one-half months of age (the end of Phase II) no longer seems "stimulus bound." *He seems to be much more in control of his own behavior.*

INCREASING STRENGTH

Another rather dramatic change in babies during Phase II is the shift from weakness to strength. Although the six-week-old baby is considerably stronger than the newborn, he is still a relatively weak creature. To prove it all you have to do is put him on his stomach and note that he can usually only manage to lift his head a few inches off the surface on which he is lying. By three and one-half months of age, however, that same baby will immediately lift and hold his head up so that it is vertical to the ground. Furthermore, he will be able to continue to hold it up and look around for long periods of time.

A baby's arms and legs are also considerably stronger at three and one-half months of age than they were earlier. Indeed, you will find that at this stage babies take great delight in exercising their new-found muscles. Phase II muscle development is accompanied by a marked weight increase resulting in a rounder-looking, sturdier baby.

VISUAL DEVELOPMENT

Still another dramatic area of change in Phase II involves vision, an area closely linked to the learning process. The Phase I infant had essentially no flexibility in his visual focusing system. Thus a target could be focused on clearly in only a very restricted range. For most Phase I babies seven to nine inches from the eyes is the ideal focusing range. By the end of Phase I, however, most babies are able to focus clearly at distances between six and twelve inches. During Phase II the full development of flexibility of the focusing system takes place in most babies. The three-and-one-half-month-old baby can adjust the focus of his eyes for objects at *all* distances, and, in fact, is slightly better at focusing on objects that are very close (three to four inches away) than is the normal adult. This is because his eyes are set more closely together than those of an adult, making the task of turning both eyes in toward a very close target (convergence) easier than it is for a grownup.

Another major visual system is also undergoing very rapid development during Phase II. This is the system that allows us to see a single three-dimensional object when we are looking at targets less than one meter (39.37 inches) from the eye. The capacity to turn both eyes in as a target gradually approaches the face is not present in the newborn, and indeed does not really manifest itself until the child approaches two months of age.

By three and one-half months of age the visual convergence system works quite well. This means that a child under two months of age —when looking at an object five, six, or seven inches away—not only has to contend with a weak focusing ability, but also has trouble keeping both eyes on the target. *I would estimate that a baby of three and one-half months of age has near-mature visual capacities.* By observing the way your baby looks at small, detailed, nearby objects at different points in the first three and one-half months of age, you will find that if he does attend to such objects before he is seven or eight weeks of age, he is likely to give them no more than a brief stare. In contrast, in the weeks to follow he will not only be much more inclined to look at small, nearby objects, but as he looks at them you will find that he is glancing from point to point along their surfaces with great skill and speed. He has become a sophisticated visual creature.

HAND POSITION AND HAND REGARD

Another development of consequence, and one that is easily observable, has to do with the baby's hands. As we have seen, the six-week-old baby generally rests with his hands in a fisted position; and the hand toward which his head is oriented is generally not actually looked at. Sometime during Phase II, however, he will start to stare at his hand, at first as described earlier in a brief double-take fashion, and then for longer and longer periods. By three months of age he may be gazing at his hands for five to ten minutes at a time. This new habit of prolonged hand and finger regard appears at about the same time as the developing visual maturity discussed above, since the child now has the visual capacity to focus clearly on and create a single image of a nearby object.

Accompanying the onset of hand regard is another interesting development. The apparently obligatory fisted position of the fingers undergoes a change at about the same time. You will find that somewhere during Phase II the fisted posture will gradually be replaced by hands held loosely clenched and even occasionally totally unflexed. What this does (most conveniently) is to provide the baby with an even more interesting visual spectacle, because the four fingers and thumb are capable of much more interesting variations in position than the fist. Therefore, during the third month of life you will see a good deal of finger movements accompanied by fascinated staring at them.

LEG POSITION

Another in the long list of striking changes in Phase II involves leg position. Sometime during the fourth month (usually by the end of Phase II) the legs will have reached such a degree of strength and musculature that they are very often held elevated. Furthermore, they seem primed to thrust out; and, if any surface happens to be available which provides pressure to the soles of the feet, those flexed legs will push against it powerfully and repeatedly. Another evidence of increased strength in the legs and the tendency to extend them when pressure is applied to the soles of the feet can be seen in the surprising ability of the baby by the end of Phase II to support much of his own weight when held upright with his feet against a surface.

CURIOSITY

While you could characterize the younger Phase I baby as a seeker of peace and quiet and the older Phase I baby as a "looker," someone with a good deal of visual curiosity, the Phase II baby is a very different being.

Increasingly, between six weeks and three and one-half months of age, the baby's hands begin to play a prominent role in his explorations. We have found that if you present a small, attractive object such as a rattle five or six inches from a child's eyes and off to his right when he is about two months of age, he will not only look at the target, but, in addition, in many cases his right fist will abruptly rise, approach the target and strike it. This so-called "batting" or "swiping" behavior is likely to first appear a week or two after the first episodes of sustained hand regard. From here on babies are no longer content to *just look*. They want to get their hands as well as their eyes into their exploratory efforts. Bear in mind, however, that in spite of their curiosity, these Phase II babies are extremely limited in their explorations by their physical immaturity. The world has to be brought near to them in order for them to examine it. Imagine for a moment that you were unable to move about, yet were equipped with a lively curiosity, and you may to some extent capture the situation of a normal three-month-old baby.

The three-month-old shows his curiosity in many ways: by his interest in your face; by his interest in his own hand movements; and by his interest in feeling various objects around him, such as his clothing and his crib sheets. One consequence of this desire to get his hands on anything within reach is that mobiles for the Phase II baby cannot be constructed of the same sort of flimsy support devices that were perfectly adequate for the child under six or seven weeks of age. In Phase II a mobile has to be put together with the expectation that it is not merely going to be looked at, but is going to be interacted with manually as well. Indeed, if it is a really successful device, it will be subjected to extensive abuse.

COORDINATION OF BEHAVIOR

As we have seen, the newborn baby comes equipped with a small number of reflexlike behaviors *which function independently of each other*, resulting in fragmented behavior (*i.e.*, the automatic grasping of a rattle placed in the palm without indicating any mental awareness of its presence). The Phase II baby, on the other hand, is considerably more mature in this regard. As we have seen, a two-month-old may take a swipe at an object placed within his reach. A slightly older child (three to three and one-half months of age) is likely to show other hand and arm behaviors at the sight of a nearby object. When the object is placed in his hand, particularly after two and one-half months of age, he is very likely to both look at it and to bring it to his mouth to be gummed. According to Piaget, these combinations of activities which occur in response to the presence of small objects show that *several action systems* (grasping, looking, and sucking) *are to some extent now coordinated*.

Another new evidence of the coordination of behaviors can be seen when the baby is between three and three and one-half months of age. A new action pattern is commonly seen—an action pattern we call "hands to the midline and clasped with mutual fingering." When shown a new, small, reachable object, the three-and-one-half-month-old baby very commonly responds by bringing both his hands over his lower chest and clasping them. (This must be a curious experience for an infant who up until now has not usually had the opportunity for one of his hands to contact the other.) Furthermore, an object *placed* in either of the baby's hands at this particular age will often be incorporated into the hands-to-midline pattern. The other hand will join the one holding the object and engage in some fingering of the target or the object. This fingering is a form of tactile exploration, and again illustrates how an object being grasped is now also examined by the other hand.

THE APPARENT INTERESTS OF THIS AGE

EXPLORATION

If there is one label to characterize a baby's major interests in Phase II it would have to be exploration. Unlike the somnolent Phase I baby, the

Phase II baby, particularly from the middle of the period on, strikes the observer with his bright eyes and increasingly alert and responsive manner. He goes about his explorations in several interesting ways.

Looking

First of all he is a looker—he is all eyes. He is particularly interested in looking at faces or pictures of faces. He is very much intrigued by small detailed objects that are not far away, and he is attracted particularly by slowly moving objects. He still is not very interested in looking at anything that is much farther than two or three feet from his eyes, but interest in more-distant objects is gradually evolving.

Feeling

As I mentioned earlier, while the Phase II baby is looking, his second exploratory means (the use of his hands) will be exercised whenever possible. Whether he is in your arms, looking up at your face, holding a small object, or looking at anything within reach, after two months of age he is likely to try to use his hands to explore the objects. He will finger surfaces once his fingers are free to do so. He will move objects back and forth, thereby getting a different view of them as well as a different feel for them.

Gumming

A third means of exploration at this age is the mouth. Gumming small objects is another favorite occupation. At first that most common small object he will gum will be his own fist. As the weeks go by, his fingers will be gummed and sucked; as a matter of fact, just about anything that can be brought to the mouth will be gummed. There are two apparent reasons for this. One is that the mouth is an exploring organ. The other is that in advance of the eruption of teeth, the gums may be tender and somewhat painful. Such discomfort can occasionally be relieved to some extent by the pressure involved in gumming things.

Listening

Another more subtle sign of exploration and interest toward the end of Phase II is that the baby now seems to begin to be interested in listening to the sounds he can make with the saliva in his mouth. This interest in sounds will become more prominent in later months.

MOTOR EXERCISE

Another emerging interest during Phase II is in sheer motor exercise. The baby is considerably more active now; and, in addition, his arms and legs and his neck muscles are considerably more substantial and powerful than those of the Phase I baby. If you place a baby on his stomach at this age, he is likely to rear his head repeatedly up to a vertical position from the surface on which he is lying, and to look about from that position. You are likely to find the three-and-one-half-month-old baby kicking at nothing when lying on his back, and you are likely to find active batting with the arms when anything battable is nearby.

EDUCATIONAL DEVELOPMENTS DURING PHASE II

GENERAL REMARKS

Unlike the Phase I baby, who is predominantly getting used to living outside the womb, the Phase II baby is beginning to familiarize himself with the external environment. In a sense, his education can be properly said to have begun. As previously mentioned, the rate of development between six weeks of age and three and one-half months of age is dramatic. Such milestones as the release from the effects of the tonic neck reflex and the grasp reflex, the maturation of visual motor capacities, and the emergence of sociability all help free the Phase II baby for further learning.

INTELLIGENCE

As we have noted, Phase II marks the beginning of the coordination of various simple action systems. We have already examined the sequence of activities. The hand is much more often successfully brought to the mouth for sucking, and gradually that hand is also looked at as well as sucked. When the baby is three months of age he will not only have found his hand visually, but he will also be bringing his hand to his mouth to be sucked—often just after having spent some time staring at it. What happens in this sequence of activities is that one object—his own hand—begins to be involved in several previously separate action systems. The hand is now something to be seen, moved about, brought to the mouth, and sucked. Shortly after the appearance of steady staring at the hand, objects that are placed in the baby's hand and grasped will routinely be brought to the mouth for sucking. In this way, objects seen become objects to be sucked, and two major action systems get thrown together. Another coordination begins to be found during Phase II: a link between hearing and looking. Things heard begin to be things to look at as well as to listen to. In other words, while the newborn does not regularly turn to the source of a sound, the Phase II baby will routinely do so. In Phase I a sound within hearing range (and that means most nearby sounds), will regularly produce at most an alerting response or some other sign of listening in the very young baby, but will not link up with his looking tendencies. The baby in Phase II, on the other hand, will both listen and turn his head to look.

There are other evidences of small amounts of learning that are taking place during this time. For example, you can expect to see a child begin to show signs that he has learned something about feeding. When the child of two and one-half or three months of age, for example, stops thrashing about or sucking when his mother appears to feed him, it is often a fairly clear indicator that he has some sense of what is coming. Furthermore, if you watch the sucking movements of your child you will notice that at about the same age, in advance of feeding, a child may begin to suck actively at the sight of his bottle, or the breast, or when he is being prepared for nursing. In these modest ways a child is behaving differently from the way he did in the first weeks of life. Such changes seem to represent a step in the growth of understanding of the world around him.

EMOTIONALITY

Social smiling

The firsts signs of *positive* emotional expression are found with the onset of social smiling. By the end of Phase II regular smiling to another person should be a common experience in the child's daily life.

What the smile means about sociability and about the baby's emotional state is considerably less clear than the fact of regular smiling to a human face. As mentioned before, it has been shown in research that with a black and white sketch of that part of the human face between the tip of the nose and the top of the head, you can rather easily get most babies of about two or two and one-half months of age to smile repeatedly. In fact, if you are very clever at designing this target, you may get them to smile more reliably to that target than to their mother's face. That fact, coupled with another to the effect that most anybody is able to get a two- or two-and-one-half-month-old baby to smile regardless of whether the baby has had any previous experience with them, suggests a rather interesting notion from the point of view of the survival of the species. It would appear that babies are designed to smile at just about any kind of sight that resembles a mother's face in these very earliest stages. Upon reflection this behavior makes sense, because a defenseless baby needs to have some guarantee of a positive response from another creature who can help assure its survival. The smile of the typical two-month-old baby is a very powerful force indeed in winning over an older human. Therefore the question of the relationship of the smiling to sociability is a bit more complicated than meets the eye.

As far as the relationship of the smile to the baby's true emotional state is concerned, again the picture is not as clear as it might seem on the surface. When an adult smiles, it is usually because he is feeling comfortable or happy. In the case of a two-month-old, however, the most we can conservatively conclude is that when he is wearing a smile he is at the very least comfortable, and at the very most experiencing a feeling of physical well-being. You do not see either laughter or high hilarity in the Phase II infant (except perhaps toward the very end of the period).

Rage

The Phase II child also reflects the other apparent emotional states of Phase I; that is, he is still capable of showing rage. Again, I doubt there is anything personal about such rage. My guess is that rage is simply a response to significant physical discomfort at this stage of life. A year from now, however, the child will be likely to express occasional anger that is clearly directed toward another person.

Concern

Phase II, therefore, is a time when only a limited number of emotional states are likely to be seen: the feeling of well-being (signified by the presence of a full smile); a feeling of neutral emotions (manifested by a sober and alert expression); feelings of gross discomfort (revealed by fussing or raging behavior); and finally, a very interesting emotional state which might best be labelled intense concern, which seems to be present when the two- to three-month-old baby is staring steadily at his own hand or finger movements. You regularly see such behavior with children in Phase II. The concern expressed during this prolonged staring does not seem to reflect worry, but rather a serious, studious interest.

MOTOR AND SENSORIMOTOR SKILLS

The Phase II infant accumulates an impressive collection of motor abilities in the period from six weeks to three and one-half months of age. Motor abilities in this phase can be discussed under two headings: those the baby brought with him at birth and which are fading out, and those which are emerging.

Inborn motor abilities
Rooting. Included in this category is rooting ability, the aforementioned skill that helps the baby to find the nipple in order to suck. This kind of behavior, which seems to be very mechanical and increasingly efficient in the first six weeks of life, remains efficient and mechanical in the early stages of Phase II. By the time a baby is three months of age, however, searching with the mouth is accomplished in a more smooth, adultlike manner.
Visual tracking. Another interesting behavior that bridges the first two phases of life is visual tracking. As we have seen, the Phase I baby has a built-in tendency to be alerted to rather large, highly contrasting objects that move slowly and slightly off his line of sight. When the very young baby looks toward such an object he is essentially centering it in his visual field. He brings the target into the line of sight where his eyes are best suited to fine visual examination. Unfortunately for the very young baby, his eyesight is not yet developed enough for fine visual inspection, so once the object is centered in his line of sight he cannot see it clearly and he therefore quickly loses interest in it. You can usually get a baby to track an object over a couple of feet, even though he is less than six weeks of age, by repeatedly recapturing his attention and dragging him along (by his eyes) a few inches at a time. During Phase II, as with

the rooting behavior, visual tracking or pursuit remains a dependable behavior; indeed, it reaches a peak of efficiency for a few weeks then gradually drops out, to be replaced by what looks like more voluntary, more adult function. The two-and-one-half-month-old baby tracks objects very smoothly as they move slowly overhead. One reason for that smoothness is that he has acquired considerably more control over his head motions; the other has to do with the aforementioned shift from apparently involuntary tracking of targets to a more controlled type of activity.

Finger position. Still another kind of motor development that spans Phases I and II has to do with the fingers. The grasp reflex and fisted-hand, both characteristic of Phase I, gradually drop out as the child moves through Phase II. By the time he nears three months of age he can put a single finger in his mouth and suck it, whereas before he was largely limited to sucking some large surface on his fist.

Tonic neck reflex. Still another extension of Phase I behavior involves the influence of the tonic neck reflex. An unusual characteristic associated with that curious side-resting posture was that the arms and legs seemed to fall into a regular arrangement dependent upon head position; so that if the infant was lying with his head resting on his right cheek, the right arm was extended and the left arm was flexed, with the left fist being held behind the head with the legs in a fencer's posture. Furthermore, if you forcibly turn the head of a Phase I baby over so that it rests on his left cheek, his arms and legs would follow suit. In other words, the right arm would gradually flex with the fist ending up behind the head, and his left arm would gradually extend with his fist held somewhere around seven inches out in front of his eyes. His legs, too, would reverse position. This interesting sort of dominance of head position over limb position drops out steadily in Phase II. As we have noted, the three-and-one-half-month-old child no longer lies characteristically in an asymmetrical pose, although he is perfectly capable of turning his head to the side if he chooses to. The three-and-one-half-month-old child is a symmetrical baby in the sense that when you look at him, he more often than not is lying with his head in the midline and his arms and legs slightly flexed.

Emerging Phase II skills

With the decrease in influence of his inborn motor systems, we find a far more able Phase II baby. You can expect, for example, that the six- to eight-week-old baby can more or less hold his head about forty-five

Three and one-half months: head at 90° position

degrees off the horizontal for a few minutes at a time. Each week that passes will bring steady improvement, so that by three and one-half months of age he should be able to hold his head so that its main axis is at about ninety degrees from the horizontal for several minutes at a time.

The other emerging motor skills of the Phase II baby were discussed in detail at the beginning of this chapter. Let me say in summary that at the end of this phase a child is a very competent visual motor creature, has good general hearing abilities (as far as can be determined), and has greater hand and body control. He is on the road toward developing the arm and leg strength he will need in the months to follow in order to maintain an upright sitting posture, to achieve a pull-to-stand posture, and ultimately to walk.

SOCIAL DEVELOPMENT

Just when the fatigue of tending the Phase I baby may be getting the average parents down to their last ounces of reserve strength, two lifesavers are likely to arrive almost simultaneously on the scene. I refer to the tendency of Phase II babies to sleep through the night, and to engage in genuine social smiling. (Additionally, some babies overcome early digestive problems at about this time as well.) The social smiling is a well-documented phenomenon. It is very clear that you can expect most children reared in their own home to begin reliable social smiling by about two months of age. Some people swear that babies are smiling regularly long before two months; but to be on the conservative side, two months, even as late as two and one-half months, is a perfectly reasonable time for you to expect such smiling to begin. Once a child engages in smiling very regularly there is no mistaking what social smiling is. It is total, unqualified engagement on the part of the baby. It has been so designed as to melt all but absolutely frozen hearts. You can easily see what an effective survival tactic it is for a young, totally dependent creature to bring with him into the world. The early smiles are not very exclusive; indeed, they are not exclusive at all. It has been shown in several research studies that these smiles are not reserved exclusively for the natural mother, nor even for a foster mother, a father, or a sibling—just about anybody can elicit them. But no matter, they are there, they are glorious, and they are to be enjoyed.

We have already commented upon the euphoria of the late Phase II child. The fourth month of life is simply a marvelous time to be and to have a baby. It is the time when photographers take pictures of young children for advertisements. The child has more chubbiness. He has usually lost any unattractiveness caused by the birth process. The result is that most three-and-one-half-month-olds not only smile a great deal, but they look quite handsome while they are doing so.

Special relationship with mother

Research shows that by three and one-half months of age a child's mother, given normal circumstances, is more able to elicit a smile from a baby, and more able to continue to elicit it for long periods of time, than anyone else. The baby seems to have begun to form a special relationship with his mother. Her smile, especially if accompanied by her voice, seems to be significantly more powerful in eliciting his smile reaction than just about anything else he will look at in his ordinary experience. Although his mother may be uniquely powerful as an elicitor of such sociability, that is not to say that the child will not smile readily to other people as well. Indeed, he is extraordinarily gregarious at this point. Most anybody who comes by can still rather easily get the child to smile to him.

Response to tickling

Over and above smiling you are likely to find children toward the end of Phase II entering a new level with respect to sociability. As mentioned before, you will find the first hearty laughter and general signs of hilarity occasionally emerging toward the end of this particular period. In addition, you probably will find that for the first time in his life the child will respond to being tickled. The fact that you cannot elicit a tickle response from a child before he is about three and one-half months of age has always intrigued me. I tend to couple it with the fact that adults cannot tickle themselves. Try it if you never attempted it before. My guess is that there is an underlying interesting fact that explains the two phenomena. I would guess that the effectiveness of the tickle is primarily dependent upon the "ticklee" perceiving that *another person* is producing the stimulation. I would say, therefore, that you cannot tickle yourself because you know that you are not another person applying the stimulation. The child younger than about three and one-half months of age may not be well enough developed socially to have reached whatever social awareness of another is necessary in order to make the tickle functional.

LANGUAGE DEVELOPMENT

The Phase II infant is still too young to understand words—indeed that capacity is still many weeks away. Earlier I mentioned that he very probably could hear well enough to discriminate words. We would expect his hearing to be approaching that of a normal adult by the time he is three and one-half months of age. He is no longer as oversensitive to loud and sharp noises as he was during Phase I. The startle response that we talked about in the first period of life is dropping out, although occasionally during deep sleep it may be triggered by abrupt stimulation. Interestingly, at about three and one-half months of age babies do get to the point where they can be conditioned. By that I mean they can be trained to respond to sound in a manner that would enable especially skilled audiometricians to determine with some precision just how well they hear. There has been a good deal of work in Russia and at Brown University that shows that conditioning techniques (which are similar to the techniques routinely used to train animals), can be applied to the human infant of three months of age. I believe that sooner or later they will routinely be applied so that we will have an accurate assessment of the hearing capacity of babies in decades to come.

The Phase II infant does emit considerably more sound than the Phase I infant. You will find when he is very excited about either you, a toy, or what he sees in a mirror, for example, he will start to gurgle and make delightful baby sounds. You may even hear shrieks of delight emerging from him in the fourth month of life. As noted earlier, another new phenomenon he will engage in is playing with the sounds made possible by his own saliva. He can entertain himself this way for long periods of time.

RECOMMENDED CHILD-REARING PRACTICES
AT THIS STAGE

GIVING THE INFANT A FEELING OF BEING
LOVED AND CARED FOR

Again, child-rearing practices at this stage are best thought about in the light of the three educational goals set down in Chapter 1. The recommendations for Phase I in regard to the first goal, assuring the baby that he is cared for, apply in total to Phase II. I would like, however, to reemphasize one point and make one comment. The point for reemphasis is that your baby, through the dozens and dozens of times each week that he experiences discomfort and cries out, probably accumulates a generalized expectation about his world. If his cries are routinely met with promptly, it seems to me reasonable that he would accumulate one kind of relatively desirable expectation about the degree of caring from the world about him. If on the other hand he is routinely not responded to (allowed to "cry it out") I would expect that he would accumulate an importantly different set of expectations. I am not talking here about a highly developed intellect or awareness on the part of the baby. It is rather difficult to talk about the real sense in which a child accumulates these expectations in light of the primitive nature of the mental capacities of the child. I do feel, however, that at some very basic and important level, these early experiences probably play a role in the cumulative growth of the sense of being cared for or loved, even though

I cannot pinpoint precisely what form of understanding or registration is involved.

The single comment about giving a Phase II infant the feeling you care is that it should be easier to do at this point than at many other points in a young child's life because the Phase II child is generally such an exciting, endearing, and lovable creature.

HELPING THE INFANT DEVELOP SPECIFIC SKILLS

As with the first educational goal, I refer you back to the general comments about encouraging specific skill development of Phase I. At the same time I would like to make a few comments specific to Phase II. Let us take the skills, in turn, that are developing during this period, against the background statement that whether you do very much at all the child is still going to acquire these skills during this particular stage of his life, although perhaps not so rapidly as he will with an appropriate set of experiences.

Head control
One of the skills that we expect to develop in this phase is head control. The child who lies on his back most of the time is less likely to achieve head control as early as the child who regularly has the experience of being placed on his stomach. To foster this development you can *place a baby on his stomach for at least one half-hour a day*, perhaps five or ten minutes at a time after meals. This will assure him of opportunities to practice head rearing and head control.

Visual skills
As regards vision, the child when placed prone for purposes of inducing head rearing is also going to be in a position to see things from different angles, and look toward some things he ordinarily would not have been able to look at. He is therefore able to engage in an interesting set of visual experiences at the same time he is practicing his head rearing. The more skilled his head rearing becomes, the farther he can look out away from his body.

Babies from six to about ten weeks are still interested in properly designed mobiles. Thus any device you might have created for the Phase I baby can be used right up until two and one-half months of age. From the time the baby begins staring at his own hand, however, he will become increasingly less content to merely look at nearby targets. More about that in a moment. Over and above prone placement and the provision of mobiles, I would suggest two other procedures to provide interesting visual experiences for children. One is the provision of a mirror, particularly from the time a child is eight or nine weeks of age. A mirror placed over the child's head, about seven inches away from his eyes, will be looked at increasingly by a baby from that time on through the next month or so. In his mirror watching, you will find a rather interesting sequence of activities. Babies tend to engage in modest flirtations and then mild love affairs with their own mirror image during this particular time of life. It is all a part of their growing sociability.

A final remark in this area concerns the desirability of using an infant seat to provide a change of scenery and to increase interchanges between mother and child. If from time to time you have the child near you as you go about your daily work by placing him in an infant seat, you will insure that he will have a variety of different visual experiences. If you use an infant seat, however, remember that until the child is about three and one-half months of age he will not be able to support his head particularly well, and you therefore are going to have to prop it up, perhaps using a small blanket on either side of the infant seat.

A general remark about these recommended visual experiences is that there is no reason to believe that any of them are especially necessary in regard to visual development. As far as we can tell, development of visual focusing and visual convergence abilities will proceed quite well irrespective of any special arrangements of the world around the child.

Hand-eye activities

The third set of specific skills to be encouraged involve hand-eye activities. As we have noted, sometime toward the end of Phase II the baby will acquire a new skill called swiping. It consists of a rather abrupt, fisted attack on any suitably designed and suitably located nearby object. I learned a good deal about this behavior in extensive research on the development of reaching abilities in young children. The Playtentials toys were designed to exploit this natural tendency on the part of children. In the Playtentials toys an object which could both be seen and touched by a Phase II baby was arranged so that it would be within range of his right or left hand. The result was that six- to ten-week-old babies spent a good deal of time watching their hands batting and feeling the surfaces of these objects. More about the specific design requirements for such materials in a later section.

How to make crib devices for the Phase II infant. The Phase I baby has no need for a mobile he can touch; when he begins to explore it will be primarily with his eyes. Since the Phase II baby becomes interested in using his hands as well as his eyes, by eight to ten weeks of age a baby ought to have objects appropriately placed so that he can easily get his hands to them—that means no more than six to eight inches away from his eyes.

Crib devices should be semirigidly supported. There is nothing more frustrating to an infant less than six or seven months of age than an attractive nearby object suspended by a string. A baby is acquiring more and more skill each day, but coping with a ring or a ball that is suspended by a four- or five-inch string is generally very difficult for him. Anyone who has ever fumbled overhead for a long string to light an old-fashioned ceiling lamp realizes how frustrating such a device can be even to an adult. We have found that using semirigid plastic—which guarantees the child that the object that he is interested in reaching for, batting, or feeling is going to be pretty much in the same place each time he goes after it—is much more effective.

Crib devices should be strong enough to stand abuse. The Phase II child, especially toward the end of the period, is becoming a surpris-

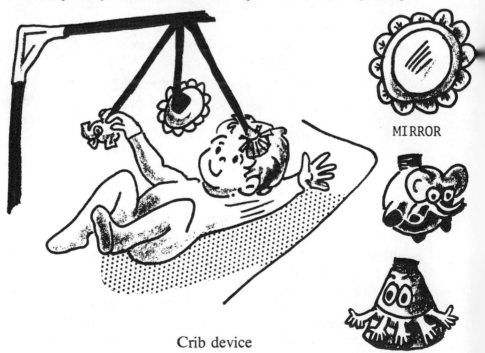

MIRROR

Crib device

ingly strong and vigorous creature. A properly designed crib device will undergo a good deal of battering and general abuse. If the toy is a good one, that battering will continue either until the child breaks the item or until he outgrows it. A crib device, therefore, for a child more than seven or eight weeks of age should be very solidly made. Unfortunately, there are no crib devices currently on the market that are suitably designed for the Phase II baby's need to explore nearby, brightly colored objects. The best device available is called a crib or cradle gym, and retails for under five dollars.

Crib devices should not produce sharp or very loud sounds, or any very abrupt changes in stimulation such as bright flashing lights. We have noted that particularly during the first half of Phase II, children are still susceptible to startles as a consequence of rather abrupt changes in stimulation. Therefore, crib devices with the above features should be reserved for when your child gets a bit older. The figure on the preceding page illustrates the design of the Playtentials crib device for this particular phase.

ENCOURAGING INTEREST IN THE OUTSIDE WORLD (CURIOSITY)

If you encourage specific skill development, using appropriate mobiles, small mirrors, an infant seat, and changes of scenery, you will find that your child will show a great deal of curiosity. Even if you do none of these things, he will display increasing curiosity in his studious examinations of his own hands and fingers, and in his visual inspection of the mutual fingering done by one hand on the other, and so forth. In other words, *it is hard to curtail the growth of curiosity.* However, should you provide effectively some of the additional experiences I have suggested, I am confident that you will see even greater growth, accompanied by many signs of enthusiasm and glee in your child.

MATERIALS YOU SHOULD NOT WASTE YOUR MONEY ON AT THIS STAGE

Rattles
A rattle is still not a good investment at this stage in life. Although a child will hold onto a rattle considerably longer in Phase II than he

would in the first weeks of life, may spend some time looking at it, and may even bring it to his mouth and gum it a little bit, nevertheless if he drops it (and he will—usually in less than one minute), he is not likely to either look for it or be able to retrieve it. All in all it is still not much of a toy.

Most crib devices

There are many crib devices on the market today. About four or five years ago a flock of toy companies entered this field in response to an increased demand from parents. I have had some experience now with several of the major toy companies and have examined a large percentage of the crib devices on the market, and it is my opinion that the vast majority of them provide negligible amounts of play value and have very little educational merit. There are several exceptions. You may find, as I have, that some of the materials toy designers put out for children of one age are inadvertently appropriate for children of another age. For example, some of the best materials for the eight- to sixteen-month-old child have been put out by one company which markets them for the two-and-one-half to five-year-old child.

CHILD-REARING PRACTICES I DO NOT RECOMMEND

I suggested in my discussion of Phase I that you beware of the abundant amount of misinformation about child-rearing that circulates. I suggested that you need not feel overly guilty if you have not provided an expensive and elaborately enriched environment for your child. This latter statement still holds true. Although there is more that you *can* do in Phase II, if you do not do very much of it you still, in my opinion, *have not done a terrible disservice to your young child.*

The second point I made during that discussion was that the idea of spoiling your child did not make much sense to me. This applies as well to the Phase II baby. I think you should respond promptly to calls for attention; try to find out what is wrong, make certain that there is no serious problem, and then do the best you can to alleviate the discomfort. Only let a young infant "cry it out" as a last resort.

A third point I made was that babies are designed to be handled, caressed, and loved, and there is no reason at all, as far as I know, why you should not indulge yourself a little in this regard.

BEHAVIORS THAT SIGNAL THE ONSET
OF PHASE III

HEAD CONTROL

When you feel confident that the baby, in an upright posture, whether he is being held or is in an infant seat, has good control of his head (such that you do not have the sense that it is going to tip and fall), you have one sign of a baby leaving Phase II and entering Phase III.

TORSO CONTROL

As we have seen, prior to about three and one-half months of age few babies can do much with their torsos. Unlike the good mobility they have acquired with respect to the head and eyes, hands, fingers, and legs, the torso remains too much for them to handle until the end of Phase II. Somewhere around three and one-half months of age you will notice that they begin turning their body up onto one side or the other. This pattern is soon followed by the capacity to turn over.

KICKING OUT

Another emerging characteristic of motor maturity as Phase III begins is the tendency to hold the feet somewhat off the crib surface from time to time and to thrust out with vigorous kicks, particularly if there is some pressure against the soles of the feet. This tendency to exercise the new-found strength in his legs leads ultimately to the infant's ability to use them for support when standing and walking.

THE SPECIAL RESPONSE TO MOTHER'S
FACE AND VOICE

Though somewhat less obvious, it should become clear that along with the growth of sociability, the three-and-one-half-month-old baby is now especially oriented toward the appearance of his primary caretaker's face and voice.

THE TICKLE, GIGGLE, LAUGH, OR EMERGENCE OF HILARITY

I have already discussed briefly the emergence of the capacity to be tickled. This phenomenon is part of a rapidly growing tendency toward euphoria and enjoyment which characterizes the Phase III baby. Although I mentioned that the Phase II baby moves into a period of high spirits, it is during Phase III that a baby is most impressive in this regard.

CHAPTER 4

Phase III _____

THREE-and-ONE-HALF

to

FIVE-and-ONE-HALF

MONTHS

GENERAL REMARKS

The three-and-one-half- to five-and-one-half-month period is a time when an interesting style of life and set of behaviors fade out. It is also a time when a remarkable quality of mood prevails. This is the last time of life when the child lives mostly in the horizontal orientation. There are still many cultures in the world where young babies are carried about and therefore held upright for large periods of the day, but in our society the first five and one-half months of life are mostly spent either with the infant lying on his back or on his stomach. From five and one-half months on, the child will spend his waking hours more commonly in a vertical orientation.

A second general comment about what is ending has to do with the baby's special concern with getting to know various parts of his body. A good example of that early introductory period can be seen in an infant's discovery of his hand, first tactually and then visually. This discovery is followed by a kind of "courtship" with the hand, culminating in the central dominance of mind over hand when the child gets to be about five and one-half months of age. In lesser fashion the child explores other parts of his body during Phase III. Sometime during this period, for example, he discovers his feet, which as far as his eyes were concerned did not exist until this point. In Phase IV and subsequently he will move on to explorations that presuppose a fairly informed and intimate relationship with his arms and legs and other parts of his body.

This is also the last phase when babies are predominantly oriented toward those things that are within a yard or so from them. Babies under five and one-half months of age do not spend much time looking across rooms or looking at scenes out the window.

A final point worth commenting upon is the tremendous geniality of the Phase III baby. The only things likely to disturb his marvelous mood are the eruption of teeth, occasional illness, and indigestion.

GENERAL BEHAVIOR DURING THIS PERIOD

The Phase III baby is likely to be awake at least half of the waking hours. This is fortunate because he has a great deal to do. While he is doing the various things we will be talking about, he will seem very happy most of the time. He will show this happiness most dramatically in the presence of other people, especially his mother, but he will also exhibit it while actively playing with materials or simply exercising. For example, if you make use of mirrors and well-designed crib devices you will find the Phase III baby occasionally having a delightful time interacting with these devices even though he is alone.

This particular age range is a period of much physical activity. In fact such activity becomes characteristic of *all* of infancy beyond this particular point. This is perhaps the time when the child shifts into high gear for the first time during infancy.

LARGE MUSCLE ACTIVITY

With respect to large muscle activity you will find vigorous activity of all the limbs to be a characteristic of Phase III. It is as if the baby simply is delighted to be alive and gets a great deal of pleasure out of sheer exercise of the large muscles (which have only recently become endowed with substantial strength). You will find the baby practicing new gross motor skills as they appear. Once he begins to turn his torso from side to side you will find that behavior to be a regular feature of his daily waking life. Once he begins to be able to turn over you will find him working very hard at this skill and enjoying practicing turning from back to stomach and from stomach to back. When he is on his stomach, you will find him repeatedly lifting his head up and holding it there for increasingly longer periods of time while he scans the world around him.

SMALL-MUSCLE ACTIVITY

With respect to the smaller muscles, physical activity is extraordinarily frequent and interesting in the area of hand-eye activities. Ordinarily Phase III will see the gradual emergence of the capacity to *use the hands as reaching tools under the guidance of vision.* The child will engage in many kinds of hand activities that lead to this important skill. While he is engaged in bringing his hands together at his midline; or mutual fingering; or exploring the clothing he is wearing, the sheet, or the fabric in the bumpers; you will notice that his concentration of gaze is remarkable. He seems to be thoroughly scrutinizing things that he is looking at and there will be an impressive alertness to his gaze.

INTEREST IN EXPLORATION

Another general characteristic of Phase III is an interest in exploration. As an infant learns to use his hands to reach, he is of course exploring. He also explores visually when he is placed prone and rears his head to peer about, or when someone approaches him while he is lying supine, or when he is in his infant seat. In addition to visual explorations, you will find evidence of a strong exploratory drive in the experimentation with his own sounds, especially when he has saliva in his mouth. This behavior is best observed when a child is unaware that you are nearby.

The final form of exploration involves the sense of touch. If you look closely you will find babies spending a good deal of time exploring how things feel, sometimes while simultaneously watching their hands, other times while looking elsewhere. Exploring through feeling takes place both with the fingers and the mouth. It is very common for held objects to be brought to the mouth and gummed.

In summary, the child of this age spends a great deal of time exercising, practicing motor skills, responding to people to the extent that they are available, exploring the sounds that he himself can make, listening to any sounds that may happen to be nearby, and, in particular, actively exploring anything that is nearby, especially his own body and hands.

THE APPARENT INTERESTS OF THIS AGE

The Phase III baby can best be described as a doer, a socializer, a *bon vivant*. He is a doer in the sense that he is far more active in all ways than he was earlier. He is a socializer in the sense that he is marvelously responsive. He is a *bon vivant* in the sense of seeming to get more out of life than human beings do at just about any other time.

VISUAL EXPLORATION

During Phase III the baby continues to show the tremendous interest he had during Phase II in the nearby visual world. He is going to be very involved with looking at and actively exploring everything within reach of his hands and feet and also everything within reach of his eyes, provided that such objects are within a yard or so from him.

MASTERY OF NEW SKILLS

Another major category of interest is that of mastery of new skills. We have remarked about the emerging gross motor skills in the area of torso control, head control, and turning over; the very important sensorimotor ability of visually directed reaching is also a focal point for activities. The Phase III child not only is interested in exploring the nearby world, but the process of mastering the skill of reaching per se has a very special power for him.

SOCIALIZING

The third major area of obvious interest is in people and socializing in general. It would appear that it is extraordinarily important for the human infant to firmly establish a relationship with a caring adult. The events of this period of life provide an almost certain guarantee that the baby will not only learn to like the nurturing adult, but also that the nurturing adult will come to feel an extremely powerful affection and responsibility for the baby.

INTEREST IN BODY FUNCTION

The fourth area of interest is one that seems somewhat unique to this age range—an apparent sheer delight in physical strength, or simple body function. Perhaps this is the time of life when an interest in gymnastics forms its roots.

EDUCATIONAL DEVELOPMENTS DURING PHASE III

In the preceding chapter I stressed the fact that parents and other child-rearers should not be stampeded into feeling guilty if they do not take elaborate (and expensive) steps to stimulate the educational development of the child in the first months of life. This remains true for Phase III. We are still in an area where there is reason to believe that *the average expectable environment contains the majority of what most children need in order to move ahead properly as far as education is concerned.* My remarks about educational practices should be taken in that light.

On the other hand, the more you know about the details of development, the better you can arrange for at least part of a child's day to be spent in circumstances that have been intelligently designed to mesh with his emerging interests and abilities. My many years of research with young children lead me to believe that a child who has spent a fair amount of the day in his second, third, fourth, and fifth months of life engaging in apparently pleasurable and sometimes even exciting experiences is more likely to be better off educationally than the child who passes the time lying in a crib or sitting in an infant seat and doing nothing more than occasionally looking, listening, or being smiled at.

THE ORIGINS OF INTELLIGENT BEHAVIOR

A baby in Phase III is not yet very intelligent according to the common definition of the word. He does not solve many problems. He is, however, moving toward being able to solve problems; and, in fact, he is moving toward becoming an intelligent being. Again, the steps he is taking have been outlined in a masterful fashion by Piaget, whose name will be mentioned throughout the text as the leading expert on the growth of intelligence.

In Chapter 3 we saw how the independent behaviors of early infancy begin to become coordinated during Phase II. This interrelating process continues during Phase III, and is highlighted by the gradual mastery of the use of the hand under the guidance of the eyes, a behavior focused on extensively by Piaget. This ability ordinarily comes in sometime during the sixth month of life, although recent research has demonstrated that a child can learn to reach as early as three months of age.

When the child is finally reaching for objects routinely (usually at about six months of age), he is demonstrating coordination of several systems of behavior. First of all, before he reaches he has to find the object with his eyes. Then he will move his hand out rather quickly and accurately to where the object is; and in a mature reach, just before the child contacts the object, he will either open his fingers or close them slightly to grasp the object. He may do any number of things with the object once he grasps it. Most commonly he will stare at it for a while. He may also move it back and forth and twist it about to get different views of it and to see what it feels like in different positions. Another typical behavior is to bring the object to his mouth and gum it.

An additional kind of behavior that a child is likely to engage in after he has grasped an object is to bring it closer to him, where his other hand may join the scene and either take over holding the object or feel the object while he holds it with his first hand. This tactual exploration is sometimes accompanied by transfers of the object back and forth from hand to hand.

We see, then, that in Phase III the child engages in more complicated and more focused hand-eye behavior than he did in the first two phases. And while he is engaging in those behaviors he is beginning to show increasing interest in the object itself. Phase I and II babies are not terribly interested in the object world. From Phase III forward, however, exploration of objects (particularly small ones that can be grabbed, chewed, swung, and batted) becomes an increasingly important occupation for infants.

EMOTIONALITY

The four-month-old child is a delighted and delightful creature. The smiling that began at anywhere from two to three months of age is now fully established, and except for those cases where a child is either ill or uncomfortable, smiling lights up his and your time for many hours every day. This is an age which firmly solidifies the baby's hold on a mother's affections. This is an age when, in addition to a broad and irresistible smile and a chronically good mood, babies show two other interesting emotional changes. For the first time you will hear your baby laugh. Laughter, and what it means for inner experience, was not terribly visible in most children until this point. But sometime during the fourth or fifth month you will find your baby regularly becoming excited and actually giggling.

Along with the emergence of laughter is another particularly interesting social and emotional phenomenon, the tickle response. We have discussed the fact that Phase I and II babies remain unresponsive to tickling. Sometime during their fourth or fifth month you will find that most babies will begin to react to a tickle. The question of why the tickle is not possible with a two-month-old but it is with a four-, five-, or six-month-old is one that has never been pursued by researchers. It is my opinion that the reason it is not functional until this age has something to do with growing social awareness.

MOTOR AND SENSORIMOTOR SKILLS

Developing motor skills

Phase III is marked by the emergence of new motor skills.
Turning sideways and turning over. Sometime during the fourth month of life the child will usually acquire the ability to turn his body up onto his side. This capacity to turn the torso from side to side is followed fairly soon by a second significant motor achievement—the capacity to

turn from the back to the stomach position, which appears toward the end of Phase III. Once this behavior appears, children practice it over and over and over again. Most children can turn from back to stomach by the time they are five and one-half months of age. Though they will become increasingly capable of turning the torso over, it will be some weeks before they are capable of pulling themselves up to a sitting posture and sitting unaided.

Kicking behavior. The third motor development worth noting at this point has to do with kicking behavior. By Phase III the leg muscles of a baby are considerably more substantial than they were earlier; indeed, he will begin to look more substantial in general. Now, for the first time, his feet are frequently held up off the crib surface while he lies on his back, whereas in the first two phases his heels usually rested on the crib surface. In addition, provided that there is some pressure against the soles of the feet, the child will get huge enjoyment out of thrusting out powerfully with his legs. This can be demonstrated in either of two ways. You can attempt to get the child to support some of his own weight by holding him erect with the soles of his feet touching a table surface or a rug, or you can provide pressure to the soles of his feet while he is lying in his crib. In the first situation you will find that he can briefly support a fraction of his weight. In the second situation you will find he will resist that pressure; and, if you hold your hands firmly against his feet, he may push his whole body away by extending his legs. The development of a powerful leg thrust is not a random or meaningless occurrence. This use of the leg muscles makes good sense in light of the fact that by nine to ten months of age the child will be pulling himself to a standing posture and cruising about while holding on to various supports; shortly thereafter he will be walking.

Arm muscle development. The Phase III baby's increasing interest in using the large muscles of his legs is paralleled by an interest in using the large muscles of his arms. You will note that his arms too have become considerably more substantial, and again, if you provide an opportunity for him to exercise them, he will do so and have a great deal of fun in the process.

Developing sensorimotor skills

The distinction between sensorimotor and motor skills, while somewhat technical, is worth noting. Sensorimotor skills involve vision, hearing, and touch, as well as muscularity.

Visually directed reaching. The crowning achievement of late Phase III in the sensorimotor domain is the mastery of the use of the hand as a reaching tool *under the guidance of the eye.* This particular talent is a very basic one for the child. It is through this skill that he will learn his first lessons about object qualities. Visually directed reaching also plays an important role in the development of intelligence. The remarkable levels to which adult human beings develop their facility to use their hands under the guidance of their eyes set man off from other animals in the same sense that language and culture do.

Eye-ear coordination. Another interesting sensorimotor change of the third phase is considerable improvement in eye-ear coordination. Earlier the child had some skill in localization of sounds, but during Phase III he becomes remarkably accurate and reliable in turning his eyes and body to the source of a sound.

Touch. A third major area of sensorimotor skill involves touch. Remember that during Phases I and II, except for the very last weeks, the child's hands were mostly fisted. Fisted hands prevent exploration of how objects feel. Once the child gets into Phase III he has use of his fingers, which he proceeds to use along with his mouth and eyes to explore the different textures, hardnesses, and shapes of materials and objects within reach.

SOCIABILITY

I have already emphasized the marvelous mood state of the Phase III infant. This mood state cannot help but make life very pleasant for parents, particularly mothers of first-born children. As noted earlier, a child's gorgeous smile is very helpful in establishing a close affectional tie with his primary caretaker. In addition, more subtle things are taking place. A child at this stage is already learning in dozens of episodes each day about responsivity on the part of his primary caretaker. If his cries of discomfort, or delight, are responded to often and rather promptly, he will get used to that kind of consequence of his own vocalizations. If on the other hand he is left to cry in discomfort repeatedly and for long periods of time, he will get used to that state of affairs as well. Babies are remarkably adaptable in this regard. Infants I worked with in a state institution gradually began to cry less and less during Phase III to the point where, by the time they were six or seven months of age, they cried rather rarely. Some parents would find that situation a desirable state of affairs. In my opinion, those children had learned that the payoff for crying was only fatigue; to me there are few sadder stories that can be told.

Capturing adult attention

One of the fundamental social skills that we have found to be a sign of very good development in three- to six-year-old children is a collection of socially acceptable means of getting and holding the attention of another person, particularly an adult. I think it is reasonable to assume that the roots of that skill lie in the experiences of the first phases of a child's life. A child's skill at getting the attention of his mother may very well be undergoing its earliest development during Phase III. In the next section on recommended child-rearing practices I will discuss this point further.

LANGUAGE

There is still no appreciable understanding of language in the mind of a Phase III baby. There is progress, however, in related areas. As noted earlier, during the fourth month of life a baby will begin to play with sound, especially in connection with the sounds he makes with his saliva in his mouth. You may notice when passing his crib that he is repeating small sounds to himself in what seems like experimental fashion. These delightful episodes are common in the fourth month of life, and will persist once they begin. A more subtle development that is likely to be taking place in the area of language has to do with the regular association of the voice of the primary caretaker with his or her presence. Ordinarily, when a mother interacts with her baby, whether it is to feed him, comfort him, change his diaper, or bathe him, she is likely to both smile and speak to him. Such behavior leads to a strong association between the mother's physical appearance, the sound of her voice, and the good feeling of being comforted. The child at the same time is learning to identify her voice, regardless of the words she uses, through its particular sound qualities. Research has shown that by four to five months of age the mother's voice can be identified from among other voices by most babies and is a very powerful provoker of smiles and attention on the part of the baby.

RECOMMENDED CHILD-REARING PRACTICES
AT THIS STAGE

GIVING THE INFANT A FEELING OF BEING
LOVED AND CARED FOR

Again, as in Phases I and II, I suggest you only let a child cry for a long period of time if you cannot avoid it. If crying persists, try to determine what is wrong and remedy the situation, comforting the baby as well. Use a pacifier if this helps.

Over and above what to do when your child seems uncomfortable, I would strongly urge you to *play with your child regularly and enjoy him*. Let him have many experiences with you where he is simply having a great time. While you are doing so, be affectionate. It may seem silly to advise anyone to be affectionate with his own baby, but some people have ambiguous feelings along these lines. Let me reinforce the notion of acting naturally and warmly with your child.

HELPING THE INFANT DEVELOP SPECIFIC SKILLS

Let me again stress my belief that even if a mother pays little or no attention to specific skill development in the first six months of life, most of these specific skills of early infancy will appear anyway. Nevertheless, I do feel that the most suitable early experiences for the child are those that are relevant to his naturally emerging skills. If you learn what they are, and can provide opportunities for them to function, I believe that on balance a child's educational development will proceed better and his zest for life will increase. Bear in mind, however, that if reaching behavior (a major specific skill) does not come in exactly on schedule, there is absolutely no reason to become concerned. Furthermore, if the child begins to reach two or three months before most children, no great significance should be attached to that event either. The story of early educational development is more complicated than that.

Intelligence

The development of the foundations of intelligence may be encouraged during Phase III by giving the child a variety of things to look at and handle. You can accomplish this first goal by supplying your infant with good crib toys, moving him about the house in an infant seat as you work, and taking him for carriage rides. This does not mean that he needs a constant change of scenery, but you should avoid leaving him in a playpen or in a crib for six or seven hours a day.

Perhaps most important to a child in regard to the development of his mind in Phase III is having appropriate nearby objects that he can examine and handle. More about such items in the section on recommended materials.

Emotionality

You can enlarge the pleasure your child has in life, and his tendency to laugh and to enjoy himself, through normal affectionate play with him. It is also a great deal of fun. Do it!

Motor and sensorimotor skills

The caretaker's main job here is to avoid *preventing* development. Swaddling a child, for example, or insisting that he stay on his stomach or his back, if done consistently, may get in the way of his practicing torso movements, arm and leg thrusts, turning over, and visually directed reaching. Crib devices that promote skill development will be discussed in the recommended-materials section.

Social skills

When your baby cries, I suggest that you respond as often and as quickly as you can in the manner described earlier. In fact you should make it a habit to respond to your child's coos and gurgles as well. He will gradually learn to associate making noise with your arrival and your presence, and with pleasure—or at least reduction of discomfort.

Language

It is helpful to get into the habit of talking to a baby, *particularly about what he is oriented to at the moment*. More about that as we get to the topic of language learning in the crawling baby.

ENCOURAGING INTEREST IN THE OUTSIDE WORLD (CURIOSITY)

If you deal with specific skill developments and educational developments in the manner described above, you will find that your child's natural curiosity will be steadily enhanced and enlarged.

RECOMMENDED MATERIALS FOR THIS AGE

MIRRORS

As noted earlier, babies first begin to become interested in mirrors at about two months of age. From earlier remarks about their interest in faces, you could predict that they will be most intrigued by that portion of their own face between the tip of the nose and the top of the head. In addition, their own face has a very special quality of attractiveness for them because, unlike the face of someone else, their image will move in a manner determined by their own movements. For these reasons a properly placed mirror is very appealing to the Phase III baby.

Avoid mirrors that are made of glass; they are too dangerous. You should also be careful to choose a mirror that is of good quality so that the image will not be distorted. A reasonably good stainless steel mirror with a minimum size of four inches in diameter and a maximum of five inches is ideal. Most important of all, remember that the mirror should be placed approximately six to seven inches from the baby's eyes. A mirror placed much more than six inches away will be relatively ineffective because the target the baby sees is twice as far from his eyes as the distance of the mirror. In other words, if you place the mirror seven inches from the baby's eyes, he will see the reflection of his own face apparently fourteen inches from his eyes. More distant objects are not as likely to attract and hold the Phase III baby's interest. A mirror positioned over a crib gives a baby something interesting to look at from time to time. Suitably placed, it can also be a useful device at diaper-changing time.

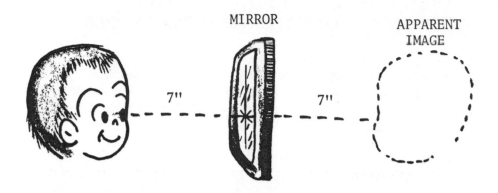

Locating a mirror for a Phase III baby

INFANT SEATS

A second kind of physical material for use at this time is an infant seat. There are many good infant seats on the market. Choose one that is not likely to tip when the baby is in it, even when he becomes active. As mentioned above, an infant seat can be used to provide a change of scene for the child several times during the day, and to keep him nearby while you work. You will also find that if a baby is in an infant seat (rather than a playpen, for example) it is easier for you to bring your face near his for friendly exchanges.

MOBILES

Very few available toys for infants are particularly well designed. Mobiles are available in great numbers, but few have appeal for babies. Their designers, as a rule, know next to nothing about what infants are really like. Uppermost in the designer's mind is the customer, and the infant is not the customer. Most mobiles and crib toys look attractive to an adult in their packages in stores, and also in the nursery as one enters the room. But put yourself in the infant's position. He sees mostly the bottoms of objects hanging overhead. Indeed, if you design a mobile with the baby's view (and preferences) uppermost, it is not necessarily going to look attractive to adults as they look at the crib. I raise this issue not only to chide a nervous industry, but more importantly to point out to you that there is a lot of nonsense in toys and you can protect yourself and your baby from being duped by learning about his rapidly changing interests and abilities.

CRIB TOYS

Phase III babies will continue to enjoy batting and feeling the safe, firmly mounted objects they interacted with in Phase II. Older Phase III infants (who have learned to reach) enjoy moving on to the next stage of hand-eye activity, which is *making simple things happen by using the hands as tools*. In the Playtentials toy line we had a simple windmill device which would spin when the baby pulled on a handle. This device was very popular with new reachers. Unfortunately, no currently available toys for this age include features quite like that item. There are many crib toys currently on the market, but very few that I can recommend. Again, the best available commercial crib toy for a Phase III baby is the inexpensive cradle gym which features a few simple objects that an infant may handle, strike, or pull.

Also in the discontinued Playtentials line was a crib kick-toy called Thumpy. Essentially, this toy was a large vinyl-covered surface on which the baby could repeatedly exert his total kicking force. It was strung between the crib uprights with tough elasticized rope so that it returned to its resting position after the baby stopped kicking or pushing

A "cradle gym"

A kick toy

it. Children enjoyed this toy simply because it allowed them to use their newly acquired leg power. You might try to make your own version of Thumpy.

MATERIALS NOT RECOMMENDED FOR THIS AGE

I advise parents to be extremely suspicious of the so-called "educational toys" for infants that are currently in vogue. This warning applies even to playthings endorsed by major manufacturers and leading "authorities" in child development. (One symptom of the lack of genuine professionalism in the toy industry is the marketing of a toy for one age group when it is really designed for another. Manufacturers are often ignorant of the play value of their various toys in terms of child development.)

There are direct-mail programs you can subscribe to for an "educational toy of the month" for infants. There are automated and illuminated "instructional" cribs for sale for several hundred dollars. There are even gadgets that feature live fish for the baby to explore visually. My advice is that you save your money.

BEHAVIORS THAT SIGNAL THE ONSET OF PHASE IV

VISUALLY DIRECTED REACHING

One of the more obvious landmarks of the emergence of Phase IV is the mastery of the use of the hand to reach for seen objects. This fundamental skill typically appears at approximately five months of age. In our research we have found that reaching ability can emerge as early as three months of age, given experience with certain kinds of crib materials, and your homemade devices can also accelerate the process. But there is no reason to be concerned (educationally or for any other reason) if reaching does not appear before six months.

By the way, it is easy to confuse batting or hands to the midline with mature reaching. The mature reach consists of a smooth approach to a nearby seen object with the fingers either opening or closing *prior* to contact with the object.

TURNING OVER AND SITTING UP

A second landmark ability to look for is facility at turning the body from supine (on the back) to prone (on the stomach) and vice versa. A third indication of graduation from Phase III is sitting without assistance. This ability is likely to be seen a bit later than reaching and turning over. It is a real step forward in the slow process of becoming free of the helplessness of the newborn.

CHAPTER 5

Phase IV

FROM
FIVE-and-ONE-HALF
to
EIGHT MONTHS

GENERAL REMARKS

Phase IV is the final prelocomotive period of life. The baby is, in many ways, much abler than he was at birth. He has greater command of his body, and his eyes and ears function on a par with those of the typical young adult. At five and one-half months of age all children who are healthy can turn their heads from left to right and pause at any point in between for long periods of time. In addition, most babies at this stage can turn their bodies from back to stomach and from stomach to back at will.

Although the baby now has significant control over his head movements, can use his hands to reach for objects under the guidance of his eyes, can localize sounds, and can turn his body back and forth, he still cannot do one very important thing: *He cannot move about*. If left on a rug in the middle of a room he is not able to propel his body any distance through space. His eyes, which for the first few months of life were only oriented toward objects that were within two feet or so, are now more inclined to attend to objects several feet away. Particularly as he spends more and more time in an upright position (in an infant seat or some substitute), his field of view is now considerably more extensive than it was.

In a sense the Phase IV baby is faced with a situation parallel to that of the three-month-old child who is provided with a mobile over his crib that can be looked at but is not suitable for reaching. He can see and is attracted to many things, but he cannot approach much of what draws him. We have what looks like a naturally frustrating situation. Midway through this phase he will overcome one major handicap. On his own, he will be able to assume and maintain an upright posture, which allows him to explore the world from a sitting position at will. Toward the end of Phase III he will overcome his other major handicap; he will acquire the ability to move about through crawling or some similar motor ability (scooting or dragging himself forward with his arms). As we have studied children over the last several years and have seen the remarkable behavior of most of them from the point they started to crawl, it has become more and more interesting to speculate on how much a child's curiosity is being primed in the weeks just prior to the onset of the ability to crawl. Although there is no firm evidence on the topic, *I suspect there is an interesting and important relationship between the building up of curiosity during Phase IV and the opportunity to satisfy it as the child first begins to move about and explore more distant objects firsthand.*

GENERAL BEHAVIOR DURING THIS PERIOD

Phase IV, like Phase III, is usually a very pleasant time for parents. There is a general continuation of chronically good humor in most children throughout the five-and-one-half- to eight-month age range. My advice to you is enjoy it while you can, because starting at about eight months, as the child acquires the ability to move about the home, the situation is going to change! You will find considerably more stress associated with rearing a baby in the months that follow, indeed in the year that follows this particular phase.

SMALL-OBJECT PLAY

What kind of a baby do we have at this time aside from his chronically good mood state? Hands and eyes still are at the center of the child's behavior. Bear in mind that the child is still physically handicapped in the sense that he cannot move about. Yet he does have a good deal of interest in exploring his world.

If you watch your Phase IV child closely, you will observe all sorts of interesting things going on in connection with his hands and his eyes. The child will be spending more and more time in an upright position. Occasionally, while he waits for you (as you prepare food, for example), you may provide him with small toys to play with. This is the age when children start showing a great deal of interest in dropping and/or throwing those small objects to the floor as often as they are placed within reach. It is also the age when infants begin to study the consequences of banging objects against different surfaces. We will talk more about this particular collection of behaviors in the section on intellectual development. Suffice it to say that small-object play is a favorite activity at this stage.

FASCINATION WITH SMALL PARTICLES

A related kind of activity, which is characteristic of this age range and no other throughout life, is a special interest in very small particles. Sometime around six months of age you should start looking for a special staring behavior in respect to little crumbs and other very small objects on the surface before an upright child. It is a rather strange-appearing behavior, probably relatable to the development of fine, detailed vision that children normally acquire at this stage of life. This very strong visual interest in small particles has been explored in some interesting research studies. In one test ball bearings of various sizes, ranging from as little as one sixteenth of an inch in diameter up to one quarter of an inch, were used to attract the attention of seven- and eight-month-old babies in the following ingenious way. Since the objects could easily be swallowed by infants, the experimenter placed some of them in a box with a clear glass top. He held a powerful magnet beneath the box so that he could move one of the metal balls by moving his magnet around beneath the box. If the ball was one quarter of an inch in size, most babies were perfectly capable of seeing it and, because of their special interest in small particles, tended to follow it with their eyes as it was moved about. As the size of the ball used was reduced, the researchers eventually got to the point where the baby would not follow the target visually or attempt to reach for it with his fingers; and at that point the examiner concluded that the child's limits of visual discrimination had been reached.

CONCERN WITH MOTOR ACTIVITY

Another general characteristic of the child at this age is his interest in physical exercise. Devotion to motor activity, and especially activity that uses newly emerging motor skills, remains typical of the entire early childhood period right on through the preschool years. We will examine the educational implications of this interest in later chapters.

Arm and leg exercise

During Phase IV major physical manifestations include very frequent powerful leg thrusts, particularly when the soles of the feet have pressure applied to them. These leg thrusts can take place when a child is either in an upright posture or lying on his back. In addition to leg thrusts, you will find a tendency to use the newly developed arm muscles for hard physical activity to the extent that the opportunities present themselves. In the Playtentials toy series we had a little trapeze arrangement that hung over the supine baby, and which he could use to pull on with great force whenever he was so inclined.

Turning over

As noted earlier, another emerging motor ability in this phase is the capacity to turn from back to stomach and back again. We have found children practicing this skill repeatedly during this two-and-one-half-month period.

Sitting unaided

The next motor skill to emerge during this period will be the achievement and maintenance of a sitting posture without assistance. You can expect children to begin practicing this particular skill sometime after they reach five months of age. By the time they are seven months of age, most children should be able to sit unaided, although others do not achieve this ability until many weeks later.*

PREOCCUPATION WITH SOUND

Another characteristic of children of this age is tied in with their growing interest in the world of sound. The same interest shown by the

---

* Although I generally expect children to crawl sometime after they turn eight months of age, it is quite possible that you will find your Phase IV baby starting to move about on the floor even before he reaches that age. Indeed, it is not unheard of for babies to be moving about by six months, and walking shortly after eight months.

Phase III baby in the sounds he produces, especially when using his own saliva, continues to grow in the Phase IV period. This involvement with sound is a prelude to the beginnings of true language learning, a characteristic of the Phase V child.

THE APPARENT INTERESTS OF THIS AGE

THE EFFECTS OF NEW-FOUND MOTOR SKILLS ON OBJECTS

There seems to be a four-step process with respect to the amount of interest a child has in small objects. The first step is essentially characterized by no interest whatsoever in objects; this is the condition of the newborn child. As we have seen, if you place a rattle in his hand the newborn will clasp it. Also, he will look briefly at certain targets that are shown to him. By and large, however, that interest is short-lived.

The second stage of the process begins when the infant is about one month old, and is revealed in more sustained visual examinations. The Phase II baby will look at his own fist or a mobile, even though his interest is confined to staring behavior.

The third step of the process is a transitional phase, during which the child's newly acquired motor skills are being tried out on objects. Now the focus of the child shifts from the motor act itself (for example, reaching for objects and batting them) to the *effect* of that motor act on objects. A good example of this particular kind of divided interest between the motor act and the object in question is what occurs when the six-month-old baby repeatedly drops things over the edge of a highchair tray and watches what happens to these objects.

The fourth step of the process, starting at about eight months and continuing for several months, is one where the motor act (reaching, batting, releasing, etc.) is now well within the ability range of the child, and therefore is accomplished rather quickly. Now the concentration is on the *characteristics* of the object. More about this fourth step in our discussion of Phase V.

The Phase IV baby is in stage three. He is especially interested in the effects of his newly acquired motor skills on objects—hence the various dropping, throwing, and banging actions that he displays with objects. Also at this time you will find that on occasion the child will become interested in the effect he can create by using his feet under visual control. The aforementioned Playtential Thumpy toy gave children the opportunity not only to push away at a big object, but also to look at their feet while doing so.

PEOPLE AND AFFECTIONATE INTERPLAY

Babies are very sociable at this point in life, and especially in the first two thirds of this phase seem to be pleasantly oriented toward just about anyone. The mother and other members of the nuclear family will be particularly favored with frequent and easy smiling. Nevertheless, you should expect an increasingly more discriminating attitude on the part of children as they go from five and six months of age through the second year of life. Over and above the simple responsivity when somebody tries to elicit a smile from the Phase IV child is the genuine pleasure he seems to get in prolonged interplay with adults. Children of this age are inclined to giggle a lot, and really enjoy exchanging smiles and sounds with their mothers. This is a time when you can begin to play little social games with children, and unless they are terribly hungry or uncomfortable for some other reason, they will be very responsive. As noted earlier tickling around the chest and under the arms will very often produce gales of laughter. Again, I think this phenomenon is symptomatic of the tremendous importance of a solid relationship with an adult figure in the first years of life.

STRANGER ANXIETY

It is very possible that as early as six months of age you will see a dramatic shift in a baby's social outlook. This change has been called stranger anxiety, and has been noted repeatedly in research literature. What it amounts to is that people other than members of the immediate family are suddenly reacted to with hesitation and then fear, rather than with the great big smile that they had experienced only a few weeks earlier. Recent research, however, has tended to cast some doubt on the universality of this kind of behavior. Indeed, I was recently somewhat embarrassed on a television program by predicting that the host, a fellow with a big black-and-grey beard, would find himself a creature of suspicion with some of our eight- and nine-month-old guests. During one program this gentleman picked up an eight-and-one-half-month-old and walked about the studio in front of the cameras, being as friendly and as physically close to the child as possible. To my chagrin, the child showed absolutely no fear.

SOUNDS

Phase IV is a time when children are increasingly interested in sounds, both those made by the people with whom they interact and those that they themselves produce. This is a good period to activate a tape recorder near the baby's crib early in the morning or at any other time in the day when the child is likely to be awake and content. There is a delightful quality to the baby's first explorations with sound.*

At the outset of Phase IV the baby will respond to sounds, but will not understand the meaning of any words. You may think he is responding to his own name, but it is more probably his familiarity with the qualities of your voice that produces the responsiveness. You can test this simply by trying a different name, of about the same length, using the same sort of general tone that you would use when you call him by his own name. In most instances you will find that he will react in the same way to the substitute name as he would to his own. Sometime toward the end of Phase IV, however, he will truly begin to respond selectively to a few simple worlds. The first words in a baby's vocabulary are almost always the same for most babies we have studied who have English as a first spoken language at home. Those first words predictably feature mother (or some variation on that theme), daddy, bye-bye, and baby.

---

* If the child spies you, he will forget his sound play because there is nothing more interesting to him than the opportunity to look at you and exchange pleasantries with you. The human face, particularly that of the mother, is at this point in time an extremely powerful attraction for most babies.

FIRST WORDS UNDERSTOOD
8 TO 12 MONTHS

Mommy
Daddy
names of family members and pets—often known
    idiosyncratically ("doody" for Judy)
bye-bye
baby
shoe
ball
cookie (sometimes idiosyncratically)
juice
no-no
wave bye-bye

12 TO 14 MONTHS

hi	hug
kitty (cat)	water
dog (doggy)	drink
cup	chair (highchair)
cracker	book
car	socks
eyes	dance
ears	patty-cake
feet	peekaboo
hair	kiss
come here	bring, give mommy, me . . .
sit down	throw the ball
stand up	brush your hair
get up	kiss me
stop that	

14 TO 18 MONTHS

milk	apple
spoon	teeth
telephone (phone)	brush your hair, teeth
keys	where is, are . . .
blanket	turn on, off the light
bed	open, close the door
cereal	go get . . .
bottle	let's go . . .
horse	find
hat	do you want (a cookie?; to get up?)
coat (jacket, sweater)	don't touch
	show me

In the first half of this phase, however, there is no significant evidence of interest in words per se, but there is a good deal of action on the part of the baby in regard to his own gurglings and the simple sounds that you can make in interplay with him. You will notice in particular that when the baby has saliva in his mouth he can make sounds that are somewhat different from his ordinary sounds. He seems to enjoy playing with those sounds (making them and varying their characteristics), either alone or with another person. One of the most pleasant experiences that new parents have with their first child is listening in on a child playing by himself with these sounds.

PRACTICING MOTOR SKILLS

Reaching

As we have seen, most babies have mastered the use of the hand in reaching by the beginning of Phase IV. Once reaching comes in, and at least for the first half of Phase IV, you can expect the average baby to reach repeatedly for just about anything that is reachable. Babies do not reach out for objects that are five feet away, even if they are large and attractive, nor do they reach for objects that are an inch from the eyeball. But offer a baby who is lying on his back or sitting in an infant seat anything graspable, and if that object is from three to eight inches away, and easily seen, you will find that in most instances he will reach for it.

Reaching is important to a child for many reasons. Not only is the use of the hand, as a reaching tool, better developed in man than it is in almost any other animal, but in Piaget's theory of the development of intelligence, reaching is seen as one of the major ways most children begin to explore the object world and build foundations of intelligence.

As mentioned before, once the Phase IV child reaches for an object he is likely either to gum it or hold it at a comfortable distance from the eyes (usually about six to eight inches), and simply look at it, or move it about.

Another commonly seen activity tied in with reaching involves bringing both hands into play. Most children of this age (at least four out of five) favor the right hand, and if an object is offered on the left side, the child may reach over with his right hand or he may take it with his left hand. If he takes it with his left hand, or if you place it in his left hand, his right hand is likely to begin either to explore the object while it is being held by his left hand, or to take the object. This pattern of both hands involved in tactual exploration under visual guidance is very common at this age, and even at times includes repeated transfer of the object from one hand to the other. Interestingly, when the object is dropped at this point in time the child will react as if he knows that he has lost something, whereas such was not the case with the two-month-old baby. Nevertheless, early in Phase IV he is not yet very adept at following the path of the drop or retrieving the object.

Turning over and sitting up

In addition to practicing reaching, babies of this age are very much into the business of practicing turning their bodies from stomach to back, and from back to stomach. By now they should be reasonably skillful at this behavior. Toward the middle of Phase IV you will begin to see them working on the problem of bringing themselves to a sitting posture. Well before Phase IV is over (by about seven months) they will acquire this ability. Each new skill will be practiced over many hours.

Crawling

The culminating skill of this phase is crawling. When babies start to crawl they sometimes do it classically, getting up onto their hands and knees and moving in a coordinated fashion using all four limbs. There are some babies, however, whose first locomotor efforts are accomplished either by scooting or by locking their arms and using their elbows to pull themselves forward, their legs dragging passively behind them. The important point here is not the style of locomotion chosen, but the fact that most children attempt to move from place to place at the first available opportunity. It is my belief that the reason they want to move has partly to do with their desire to exercise new motor skills. But even more, it is due to a burning curiosity to conduct firsthand investigation of the many things they have been able to see for several months.

With regard to the devices that are usually called walkers, I do not have any particularly strong opinions except to say that if they are properly selected I think they may allow the child to begin to exercise his curiosity a bit earlier than he might ordinarily. Many six-month-old babies can use walkers reasonably well, although they seem to have difficulty moving forward at first, and no doubt the walkers help to develop muscles and the technique of leg extension. But there are also some drawbacks to be considered.

You should be very careful in the selection of walkers because of wide variations in quality. Some are well made and stable; others are not. Some may allow the child to pinch his fingers or legs in the walker itself; they should, of course, be avoided. Furthermore, a child in a walker will probably know even less about the potential hazards of moving about rooms than the child who is crawling for the first time. One example of possible dangers involved is, these children are not at all aware of the consequences of pulling on an electric cord that may be hanging from an ironing board. If you use a walker you are going to have to be particularly careful about the child's safety.

EDUCATIONAL DEVELOPMENTS DURING PHASE IV

INTELLIGENCE

Experiences at this age play a fairly basic role in the formation of the roots of intelligence in the same sense that they have since birth. Again, the main source of my comments is Piaget's work on the development of intelligence.

INTEREST IN OBJECTS

In Phase IV the child seems to be gradually shifting the focus of his interest from his own motor skills to the objects that he interacts with. I pointed out that in the dropping, banging, and throwing behavior of Phase IV you have good examples of events that reveal a beginning of serious interest in the effects of motor actions on the objects involved. A classic example of this interest occurs when the seven-month-old drops a spoon from a highchair and then looks carefully to see where it went.

Interest in cause and effect
A second interesting aspect of the development of intelligence in Phase IV is the child's beginning interest in causality (cause-and-effect relationships). The aforementioned Playtential windmill fan allowed a child to use his new reaching skill to make something happen. When the baby pulled on a miniature subway strap, a spinning action was activated, causing a wheel above the strap to revolve. The speed at which the wheel would spin depended on the strength with which the handle was pulled. To make the toy even more attractive, the wheel featured interesting little facial patterns with exaggerated eye and hair areas, and was equipped with vaned plastic wings. These vanes were brightly colored, and outlined the wheel as it revolved. Our hope was that if the baby spun the wheel rapidly enough, he might get a little breeze on his face as an added feature. This particular device proved to be very interesting and exciting to many a child who had just learned to reach.

This interest in making simple things happen is a theme which begins to gather momentum during Phase IV, and grows throughout the next year or so in the child's life.

From Phase IV on through the second year of life a child will spend a lot of time getting to know what happens as a result of the many kinds of actions that he becomes able to perform. In a few months he begins to explore what happens when he pushes a large ball or a full-size door. He will also show characteristics of the researcher in repeatedly flipping a light switch and looking up to see the consequences, and also in his fascination with simple jack-in-the-box toys.

Another closely related theme (one which Piaget talks about) is the appreciation of time and sequences of events. Every cause-and-effect relationship involves some sort of temporal order or sequence of events in time. The baby pulls on the windmill of the Playtentials toy; this is followed by movement on the part of the vaned wheel. The baby drops an object from his highchair at seven months of age, and then looks at the consequences. There is no reason to assume that a newborn child has any understanding of either cause-and-effect relations or the time relationships between events. Yet it is clear that later on during infancy he learns the fundamentals of such relationships in the course of the simple activities that all babies experience during this period.

Memory

Another topic of special interest in examining the growth of intelligence is memory. The most common approach to the study of human memory involves asking the people you are working with to tell you about events they have experienced in the past. This procedure obviously cannot be used with infants. But in some of the films that Professor J. McVicker Hunt has produced* illustrating Piaget's theory of the early growth of intelligence, the topic of memory is ingeniously explored. There is a film called *Object Permanence,* in which the task of the year-old baby is to find a small toy that has been hidden under a scarf or some other piece of fabric. The year-old baby usually does not have much trouble whipping that scarf off the toy and finding it; but if there arc three scarfs on top of the toy, the twelve-month-old baby very often pulls off the first scarf and then seems confused and gives up. The two-year-old baby, on the other hand, will continue to pull scarfs off until he finds the toy. While one cannot be certain, it is reasonable to assume that the persistence of the image of the missing toy is greater in the mind of the two-year-old child than it is in the case of the one-year-old or younger child.

It would appear that persistent images—or memory—are necessary in order for the child to stick to the task and to finally get the item he is after. There is reason to believe that the child in Phase IV has a very limited memory of this sort. Even if the seven- or eight-month-old child is presented with an object, plays with it, enjoys it, and then has that object hidden before his very eyes under a scarf, the chances are not very good that he will seek it out. The child's memory development is probably quite limited in Phase IV, but it is progressing.

---

* With Ina Uzgiris of Clark University, Worcester, Massachusetts.

EMOTIONALITY

As previously mentioned, the emotional tone of most babies, especially during the first half of this phase, is one of contentment or delight. This is especially true in terms of interpersonal relations. This is also a time when children exhibit rather abrupt mood changes. A baby who is crying can often be easily induced to stop crying and to start smiling, even laughing. This capacity to move quickly from one mood state to another is rather remarkable, and it is probably somewhat related to the baby's lack of memory.

MOTOR AND SENSORIMOTOR SKILLS

Motor skills that are routinely appearing in Phase IV have already been listed and discussed to some degree. Motor development plays a very important instrumental role in early education.

As a child acquires each new ability, he gains additional freedom to become educated, because he is gradually shedding limitations he was saddled with at birth. The activities of dropping and throwing objects, and what these activities teach about object qualities and the physics of objects, are much easier and better entered into, for example, once the child can sit unaided. After all, lying on his back or even his stomach does not allow him to drop objects very far, or to throw them very well, or to monitor their movements. Again, once the child starts crawling the opportunities for learning become considerably greater than they were until that point in time.

SOCIABILITY

We have already remarked under the section on emotionality that it is during times when the child is interacting with others that he most often reveals his capacity for hilarity and pleasure at this phase. We have also noted that as Phase IV draws to a close, the child will begin to stop feeling affection for *all* people. He will start to narrow down to the nuclear family as preferred people, and he will become shy or apprehensive with others at times. His disposition may also be marred by the pending eruption of teeth.

LANGUAGE

Somewhere toward the end of Phase IV the baby's first words will begin to have actual meaning for him. By this I mean that the word "bottle" will signify a bottle, or something that looks like a bottle, and nothing else. Also the baby's own name means *him* rather than anything or anyone else; and "Mommy" or some reasonable facsimile means only his mother rather than his mother and his father. By referring back to page 84 you can see just what these first words are likely to be.

The Phase IV baby is not likely to understand even the simplest instructions, but very soon he will. Once he starts to learn language you will witness a remarkably interesting process. The rate at which he will acquire ability in this area is breathtaking, particularly for parents who experience it for the first time. However, one caution. Although he may acquire tremendous skill very rapidly over the next year or so, he may very well not *say* anything at all during that time. It is not unusual for children not to utter words until they are one and one-half or even two years of age. What you should watch for is how rapidly they are learning to *understand* words, phrases, and grammatical structures.

RECOMMENDED CHILD-REARING PRACTICES
AT THIS STAGE

GENERAL REMARKS

I have characterized Phase IV as the last period of infancy during which you will be living with an essentially stationary creature. It should thereby be enjoyed as the lull before the storm.

Prior to eight months of age there is, of course, difficulty of one sort or another. Some infants go through problem periods during their first months that are lumped under the title of colic. Other infants may not sleep through the night, especially during their first six weeks. Some infants experience discomfort associated with precocious teething. But from eight months on, the difficulty one experiences in child-rearing is of a somewhat different order. Once the baby starts to crawl about the home you are going to have much to cope with, both in terms of the very real dangers he exposes himself to and *in terms of the possibilities of missing the boat on one or another important educational process.*

GIVING THE BABY A FEELING OF BEING LOVED AND CARED FOR

Assuring the Phase IV child that he is cared for can be pursued in ways similar to those that I have recommended for the preceding three phases. Perhaps the only difference of consequence in this particular phase is that affectionate interplay with the baby now is even more rewarding than it was before, thanks to the Phase IV baby's greater responsiveness. Furthermore, you can use the interplay to focus the child's interest on various events. If, for example, while changing the child's diaper you talk about the process, referring to the diaper pins, powder, and Pampers or whatever, you will on the one hand begin to help him form linkages between words and things, and on the other hand begin to focus his attention on sequences of activities. If you engage in a peekaboo game, or point out something about his own feet (which he has, after all, had relatively little experience hearing labeled), you may help to reinforce his basic curiosity.

HELPING THE BABY DEVELOP SPECIFIC SKILLS

Language

As we have seen, language development begins in earnest during this phase for most children. I would suggest two kinds of activities on the part of child-rearers in regard to the encouragement of early language development.

Talking to your child. During Phase IV you should get used to talking to your child, doing so in a manner that is functionally effective with someone of very limited language skills. The talk should be concrete, not abstract. You should not refer to events that took place yesterday or may take place in the future, nor should you talk very much about ideas to a child of this age. There is nothing intrinsically bad about language in those domains, but most of it will go over the baby's head. You and the baby are much better off if you will concentrate on tying your language to the here and now, talking about the sock that you are putting on, or the toy you are holding before the baby, or some feature of your face or the baby's fingers.

When speaking to a Phase IV child, refer as much as you can to things that are actually present and perceivable by the baby. If you get into the habit of such talk, it will be useful to the baby. In addition, you will avoid the tendency of many adults to say very little to their babies until such time as the baby shows that he is a linguistic creature by substantial speaking. If you wait for children to make it clear to you that they are linguistically able by speaking, you may find that you have to wait until the child is a year and one-half or two years of age. Yet we know that many children learn their first words before they are eight months of age, and have a receptive vocabulary of several dozen words by the time they are a year old. It is understandable why some people do not speak very much to a baby who is less than a year and one-half old. Monologues are not very rewarding. Unfortunately, however, if you both remain silent, the baby will be missing an opportunity to learn language.

Reading aloud. The second way you can begin to provide opportunities for language development is to read simple stories to your baby *just before he falls asleep.* Although not mandatory, listening to stories is probably useful to some children, and story reading is consistent with the notion of a close relationship between mother and child. I suggest that the stories be read at bedtime because as the child moves out of Phase IV he is going to be harder and harder to corner. You will have a great deal of difficulty getting his attention for any length of time. Trying to read a story to him is not often going to be successful. If he is quite sleepy and is lying in his crib or in your lap, during the day or in the evening, you will find him a much more receptive listener. It is at times such as these that I suggest you try simple storytelling. Do not assume that he has much in the way of an elaborate vocabulary or capacity for dealing with complicated ideas. The stories should be very simple until he gets to be about a year and one-half old.

Motor skills

Motor development is dramatic in Phase IV and it will proceed pretty much on its own. You can, however, facilitate progress somewhat and you should at least be advised as to what is happening so you do not inadvertently impede it. Once again, the central skills that are emerging are torso control (turning over), the ability to sit unaided, some form of crawling, and continued leg development in the form of increasingly frequent and powerful leg extensions.

There is little you can do to encourage the development of torso control or the ability to assume a sitting position. I do, however, *strongly urge you to provide opportunities for the baby to acquire the ability to move about.* This means getting into the habit of putting the child on the floor, preferably on a blanket, and clothed in such a manner that he is not likely to get splinters, or otherwise injure himself, then letting go. If you make extensive use of a playpen or a crib, jump seat, highchair, play-and-feed table, or any other device that effectively prevents him from crawling, you will, of course, reduce several problems caused by the new mobility, but probably do so at the expense of the baby's development.

A crib device along the lines of the Playtential Thumpy toy will provide opportunities for a child to practice kicking at this point. He will also enjoy being held in an upright position with the opportunity to push against some solid surface. Walkers and jumpers are popular with Phase IV babies, but as I said earlier should be used with caution. More about these in the sections on materials.

Intelligence

There are many ways in which you can encourage your child's intellectual growth at this stage.

Providing suitable small objects. As we have seen, this is a period when children enjoy dropping, banging, and throwing small objects for the very first time. In order to pursue these perfectly natural processes, children need access to a fair number of droppable, throwable, bangable objects. Bear in mind that these objects should not be too small. Anything much below one and one-half inches in any of its dimensions might very well get stuck in the child's throat. Beware as well of very small parts of larger objects that could break off.

Exposure to small mechanisms. Another area in which the Phase IV child shows interest, as noted earlier, is in how things work, or cause-and-effect mechanisms. You probably will begin to see some interest in the working of light switches at this point. If you operate a light switch, directing a baby's attention to what happens to the lights in the room, you will begin to see a dawning of interest. He will also show interest in the jack-in-the-box toys during Phase IV.

Setting up simple problems. The Phase IV child also shows increasing interest in solving simple problems. The first problems that he is likely to be able to cope with at this stage may involve moving something out of his way when he is trying to procure an object. The baby on his stomach at six or seven months of age is usually capable of reaching out with one hand while supporting his upper torso with the other arm or elbow. If objects are in the way he will become increasingly sophisticated about moving them aside in order to get what he is after. Although during Phase IV out of sight is still out of mind, you can begin to play hide-and-seek games with him, using your own face or any small object in which he may show an interest.

In summary, then, by providing a goodly number of small objects and allowing your child to indulge himself in dropping, banging, and throwing, as well as performing other simple actions with them, you will be feeding one process of mental growth. By giving him some exposure to the way simple mechanisms work, you will be nourishing another process. And by setting up very simple problems for him, those that involve an occasional easy-to-surmount obstacle in the way of his procuring some desirable object, or in little hide-and-seek games, you will be providing a third kind of input to mental growth.

Hide-and-seek

ENCOURAGING INTEREST IN THE OUTSIDE WORLD (CURIOSITY)

In your use of language during your friendly give-and-take with the baby, and in the provision of small objects and related materials for the child, you will be simultaneously encouraging and broadening the growth of his curiosity.

RECOMMENDED MATERIALS FOR THIS AGE

CRIB DEVICES

I have already mentioned the kind of crib kick-device that I know is enjoyable to children in this age range. The baby's interest in simple mechanisms can be fed by directing his attention to the various mechanisms you routinely use, such as water faucets or stoppers in a tub or sink. In addition, there are a few toys on the market which can be suspended above the supine baby and will give him a chance to activate simple cause-and-effect mechanisms.

In selecting crib toys for the Phase IV baby, you should look for devices that are relatively easy for the child to operate. Toys that provide the child with a large and relatively stationary object to pull on are within the child's capacities, and should give him pleasure.

MIRRORS, STUFFED TOYS, AND BALLS

The Phase IV child shows a declining interest in his own mirror image, but the use of mirrors above the changing table or the crib is still advisable. There are quite a number of stuffed toys available for a child of this age. I do not see anything particularly wrong with them, but you should not expect a baby of this (or any other) age to spend much time with a stuffed toy. He may occasionally look at it or gum it, but it is not likely to occupy his attention for long. Toward the end of Phase IV it is wise to start providing your child with balls of various sizes. The child who can move about is a child who becomes particularly interested in balls, partly because they can be made to travel so far with such a little effort on his part, and partly because they are things to be retrieved and as such fit into his growing capacities to move about and to handle objects.

OBJECTS TO COLLECT

Many materials that will keep your child interested for a relatively long time at this age can be procured free of charge. If you allow a child from the time he is five or six months of age to spend a good deal of time on a blanket on the floor with a variety of small objects and a few containers to put them in, you will find he will spend a good deal of time exploring those objects and practicing simple skills with them. These objects should be from two to five inches in size. Some should have fine details to be fingered and looked at because of the particular interest of children of this age in small visual detail. They should be many sizes, shapes, and textures. Also provide the baby with a container or two into which to put these objects and out of which he can pour them. This interest in exploring small objects and in practicing simple skills on them is directly at the center of the educational process at this age and will stay there for a good year. You might just as well begin to encourage it at this point.

STACKING TOYS

Beyond this concept of a collection of different types of small objects, you might begin to exploit the tendency of the baby to want to put objects into and out of each other. You can, for example, provide plastic cups that will nest. As long as they do not stick together you will have toys that are suitable for a child of this age. There is a widely available commercial toy that is good for this purpose. It consists of several plastic doughnuts of different colors and sizes, and a tapered wooden base. The doughnuts can be stacked onto the base according to their size. This and similar stacking toys are available for relatively small amounts of money. Bear in mind, however, that the child's talents are as yet still quite modest. Do not be surprised if something that seems trivially easy to you is very difficult for him.

INFANT SEATS

I recommend the infant seat for use at this stage because it gives you an opportunity to have the child near you during the day, facilitating affectionate interchanges. Bear in mind, however, that as the child nears the end of Phase IV the infant seat will become less and less appropriate because he will be impatient sitting in it for very long and because he will get to be big enough so that it becomes somewhat unstable and possibly dangerous.

WALKERS

Walkers for infants have good and bad features. A good feature is that they permit an activity that fits naturally into the child's tendency to want to move about the home, to explore firsthand situations that he has seen from a distance. They also fit naturally into the child's desire to exercise his leg muscles, particularly if the distance between the bottom of the seat and the floor is just right. Nevertheless, the bad features must also be considered. The child in the walker is a child who not only can explore, but who can endanger himself much more easily than the child who is unable to move off a blanket in the middle of the floor. Therefore it becomes very important that you supervise your child closely if you let him use a walker. It is too easy for a child of six to seven months of age to injure himself seriously in a walker by pulling things down onto himself, or by stepping on materials that are unsafe, or by reaching with his hand into areas that are unsafe. Also be sure to choose a walker that is well made and stable and will not pinch your child's fingers or legs. In short, if you want to use a walker, fine, but be very careful.

MATERIALS NOT RECOMMENDED FOR THIS AGE

Under this heading I am obliged, again, to lump most commercially available toys.

BUSY BOXES

There is an interesting story about the now-legendary busy box that I like to tell. Busy boxes have been available commercially for some time, and they have enjoyed a good deal of popularity. But busy boxes are not very interesting to infants. By this I mean that if you watch a fair number of infants repeatedly, you will find that beyond the initial exploratory interest they show in any new object, they rarely spend much time with the toy in the weeks that follow its introduction. Busy boxes usually do have a few cause-and-effect mechanisms. There is usually a small squeaky horn; there are spring-loaded devices that make sharp sounds when an object is pushed along a track; there are colored balls or wheels that flash alternating colors when they are rotated; and there is the ever-present telephone dial mechanism. The fact is that none of these objects is very appealing to an infant at any stage of his development. An inexpensive eighteen-inch-diameter plastic beach ball will provide twenty times the number of hours of enjoyment than any current commercially made busy box. Infants seem to demand more variety in terms of feedback than they get as a result of the actions of busy box items. One of the reasons a mirror is so interesting to a young child is that he never sees exactly the same thing twice. Even simply changing the expression on his face produces a different visual feed-back. But when he pushes a little button that produces a horn squeak on so many available infant toys, all he ever gets is the same old horn squeak. It just is not enough. The reason such toys have sold so well in the past is simply because they have not had any competition.

Interestingly, one of the best of the toy companies has just moved into this field and has started to market a more elaborate busy box than the older one on the market, again not realizing that neither toy has much play value. Nevertheless, the new toy is selling better than the old toy and the new company is making money on it.

There have been some high-powered, very ambitious toy companies in the infancy field over the last few years and one of them has advocated that you purchase a reasonably expensive device to help your child crawl. I strongly urge you to forget this one. The idea is to lay the child on a piece of heavy-duty plastic with rollers under it and encourage him to propel himself with his hands and feet. As far as I can see, children very rarely enjoy this toy at any age. It is fairly expensive, and it just does not have anything to offer beyond a rather imaginative name.

JUMPERS

The jumpers that became popular a few years ago, featuring a canvas seat or swing suspended by a spring-loaded support hung from the top of a doorway, are controversial today. People in pediatric orthopedics have remarked that they really feel there is a danger to the growing bones of an infant from a jouncing injury that is sometimes involved. Since I am not a physician, I cannot comment firsthand on this device. From a play-value viewpoint I would say that a properly designed toy of this sort would be enjoyed by most children in this particular age period. But I would certainly recommend that you check it out with your pediatrician before you use such a device.

PLAYPENS

Finally we turn to the topic of playpens. Playpens have been sold in huge quantities in this country for some time now. They certainly play a valuable role as a way of preventing certain kinds of accidents with young children, but I strongly urge you to consider other ways of preventing such accidents. The main reason I say this is that children are usually put into playpens when they first begin to move about. The very word "playpen" means that you are penning a child in to play in a restricted area. You pen him in to either stop him from moving about or to protect him from other children. We have watched hundreds of babies of all ages in playpens for hours at a time and we have come to one simple conclusion: *There is no way of keeping most children from being bored in a playpen for longer than a very brief period of time*, perhaps ten to twenty minutes.

It is my view that to bore a child on a daily basis by the regular use of a playpen is a very poor child-rearing practice in terms of the child's educational needs. The same principle applies to the use of cribs, jump seats, highchairs, and play-and-feed tables, to the extent that any one of these devices is used for the purpose of restricting the child's movement about the home. I will discuss this situation in greater detail in the next chapter, as we move fully into the phenomenon of exploration of the home by the crawling baby. Basically I believe that caging your child as a way of saving work and aggravation, as well as preventing accidents, is the wrong way to go.

BEHAVIORS THAT SIGNAL THE ONSET OF PHASE V

LOCOMOBILITY

Locomobility, the ability to move the entire body through space, usually through crawling, is one of the most dramatic and consequential new behaviors of infancy. It emerges at about eight months of age, and plays a very large role in the story of how to educate an infant. Locomobility and its repercussions will be discussed in detail in the next chapter. If you leave the Phase IV child (certainly in the early stages of that period) on a blanket in the center of a floor, he will very probably be in the same place, give or take a few inches, when you return five minutes later. The Phase V baby, who can crawl or scoot about, definitely will not be in the same place very often after five minutes. There is no mistaking this new behavior. When the baby can crawl or move about in any manner beyond a few inches or so you will know it. Some babies do not begin to move any distance of consequence immediately. For other babies there is a period of a few days when they may be able to move back and forth a few inches, perhaps even a foot or two, before they enter into that period when they can move across a room. At any rate, once locomobility has begun, you have entered Phase V—so brace yourself.

THE UNDERSTANDING OF THE FIRST WORDS

As babies enter the eighth or ninth month, the first few words begin to have meaning for them. We have noted that the first words that are likely to cause unmistakable signs of recognition on the part of the baby are such words as "Mommy," "Daddy," "bye-bye," and "baby." You can tell if the word "Mommy" means *mother* by having someone else, usually the father, ask the child where Mommy is. If you keep asking, "Where is Mommy?" when she is nearby and when there are one or two other people to choose from, and if the baby turns toward his mother and smiles when he does so, then you begin to get a reasonably reliable indication that the word is linked to his mother. Although it may not be exclusively linked to his mother, it might be used for any creature that generally resembles his mother.

Soon thereafter children begin to understand simple instructions. One of the first is commonly found, for obvious reasons, to be, "Wave bye-bye." Waving bye-bye is generally an easily identified activity; when children begin to do it on command and with some regularity, it is reasonable to assume that they have linked those words to a particular behavior pattern. Other typical simple instructions that are part of the early repertoire of a child are "Stop that," "Kiss me," "Sit down," "Get up," and "Come here."

A *POSSIBLE* CHANGE IN BEHAVIOR TOWARD NONFAMILY MEMBERS

This sounds like an unusual title for an emergent behavior, and up until very recently I perhaps would have simply said, a change in behavior toward nonfamily members. However, the results of recent research force me to hedge the statement. Eight months has traditionally been considered to be an age at which babies exhibit rather striking fear reactions to nonfamily members for the first time. Closer inspection of the phenomenon, however, suggests that this so-called "stranger anxiety" is not universal, nor always intense. Nevertheless, from this point on the child's social sophistication increases steadily and is fascinating to observe. During the second year of life, for example, the child's entire world will revolve around his primary caretaker (usually his mother). He will then gradually move off during the third year toward a beginning interest in socialization with children his own age.

The first eight months of life by and large can be characterized as a period wherein the baby is maximally attracted to all other people, and for very good reason—survival. Somewhere in the vicinity of eight months of age that process comes to an end. The child usually starts to become more selective as he begins to really form a unique attachment relationship. At about this time you will probably begin to notice a slight wariness in the baby's behavior when someone not in the nuclear family comes close to his face, and do not be surprised if that wariness changes to outright screaming. This change in behavior, starting at about eight months of age, is again a sign that signals the emergence of Phase V.

CHAPTER 6

FROM EIGHT

to

FOURTEEN MONTHS

of AGE

GENERAL REMARKS

THE SPECIAL IMPORTANCE OF THIS PERIOD OF LIFE

With the onset of Phase V, the parent assumes a new, challenging, and considerably more significant role. Whereas most families in this country today get their children through the first six to eight months of life reasonably well educated and developed, I have come to the conclusion that *relatively few families, perhaps no more than ten percent, manage to get their children through the eight- to thirty-six-month age period as well educated and developed as they can and should be.* This statement underlies my dedication to the subject of education in the first years of life.

Not all professionals agree with me. There are people in child psychiatry, for example, who think that the first weeks of life are the most important and that prospective parents must be educated in the best way to establish a healthy mother-child relationship. My response is that I am as much an advocate of love and a close emotional relationship as anybody, but I do not believe that there really are very many parents who do *not* establish a good solid relationship with their children in the first months of life.

There are, of course, exceptions. Tragically, every day of the year some small fraction of our families is doing an apparently abominable job with young children. There are children who are abused physically, children in family situations so burdened with problems that neglect takes a heavy toll, and of course there is the special case of children afflicted with disease or physical anomalies. But my remarks are not addressed to these extreme cases. They are addressed to the ninety percent or more of our families who do not have to cope with such extraordinary difficulties.

103

There is a good deal of information that suggests that sometime during the middle of the *second* year of life, children begin to reveal which way they are headed developmentally. Most children of this age begin to produce performances on achievement measures that increasingly represent the kinds of levels of achievement they will be reaching and attaining in the years to follow, including the school years. Put another way, in the earlier phases—I through IV—and at the beginning of Phase V as well, what a child scores on tests of intelligence, motor ability, language, and social skills does not seem to bear any meaningful relationship to what he will score on similar tests when he is two or three years of age. The only exception to this concerns the children in the five percent group who look seriously weak from birth and who, in tests during the first year of life, consistently score very much below most of the population.

The fact that test scores in the first year of life generally have no predictive power is an old, very well-established finding. It is a finding that people who emphasize development in the first months of life have great difficulty explaining away. To be sure, there is always the possibility that problems created in the first months of life may not reveal themselves until considerably later in the child's life. Nevertheless, there is also the real possibility that what people are claiming as problems in the first months are not indeed so very important. My own feeling is that *the reason we do not see dramatic evidence of poor development in the first year of the lives of most children who will do poorly later is simply that they have not yet actually developed the deficits*.

Groups of children who go on to underachieve in the elementary grades almost never look particularly weak in terms of achievement at one year of age, but only begin to lag behind as a group sometime toward the end of the second year of life. Such children, on standardized language and intelligence tests, for example, will pretty clearly reveal where they are headed educationally by the time they are three years of age. In report after report—whether from low-income urban American children or from children from low-income homes in Africa, India, or other places around the world—the pattern of findings is pretty much the same. These disadvantaged children make a fairly good showing during the first year of life on standard baby tests like the Gesell, even if they have not had the best of nutrition, and even if their parents have had little

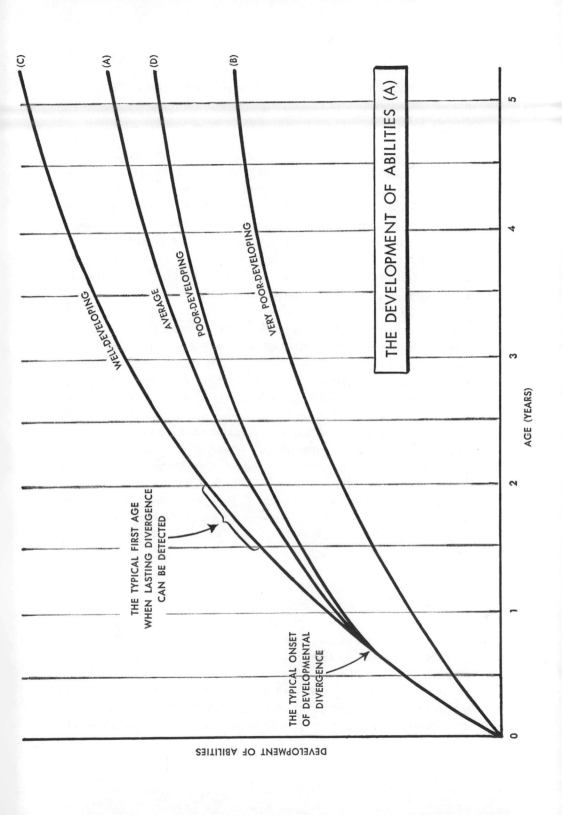

THE DEVELOPMENT OF ABILITIES (A)

DEVELOPMENT OF ABILITIES

AGE (YEARS)

(C) WELL-DEVELOPING
(A) AVERAGE
(D) POOR-DEVELOPING
(B) VERY POOR-DEVELOPING

THE TYPICAL FIRST AGE WHEN LASTING DIVERGENCE CAN BE DETECTED

THE TYPICAL ONSET OF DEVELOPMENTAL DIVERGENCE

or no education. It is not until they reach the middle of the second year of life, at the earliest, that scores begin to slide. Subsequently, it is all downhill. That is, it is all downhill for such *groups* of children, not necessarily for every *individual* child within those groups.

It is very important to point out that many low-income children are *not* underachievers. Vast numbers of these children, both in this and other countries around the world, develop just about as well as any children during the first two years of their life. Many do average or above-average work from the elementary grades right on through graduate school. To be born into a low-income family is very far from being a guarantee of academic underachievement.

What I have described is complicated, emotionally charged, and highly confusing. Perhaps it is best to summarize this situation with a graph (page 105).

Curve *A* represents development for most children. In this figure I am referring to overall ability—not just to performance on an IQ test, but to all the major abilities of the young human, including his social and language skills. This curve *(A)* refers to the average child from birth all the way through five and one-half years. You will note there is a secondary curve *(B)* that starts low. That curve represents the five percent of the population that for one extreme reason or another is in large trouble right from birth or shortly thereafter. That group stays in large trouble. Note that starting at about eight months of age I have sketched in two additional curves *(C* and *D)*. One moves up more rapidly than the average; the other falls back as compared with the average. Note that at about eight months of age, the divergence of *A*, *C*, and *D* begin.

THE EFFECT OF REARING CONDITIONS
ON DEVELOPMENT

Let us move on to a subsidiary point which I want to keep separate in an attempt to avoid confusion. During the ten years I spent studying the role of experience in the development of children in the first six months of life, I learned many interesting things concerning the rate of development as a function of different kinds of experiences in those early months. Through experimentation with physically normal children, I became convinced that the rate at which children acquire abilities in the first six months of life, at least in regard to visual motor skills and foundations of intelligence, can be modified rather dramatically by the manipulation of rearing conditions.

It has long been known that you can easily prevent a child from reaching any significant level of development in the first six months of life. What we also learned in our ten years of research was that if you provide certain circumstances for the young child in those first months of life, he can achieve some kinds of skills considerably earlier than what is typical for the average child—indeed, in some cases even earlier than the precocious child.

Take the skill of visually directed reaching which, as we have seen, is normally acquired at about five to five and one-half months of age by children in this society, as well as in most others that have been tested. Our studies, in which we provided objects for children to look at, bat, feel, and play with, starting from when they were three or four weeks of age, resulted in the acquisition of mature reaching at about three months of age. Not only is this a considerable acceleration of the acquisitional process, but, perhaps more important, the children involved had a marvelous time engaging in these activities. During the fourth month they were full of enthusiasm, giggled excitedly, played with the objects around them, looked happily into a mirror that we had placed overhead, and did a good deal of vocalizing. You can see how this kind of pleasurable and occasionally exciting play fits into the aforementioned goals of supporting the development of specific skills while nurturing the zest for life and curiosity of a child. The children who went through those studies seemed to be spirited and terribly interested children at six and seven months of age, much more so than children who were like them at the outset but who had not gone through those particular experiences. It was from those research studies that we were able to generate the commercial line of toys, Playtentials.

What all of this adds up to is that we now have information at hand which will enable us to provide future children, at least in principle, with circumstances that are more suited to their earliest needs and interests than the circumstances to which they are normally exposed. It also means, very probably, that what we now call a normal rate of development will be considered—thirty or forty years from now—to be a slow pace. As you look at the following figure (page 109) you will see that in addition to the same curves that appear in the preceding one, there is an additional curve that suggests the course of accelerated development of children in our research studies in the first six months of life. This curve goes on to become curve E, which suggests what optimal development might look like fifty years from today.

But let us get back to today. In the research of the last several years we arrived at another telling conclusion. In addition to the notion that somewhere between the first and third birthdays children are beginning to reveal where they are headed in later years, we have come to the conclusion that *to begin to look at a child's educational development when he is two years of age is already much too late, particularly in the area of social skills and attitudes*. We find the two-year-old is a rather complicated, firmly established social being. We find it not uncommon that a two-year-old is already badly spoiled and very difficult to live with, or in more tragic situations, alienated from people, including his own family. We have seen these phenomena over and over again. On the other hand, we rarely see an eight-, nine-, or ten-month-old child who in any way seems to be spoiled or particularly well differentiated socially. Up through Phase IV a child is, comparatively speaking, a very simple social creature.

You can trace your child's evolution as he goes from eight to twenty-four months of age by keeping a step-by-step journal and taking movies of him, preferably sound movies, if possible. This will confirm the fact that the twenty-four-month-old child is as different from the eight-month-old as the eight-month-old is from the newborn. Human growth is a remarkable process.

From the above discussion you can see that the period that starts at eight months and ends at three years is a period of primary importance in the development of a human being. And the period eight to fourteen months of age is the first major phase of that exciting time span.

Educational goals

Over the years three useful ways of describing educational goals of the period from eight months through three years have emerged. One deals with the child's major interest patterns. We have found that all healthy eight-month-old children seem motivated by three major interests aside from the fundamental physiological needs such as hunger, thirst, freedom from pain, etc. These three major interests are: the

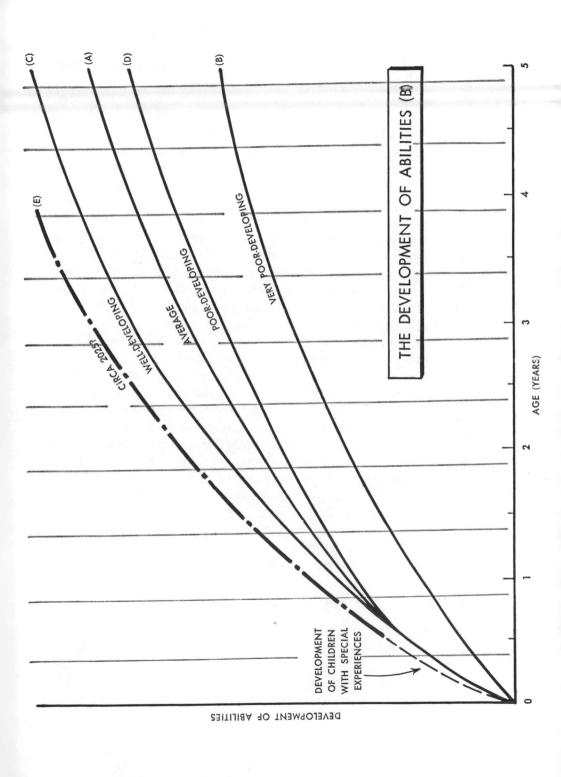

THE DEVELOPMENT OF ABILITIES (B)

DEVELOPMENT OF ABILITIES

AGE (YEARS)

(C)
(A)
(D)
(B)
(E)

CIRCA 2025?

WELL-DEVELOPING

AVERAGE

POOR-DEVELOPING

VERY POOR-DEVELOPING

DEVELOPMENT
OF CHILDREN
WITH SPECIAL
EXPERIENCES

primary caretaker, exploration of the world as a whole, and mastering newly emerging motor abilities. These interests have obvious specific survival value. They start out vigorous and in balance in all healthy eight-month-old babies. When development goes well, they each grow steadily and the balance is maintained. Very often, however, they develop unevenly between eight and twenty-four months of age, and the results are mildly or severely debilitating. Guiding the balanced and rich growth of these primary interests will be discussed in later sections.

A second way of discussing educational goals is to talk of emerging competencies of special importance. These competencies are by no means guaranteed to develop well. I'm referring to the pattern of intellectual, linguistic, perceptual, and social competencies our research has found typical of beautifully developed three- to six-year-old children. These processes sometimes overlap with the processes to be discussed under the other ways of dealing with educational goals. They will be dealt with repeatedly throughout later sections of the book. At this point, I would like to single out three social competencies that emerge in Phase V for special mention. Toward the end of the first year, children begin to realize older people can be helpful. They begin to deliberately seek assistance from them. This behavior we call using an adult as a resource. Shortly after the first birthday, two other very important social potencies emerge. Seeking approval for a simple motor achievement or for a "cute" behavior seems to indicate the first feelings of pride in achievement. Finally, at about the same time, children begin to manifest simple make-believe or fantasy behavior. Common examples are "talking" on a toy telephone or pretending to be driving a toy truck, car, or airplane. Each of these emergents seems to play a special role in educational development. More on this topic will follow.

The third way is to emphasize four key goals which are commonly accepted by most people knowledgeable in early human development. These goals are language development, the development of curiosity, social development, and nurturing the roots of intelligence.

Language development
We have seen that while children may respond to words in some simple fashion during the first six or seven months of life, there is no indication whatsoever that they understand the meaning of those words. Their response is really an affair that involves the sound qualities of the words—the association of the particular patterns of a mother's voice, for example, with the pleasure in her presence. But they do not respond

differently to their own name or to some other name. They do not know, for example, that the word "Mommy" means only one person. But at about seven or eight months of age they begin to learn language.

By three years of age, experts estimate that most children understand most of the language that they will use for the rest of their lives in ordinary conversation. Notice I said most children *understand* most of the language they will use in ordinary conversation. There is an important difference between the growth of *understanding* language and the growth of *producing* language. Children begin to learn to understand language earlier and at a more rapid rate than they learn to use it orally. The first five or six words should be fairly well understood by the time a child is nine or ten months of age. But he may not *say* five or six words until he is two years of age or even older. Nevertheless, in both cases he may be a very normal child.

Language, like so many of the issues we will talk about, is interrelated during the first years of life with other major developments. There is no way that a young child can do well on an intelligence test at three or four years of age, for example, unless his language development is good. You can usually predict a child's IQ once he gets to be three or four years of age with reasonable accuracy from any reliable assessment of his language skills.

Over and above language's fundamental role in the development of intelligence, it plays an extremely important part in the development of social skills. So much of what transpires between any two people involves either listening to or expressing language. And so, in a very significant way, good language development underlies good social development.

The development of curiosity

Just about everyone knows that kittens go through a stage during which they are incredibly curious. We also know that monkeys and puppies are similar in this regard. Indeed, it appears that almost all young mammals go through an early period when they are consumed by the need to explore. This is even true, I learned recently, of young horses. We have never really pinpointed such a stage with man before, and I think this is simply because the people charged with the responsibility of doing research on early human development have left much of that research undone to this point in time. We believe, however, that we have filled this informational gap through extensive home observations of a wide variety of children.

We have never come across an eight-month-old child who was not incredibly curious. We have never come across an eight-month-old child who needed to be reinforced for exploration of the home once he could crawl. Bear in mind that to have a very strong exploratory drive is vitally important for humans in that unlike most other animals, humans go through a very long developmental period, and come equipped with fewer instincts than other animals with which to cope with the world.

Nothing is more fundamental to solid educational development than pure uncontaminated curiosity.

Social development

The two-year-old child is an extremely complicated and sophisticated social creature. His social world, for the most part, revolves around his primary caretaker (who is usually his mother); and ordinarily he has worked out with her an extraordinary contract full of ifs, ands, and buts which describes a great deal about the various possibilities for him within the home. He has learned specifically what he can and cannot play with in each room in the home. He has learned how much he can get away with with his mother. He has learned whether or not she is a generally friendly person. He has learned all the subtle cues that help him to identify what her mood state is at any given moment. He has usually learned a whole other set of information about his father and about siblings, particularly those close in age to him. He may have, at age two, developed into a delightful human being who is a pleasure to live with, a mini-companion good for all sorts of genuinely pleasant experiences; or more sadly, he may have developed into an overindulged child who constantly badgers his mother, particularly if there is a younger child in the home. He may become, in other words, extraordinarily difficult to live with and regularly unpleasant. Even sadder is the case of the child who at two has been consistently turned off by people, who has learned to be an isolate, one who has never had the pleasure of a free and easy rewarding relationship with another human being.

These are the three major patterns we have seen. There are all sorts of variations on these themes, but it seems to us that the process which leads to one or another of these states, or something similar to them, begins in earnest somewhere around seven or eight months of age.

Nurturing the roots of intelligence

As we have seen, in Piaget's system the child of eight months of age has turned a corner wherein he leaves behind his early introduction to the world and to his own basic motor skills and starts to focus on the world of objects. The year or so that follows is a period of active exploration of simple cause-and-effect mechanisms; of the movement patterns of objects; of their texture qualities, shapes, and forms. This is an incredibly rich time during which the child's mind is undergoing basic development with respect to the prerequisites of higher forms of thinking. Surely, as far as education is concerned, few things are more central than the substructure of sensorimotor explorations upon which higher levels of intelligence are built.

In my opinion, *every one of the four educational goals and processes is at risk during the period from eight months to two years*. What do I mean by *at risk?* I mean that unlike the achievements of the first six or seven months of life, which I propose are more or less assured by virtue of their simple requirements and the characteristics of the average expectable environment, the educational goals of the eight-month to twenty-four-month period are by no means assured. It is not at all inevitable that a child will learn language as well as he might. It is not at all inevitable that he will have his curiosity deepened and broadened anywhere near as well as he might. It is not at all inevitable that his social development will take place in a solid and fruitful manner. And it is not at all inevitable that the substructure for intelligence will be built well. Indeed, I must repeat that on the basis of all I have learned in close to two decades, no more than one child in ten achieves the levels of ability in each of these four fundamental areas that he could achieve.

OBSTACLES TO OPTIMAL ACHIEVEMENTS IN THE FOUR FUNDAMENTAL EDUCATIONAL PROCESSES

As I see it, there are three kinds of obstacles to successful educational development in the eight- to twenty-four-month age range. They are ignorance, stress, and lack of assistance.

Ignorance
Typical young parents are quite unprepared for the responsibility of educating their first baby. As noted earlier, we do nothing in this country, in a systematic way, to educate couples for the responsibility of parenting young children. Even if we did, there would be yet another fundamental problem, the fact that we simply did not have enough useful information.

We know, of course, when the typical baby starts to walk, to sit unaided, to wave bye-bye, and so forth. But sophisticated, extensive, and detailed information about the growth of the young human, and especially about the causes of good or poor growth, has been in remarkably short supply in spite of all the opinions and all the words that have been written on the topic. The problem is simply that the people who are supposed to produce the information—that is, psychological and educational research people—while acknowledging the importance of the processes developing in the first three years of life, have not, for one reason or another, developed the necessary knowledge. After all, if you wanted to do research on a very young child, up until very recently the only way you could do it would be to go out to his own home or to make an appointment for him to come into your office or your laboratory. Going out to the home is a relatively inconvenient affair. It is also an extremely inefficient way to do research. It is much easier to have a group of college sophomores beating a path to your laboratory, where they can be researched upon for thirty minutes at a time. Studying a child in his own environment not only necessitates transportation to and from his home, but more important, does not provide conditions good for this kind of research. The college sophomore coming into a psychology laboratory to be a subject does not bring his parents along. He is not overly apprehensive about what might happen to him, and he has been conditioned for many years to do what he is told, particularly when he is told to do something by someone with high prestige or someone who is going to give him a grade in a course. Furthermore, there are so many different kinds of children. It is not scientifically proper to make general statements about children on the basis of one middle-class Protestant child. Samples must be drawn from all the major types of children, depending on the particular topic under study. And, of course, on one day a child of two years of age may do one thing in a test situation or in his spontaneous behavior; the next day, or even an hour later, he may do something else. You cannot assume that if you have gone to a home one, two, three, four, or five times that you have gotten a fair sample of a child's behavior.

All in all, it is not surprising that the actual basic building of a science of human development has made so little progress in spite of hundreds of millions of dollars poured into the enterprise by the federal government and private foundations. In spite of the fact that during the last ten years or so this situation has been improving, as I look about my office at the several hundred books on young children that line my shelves, I know that parents cannot find in them the basic information they ought to have.

Such a situation, by the way, is an ideal one to stimulate all sorts of misinformation to be offered to the public, and indeed, you can find many programs in existence which purport to help the parent in this regard. Scratch the surface of the programs, however, and look for the basis on which the recommendations about child-rearing are made and you will generally find that the basis is very shallow. There are a few exceptions. By and large, up until very recently, if you wanted legitimate information about raising a very young child, I frankly think you would have been better off asking an intelligent well-put-together mother of four or five children than if you had tried almost any other approach to the problem.

The problem of stress
Not only are families unaware of what they should know about early human development, but in addition they are put under a fair degree of stress in trying to do their job. When I say *they,* I am referring for the most part to the young mother, because by and large she is the one most likely to have the almost-total responsibility for a baby's upbringing. Major stress occurs routinely when the baby starts to crawl about the home, because he is then actually in physical danger. He is in danger because houses are not ordinarily designed for eight-month-old crawling babies; because babies are incredibly curious about everything they see and can reach; because they use their mouths as exploring organs; because they do not know very much about the characteristics of objects and about physical dangers; and because they are inadequate masters of their bodies.

What it all adds up to is a worried parent, and rightly so. The period from ten to thirty months of age, for example, is the time when something in the order of eighty percent of all reported accidental poisonings involving children take place. Remember that the child, when crawling about the kitchen, the living room, the bedroom, or the bathroom for the first few times, finds everything new. He has seen some of these things from a distance but he has never before been able to come up close to such intriguing objects as the shut-off valve behind the john; bits of beautiful, shiny glass from a broken jar that happened to fall in an out-of-the-way place; and interestingly frayed sections of lamp cords.

Babies do not know which physical objects are sturdy enough to support their weight and which will fall if leaned upon. And babies have poor memories at this point. There is nothing of more universal appeal to a ten-month-old than a set of stairs. Put him at the bottom and you can bet money (with confidence) that he will attempt to climb. Some ten-month-olds are pretty good at climbing three, four, or five stairs. Very commonly they will then pause, and in the moments that follow they may be distracted, perhaps by a mark on the bannister that captivates them or by a small toy left there by another child. This may cause them to forget where they are and simply turn around and fall down the stairs. No wonder anyone who is reasonable and loving worries about the safety and well-being of the child who is crawling about the home for the first time.

In addition to the stress from the worry about physical danger, there is also the stress from the extra work that a child of this age produces. If you give him a chance to roam about the home, you will find yourself spending more time during the course of the day straightening up the house, particularly if you or your husband happen to be compulsive about household neatness. Babies create clutter. It is as natural as breathing. A cluttered house with a ten-month-old baby is, all other things being equal, a good sign. In fact, an immaculately picked-up house and a ten-month-old baby who is developing well are, in my opinion, usually incompatible. If more husbands were aware of this contradiction, it would save a lot of grief.

Another source of stress at this time has to do with the actual damage a young child can do to a home. Babies of this age are not exactly graceful, nor are they aware of the value of objects. From time to time costly breakages may occur.

A fourth major source of stress which is extremely important has to do with ill feelings from older siblings directed toward the baby, particularly when the older sibling is a first child and less than three years older than the baby. It is extremely common to find deeply rooted feelings of anger and outright dislike on the part of the older sibling for the baby. This may express itself in nasty behavior to and even physical battering of the younger sibling, which at times can produce serious physical harm, and in many other ways which are difficult for most mothers to tolerate. We have found over and over again that when we begin to talk with mothers of five- to eight-month-old babies about that child's educational development, they pour their hearts out to us about the difficulties they are having with the two- or three-year-old. They simply cannot attend to the problems of the younger child until we give them some sort of assistance in coping with the havoc that is created by the older child. This is a problem which we will deal with in more detail later.

The final form of stress to the system has to do with the negativism that emerges with most children in the second half of the second year. Although the eight- to fourteen-month-old baby creates a good deal of stress because of the aforementioned reasons, there does not seem to be anything personal in his behavior. He is simply acting in accordance with his nature, rather than deliberately trying to aggravate or stress his parents. Not so the child of fifteen or sixteen months of age. It is perfectly normal for such children to begin to vie for supremacy in the home with the primary caretaker. Resistance to simple requests becomes very common at this time, and some parents find this behavior extremely difficult to take. This is an age when you see the spectacle of a young mother in a dawn-to-dusk struggle with the one and one-half-year-old child, trying somehow or other to regain control over the situation. If there is more than one young child around this can be a very trying time for a young family. We will go into more detail on this topic in the next chapter.

Lack of assistance

The final obstacle to facilitating optimal educational development has to do with the fact that by and large young parents have to go through these processes alone. Very often the mother does not even have the benefit of a sympathetic husband, and has to cope with his dissatisfaction during this period on top of everything else. Pediatricians vary in the degree to which they provide support; the ones that do provide intelligent support are revered, at least in my acquaintance. Very often, however, the pediatrician does not have any extensive background in these topics and is ill equipped to cope effectively with this part of his practice. The public educational system is gradually beginning to consider whether it should try to lend a helping hand, but by and large there are very few programs where educators assist parents in this situation. Occasionally public-health nurses, visiting nurses, home-study people, and child-study-association people provide some support. Indeed, there are even occasions where a young mother is on good terms with her mother or mother-in-law, in which case she can profit from the wisdom that experience and good sense often present in the minds of practiced mothers. By and large, however, the typical young family—and particularly the mother—has to go it alone.

GENERAL BEHAVIOR DURING THIS PERIOD

THE REMARKABLE CURIOSITY OF PHASE V

As noted earlier, at about eight months of age babies enter into a period that closely parallels the peak period of curiosity in the young of other mammals. One cannot help but be impressed by this curiosity, which shows itself in a love of physical exploration as soon as a baby can move his body through space. This behavior is highly predictable except in those children who are ill or seriously damaged.

It seems logical that in the course of the hundreds of hours prelocomotive children spend looking about at distant, unreachable objects, they build up quite a head of steam with respect to an interest in exploring the rooms within which they live. Regardless of whether or not such speculation is true, you can expect the crawling infant to explore if given the chance. If you have an eight-month-old child who shows no interest in exploring the environment, I would urge you to see your pediatrician or other health specialist to find out whether he is seriously ill or has some sort of physical handicap.

Things that most adults would find totally uninteresting absorb a baby. Do not be surprised if you find your child swinging a kitchen cabinet door several dozen times for several dozen consecutive days. Do not be surprised if small pieces of dust that are picked up from the floor intrigue him. Do not be surprised if he is fascinated by the cellophane wrapper from a package of cigarettes. At the same time, of course, razor blades will interest him, along with anything else that he can inspect closely, particularly if he can handle the object and bring it to his mouth. You can therefore sense the dual nature of curiosity. It is the motivational force underlying all learning and development and achievement; at the same time, it is the source of many childhood accidents and tragedies, and certainly causes a great deal of normal anxiety on the part of parents.

"Why? Because it's there."

MOTOR EXERCISE

The incredible curiosity of this period is accompanied by a continuing and very solid interest on the part of the baby in mastering the use of his body.

From eight to fourteen months of age, new motor skills of a very important kind continue to come in; it is the nature of the baby to practice every one of those skills repeatedly until he gets them right.

Crawling and climbing

The first motor skill of Phase V, as already mentioned, is some form of crawling. This initial locomotive skill is followed by the ability to get higher in space, a skill which takes two forms. The first of these is the initial ability to climb; the second is the ability to pull oneself up to a standing posture.

The ability to climb is an extraordinarily interesting and momentous affair. It generally appears in two stages with infants. The first stage emerges somewhere between eight and twelve months of age, when children can climb relatively modest heights, usually limited to about six inches at a time. You may find a child managing to ascend a low ottoman, for example, when he is eight to ten months of age. He finds this capacity to get up off the floor very exciting, and he will practice it over and over again. This, too, is slightly dangerous for him in that his ability to maintain his balance is only marginal, and his judgment as to where his behind will land, if he turns to sit, is not particularly good. In addition, as noted earlier, his memory leaves something to be desired. Therefore there is a strong likelihood of a daily fall or two as a result of this new-found ability to climb.

Sometime in the vicinity of eleven or twelve months of age, a baby acquires a second climbing skill, the ability to climb as much as a foot or so at a time. The result of this ability is that he will be able to get up on the living room sofa and from there he will generally be able to climb onto the arms of the sofa and then onto the top of the sofa back. Given this new range, he can climb onto a kitchen chair, from the kitchen chair onto the top of the washing machine, on over to the top of the stove, and onto the counter. This two-step process, again, seems to happen with all infants, and you can see immediately that it has important consequences for a child's safety as well as a payoff in the excitement of new places that he can now reach and explore. Obviously, at this point, when he is capable of climbing twelve-inch units, you have to take special precautions with poisonous and other hazardous substances.

Standing and cruising

In addition to the baby's climbing ability, another early achievement during this period is pulling himself to stand. He will pull himself to stand against a piece of furniture, or even against your leg, using your slacks, your skirt, or any other article of clothing that is handy for support. This pulling to stand is followed fairly soon by an activity called "cruising," which consists of careful moving about on two legs while holding on to one or another supporting object. Cruising, as you might imagine, is then followed, usually at about one year of age, by unaided walking. Unaided walking is followed by running and also, at about thirteen or fourteen months of age, the capacity to straddle small four-wheeled objects and drag them about. These are the primary motor acquisitions having to do with the large muscles of the body. They mean a great deal to a child, and he will spend a great deal of time practicing them.

STARING BEHAVIOR

During our extensive observations of all kinds of children in the Phase V age range, we have been struck by the surprising frequency of a behavior we call staring or gaining information through vision. We find in observations of a fair number of different kinds of children that the single most frequent activity of the age, other than sleeping, is simply looking at one or another object or scene. If you study your child (when he cannot see you) for any length of time, you can see for yourself that your Phase V baby is a "looker." He stares a lot. My colleagues who study infrahuman primates, the great apes and monkeys of various kinds, tell me that the young of those species also spend a great deal of time looking at objects, at other monkeys, and so forth. All babies spend a substantial fraction of the time looking at their mothers or other primary caretakers. At other times they will look at objects just before or just after a more active exploration of them. They also like to look out the window. They will look at other children playing at a distance. We find about twenty percent of all waking time in the age range from eight months to three years is spent staring at one thing or another.

THE FIRST RESPONSES TO WORDS

The Phase V baby, week by week, will reveal greater and greater interest in and understanding of words and phrases. You will begin to find you have a companion in the sense that the young child is becoming more of a person, more of the kind of creature you have been used to as you ordinarily deal with other humans. His first understanding of words will reveal itself in the compliant behaviors of this period. Increasingly, children will tend to respond when you call their names; will tend to look toward other members of the family whom you are addressing; will tend to go along with simple requests to throw a kiss, stop a particular activity, or retrieve an object. You should not yet expect a great deal of talking by your child. A few children do begin to talk before their first birthday, but not many. The picture will change by the time the child is one and one-half years or so.

INCREASING INTEREST IN MOTHER

From eight months right on through two years, babies under most circumstances reveal an extremely strong orientation toward the primary caretaker, who in most instances is their mother. This is one of the very basic dominating forces in a child's life, and more will be said about it in a later section. Suffice it to say that from eight to fourteen months of age you will notice a steadily increasing orientation toward the primary caretaker, featuring at about eleven or twelve months of age the first clear requests for assistance from that person. These first requests are often for more milk or other food, and sometimes for help if, for example, the child is stuck climbing.

ACTIVE INTEREST IN SMALL OBJECTS

As noted earlier, the eight-month-old child very often will show a striking interest in tiny particles. While he is sitting, playing at a feed table or highchair, or even on the floor, you may notice a scrunching-up of the forehead and an intense stare at small items, some of which you cannot see from a distance. On closer inspection you may find the child concentrating on some cracker crumbs, or perhaps on a small bug. My guess is what you are seeing is the result of two processes reaching maturation: the capacity to really see very fine detail accurately, and the increased capacity to explore that fine detail because of the new-found abilities of sitting up and locomoting. This interest is linked to the more general but equally deep interest in the exploration of the qualities of small objects. From eight months until two years of age, and increasingly so during Phase V, children universally spend roughly twenty percent of all waking time in active exploration of small objects. That active interest takes two forms, at least according to the definitions we use in our work. One is exploratory behavior where the child explores all the attributes of any new object he comes across. That exploration includes bringing the object to the mouth for gumming, banging it, striking it, throwing it, turning it around and staring at it from different angles, rubbing it against things, and so forth. He will try out a wide variety of actions on the object; this diverse collection of behaviors we call exploring.

The second major type of exploration is what we call mastery experiences, the practice of simple skills on objects. If the object has a base so that it can be stood up and then knocked down again, you may find the child practicing standing it up and knocking it down. If it is a crayon, you may find him rolling it back and forth and watching the motion. There are many simple skills that children practice on objects at this particular point in time. Earlier I mentioned that at this age children stare a great deal; one of the ways of interacting with small objects is to simply stare at them, often in combination or alternation with practicing simple skills on them.

As we have seen, children have a peculiar fascination with collections of items, particularly if they are irregularly shaped and have fine detail. One of the simple skills they practice as early as Phase IV is the emptying of objects out of containers, one at a time. Once those objects are all emptied out, they may very well be systematically returned, one at a time, with a child pausing to examine them as he does so.

MOUTHING OBJECTS AND OTHER MATERIALS

At this time, the mouth continues to be a prominent organ for exploration. You can also expect that, with most children, new teeth are erupting or about to erupt. As a result of both factors, it is extraordinarily common for objects to be brought to the mouth at this age, often with unfortunate consequences in terms of the child's safety.

CLUMSINESS

In spite of the fact that abilities are emerging rapidly, you must not forget that children at this age have a good deal of baby fat and are not terribly skillful. You will notice, however, that by and large they are surprisingly careful about themselves. It is my estimate that ninety percent of the children of this age are careful climbers, and are careful as well in a variety of other motor activities and situations, at least with respect to their own clumsiness. Nevertheless, there is that one child out of ten who seems to be bent on self-destruction, and I have seen him too often not to tell you to watch him closely.

FRIENDLINESS

The eight- to fourteen-month-old baby, particularly during the early stages of this phase, is a very friendly child. He may be causing you all sorts of grief, extra work, and anxiety, but he is not doing this on purpose. The difficulties he creates are simply natural accompaniments of this particular stage of his development. You will be rewarded over and over again with gestures of affection and wide, sincere smiles. You may, if you are lucky, be hugged and kissed spontaneously, as well as on command. Enjoy this friendliness while it lasts, because you may well find that with the onset of Phase VI things take a turn for the worse.

ANXIETY AND SHYNESS WITH STRANGERS

The friendliness referred to above is chiefly for the primary caretaker and other people whom the baby sees every day. During this phase you should find the child normally becoming less and less gregarious. Two trends account for this decrease in general gregariousness or sociability. The first is a growing intensity of interest on the child's part in learning precisely what he can and cannot do in the home or other living area. The second is his interest in beginning the process of learning who he is. This double interest is a consuming one, and it can best be pursued via the primary caretaker. At the same time the "hail-fellow-well-met" quality of the child during the preceding phases, particularly between three and eight months, is gradually receding. It is as if he has made his choices. He has usually concluded (though not consciously) by eight months of age that his security lies with his mother or with some other primary figure in his life. He remains relatively friendly with other members of the nuclear family; but outsiders, even those as close as grandparents who do not live with the child and do not see him every day, are treated during Phase V with growing apprehension and shyness. This apprehension and shyness is less obvious in the child's own home or favorite living area than it will be when he is in a strange environment. Put him into the home of the grandparent and you will find more often than not that he will seek out his mother for security and tend to stay with her. This kind of behavior is normal at this age and will persist until the child reaches at least two years of age.

BEHAVIOR WITH SIBLINGS

Two types of situations are involved here, and they require separate discussion. The first is the situation where the child has a sibling who is three or more years older; the second is where the child has a sibling less than three years older, and therefore not much more than an infant himself.

Interaction with a sibling three years or more older
We have seen over and over again that the older sibling tends to treat the Phase V baby with affection and interest, on those occasions when he or she has a chance to interact. Somewhat surprisingly, under most circumstances siblings this much older than the infant do not spend a great deal of time with the baby. They have entered into a period of life where they are much more oriented to children their own age than was the case in infancy, and they are much more inclined to play with peers than with an infant brother or sister. The baby's most common experience with such an older sibling therefore involves watching the older sibling doing something alone or playing with his friends.

Interaction with a sibling less than three years older
In the case of a baby with a sibling not much older than himself, the situation is different in what I believe to be very important ways. The older child in this situation—especially if it was a first child and especially if he or she was somewhat overindulged (all of which happen together rather commonly)—can be expected to feel and show genuine resentment and dislike toward the baby. This behavior, while very unpleasant to witness and live with, is so common that it must be considered normal. It also should be anticipated and must be coped with by the family.

The result of the resentment and occasional dislike felt by the older sibling toward the younger child is that from time to time he will act aggressively and selfishly toward the baby. The older child may hit the baby now and again, may throw the baby down, and may take toys away from him. The severity of this problem seems to be very directly related to the age gap between the children. The closer in age the two of them are, the more frequent and intense the hostile behavior from the older child to the young one during Phase V.

Your younger baby will probably learn during Phase V how to cope with his older sibling, how to defend himself, how to avoid getting into difficulty, and sadly but truly, *how to behave in a manner similar to the aggressor.* If you watch the interchange without actively interfering with what is happening, you will probably find that for the first half of Phase V the younger child is on the receiving end of the situation, helplessly accepting whatever abuse the older child wants to shower upon him, without knowing how to cope with the situation. After two or three months of simply taking whatever the older sibling has inflicted upon him, you will find the baby starting to shift ground. Between eleven and twelve months of age you can expect him to begin to object rather vigorously to aggressive behavior by the older child. This is coincidentally the first point at which the child will be deliberately turning to you for assistance, and this will be one of the areas in which he does so. A third stage will develop within Phase V when the baby unfortunately begins to use upon his tormenter some of the tactics that the tormenter had used upon him at the beginning of this phase. By the time the younger child reaches thirteen or fourteen months of age you no longer will be able to assume that if there is difficulty between the two of them, it was invariably initiated by the older child.

We will talk more about interaction between siblings in later sections. Suffice it to say, *I believe that spacing children at least three years apart is an extremely good idea.* I might add to this somewhat distressing picture the notion that there will be times when the older child will treat the younger child with genuine affection, but do not be surprised if such events get to be fewer and fewer in number during the Phase V period.

THE APPARENT INTERESTS OF THIS AGE

We have found it useful to characterize the central interests of this age in the following manner: a social interest in the primary caretaker, an interest in exploration of the world in all conceivable ways, and an interest in practicing new motor skills. These are the three areas of concentration most germane to educational achievement.

INTEREST IN THE PRIMARY CARETAKER

I have been very much excited by what I observed as children progress from eight months to about two years of age in the area of their interest in the primary caretaker. The topic of attachment to another person has been a popular one in child-development research over the last decade; and by other labels, has been a popular one for many, many years. Popularity does not always produce wisdom, but I think in this case we have learned a great deal about the details of the process of attachment in the early years of life.

We know for certain that the newborn human literally cannot survive without a relationship to a more mature, more capable human. I am talking here about simple survival. A newborn baby is helpless. Physical survival is impossible unless somebody provides for him. We talked earlier about the various assets babies have during the early months of life that seem to heighten the probability that someone else from the species will come to love them deeply, to care for them, to nurture them, and to protect them. A new phase of the ongoing development of that relationship begins in earnest at about eight months of age.

Between eight and twenty-four months a good deal of the child's waking activities will revolve around his primary caretaker. He will watch her actions for a substantial portion of each day. He will use her as a haven whenever he is feeling distressed. He will use her to assist him whenever he can, increasingly from about ten months. He will learn from her, in an apparently very necessary way, what he can do and what he cannot do while living in his particular world. He will learn, for example, whether he can pull on the curtains, climb on furniture, climb on his own or his mother's bed, touch the plants in the living room, or move out onto the porch. He will learn literally thousands of specific answers to questions that will arise as he goes about his explorations. He will learn something about his mother's disciplinary style, and by the time he is thirteen or fourteen months of age he will have become rather sophisticated in all of these areas. He will learn that if she is a talker, rather than a doer, her threats are only words and will not be quickly followed by action. He will learn how to determine whether or not she means business. He will learn, albeit imperfectly, whether she is the kind of person who gives him undivided attention or divided attention; whether if she gives him an instruction or an admonition while she is on the telephone he need immediately toe the mark, or can be assured that she will not follow up.

By the time a child is two years of age, and often much earlier, he will have established a very elaborate and detailed social contract with his primary caretaker. I personally believe that contract is relatively hard to subsequently alter or modify against its established direction. I think that what children acquire in that first two years is the first set of social skills and attitudes they will begin to use with all people—with other family members, and with other children as they enter into true peer relations.

As noted earlier, I do not think you can spoil a child in the first eight months of life, but surely you can between eight and twenty-four months of age. I believe one of the greatest opportunities parents have to influence their children is through the quality of their interactions, starting particularly at about eight months of age. You can observe a drying-up of interest in the mother at this point if certain conditions prevail. If, indeed, a child of this age is prevented from having a free and easy exchange with his mother or some other primary caretaker in the months that follow, and if, for example, he is provided with all sorts of interesting toys and areas to explore, you may find him showing less and less interest in people and more interest in objects. But given most circumstances, the interest in people will not only be strong and growing throughout this period, but may very well overpower the interest in objects. More about that later.

INTEREST IN EXPLORATION OF THE WORLD

As I have remarked several times earlier, the child at eight months of age is an explorer. He wants to see everything, touch everything, and bring everything he can to his mouth. This interest is visible in his active exploration of any area to which he is allowed access. You will find that there is absolutely no need to reward him for exploring and learning. He will do it for the sheer joy of it. I have mentioned in the preceding section a particular fascination with the world of small objects. You will find that he is interested in the controls on the television set, on the radio, and on the stereo. He is interested in doorknobs and the contents of kitchen cabinets and pantries. He is interested in particles of dust, leaves, and just about anything he can make contact with.

The Phase V child's deep natural interest in the object world has several important ramifications. One is the role this interest plays in deepening his curiosity and in promoting the development of intelligence. Another is the role it plays as a *balancing agent* against the interest in social relations with the primary caretaker. (In fact I believe that the Phase V child at about eight months of age starts out with his three main fields of interest in balance, but there is no guarantee that they will remain that way in the year or so that follows. Furthermore, when the balance is lost or, more commonly, distorted, I believe the educational progress of a child tends to become less than ideal. One common way in which the balance is thrown off is if the normal focus on the mother tends to expand at the expense of the other two interests.)

The final point to be made concerning the Phase V child's interest in exploration is the apparently universal appeal of water play and the apparently perfect suitability of the toilet bowl to serve that interest. Along with the interest in climbing stairs, interest in pulling themselves up to stand near the bowl and playing with the contents therein seems to be as common in the lives of children as just about anything we have seen.

INTEREST IN PRACTICING NEW MOTOR SKILLS

In the preceding section I described the sequence of emerging motor skills, starting with crawling and moving up through climbing. Phase V children will spend many, many hours practicing their new-found ability to move through space in all directions. Again, one of the most common interests at this stage is in climbing stairs. It is amazing what a hypnotic power steps have on the very young child.

EDUCATIONAL DEVELOPMENTS DURING PHASE V

I would like to preface the ensuing discussion by reemphasizing some points made earlier. First is my belief that the educational developments that take place in the year or so that begins when a child is about eight months old are *the most important and most in need of attention of any that occur in human life*. Absolutely basic educational foundations begin to develop in a very important and fundamental way as soon as a child starts to crawl about the home and simultaneously begins to master language. The four basic educational foundations discussed earlier in this chapter are now central in determining what a human being will become.

Again I would like to emphasize my belief that solid development of the above-mentioned foundations *is by no means assured*. The responsibility for the quality of the educational outcome for most children rests with their own families, and more specifically with their mothers; as we have seen, parents are not routinely prepared for the job, nor are they given very much assistance to do the job well. Once more, my view is that not more than two thirds of our children currently get adequate development in the areas dealt with here, and no more than ten percent of our children do as well as they could during the first three years of their lives. This state of affairs may be a tragedy, but it is by no means a twentieth-century tragedy. *In the history of Western education there has never been a society that recognized the educational importance of the earliest years, or sponsored any systematic preparation and assistance to families or any other institution in guiding the early formation of children.*

LANGUAGE DEVELOPMENT

This was dealt with extensively on page 110. Let me stress again that language is absolutely central to the development of intelligence, and that a child doing well linguistically has a solid asset in his attempts at becoming a well-rounded human being.

THE DEVELOPMENT OF CURIOSITY

I have discussed the importance of curiosity for the Phase V child on page 118. Here I should only like to reemphasize my belief that curiosity *can* be broadened and deepened by intelligent child-rearing in this period, but that relatively few families do the job as well as they can and should.

SOCIAL DEVELOPMENT

As we have seen, children two years of age can have evolved into delightful companions who have free and easy social relationships, and who at the same time have maintained a profound curiosity about the world at large. Or they can have developed into beings whose world revolves almost exclusively around an older adult (usually the mother), in a manner such that the mother is badgered from morning to night by a kind of consuming desire on the part of a two-year-old to monopolize her time and attention. This latter type of child very often has lost basic intrinsic interest in objects and materials, and now sees a new toy only as a tool for manipulating the mother. Sad as this state of affairs is, it is sadder yet to see a child who by two has learned that his mother is not a generally approachable human being; who has learned that he had best stay out of her way unless she shows obvious signs that the coast is clear, that she is in a good mood, and that she would like him to approach. We have seen children systematically turned off from their primary caretakers by repeated rejections during Phases V and VI. This particular pattern is tragic to see, and when it is accompanied by a lack of interesting physical materials and locations you get the saddest situation of all, a child who seems to be somewhat empty at two years of age. I believe poor social development can be avoided fairly easily. When this aspect of development goes well, it is deeply rewarding. More about how to achieve the desired pattern will follow.

Earlier, I listed three important emerging social competencies of special importance. They are: using an adult as a resource, showing pride in achievement, and engaging in make-believe or role-play behavior. From our research these new behaviors seem to be very important from an educational standpoint. Again, a discussion of how to encourage optimal development will follow.

NURTURING THE ROOTS OF INTELLIGENCE

I have described a powerful and near-universal urge in eight-month-old children to explore the world. This urge is the motivating power underlying the acquisition of intelligence. That force can be deepened and broadened by effective child-rearing practices, or it can be made more shallow and/or more narrow by inadequate child-rearing practices.

Growth of learning-to-learn skills

I have already expressed my belief that the underlying motivation to learn is as important as just about any other factor in regard to a child's educational well-being. In addition to that underlying urge is the collection of learning-to-learn skills that children are building during Phases V and VI. Piaget has described the exciting and fundamental events of this age; our own research on dozens of children as we watch them develop during this period adds many details to the story.

Learning-to-learn skills come easily to the child who is given a chance to explore the world, as well as encouragement and assistance by adults. Children do not build products of any consequence in this particular phase, nor will they until they are two years of age or more, but they are learning prerequisite skills. You will not find children drawing pictures, for example, but you will find them learning to handle small devices like those they will use later to write. You will begin to see signs of an interest in scribbling toward the end of Phase V, and children practice fine motor skills throughout this period. The multitudinous efforts directed at getting to know the characteristics of objects—whether they bounce or roll, whether they plop or slide—will later be used in the construction of products such as towers, ships, trucks, and scenes that feature dolls, animals, and buildings.

The retrieval skills that children are learning when they roll or throw a ball and then seek and reclaim it are also in and of themselves prerequisite elements in the more complicated and elaborate creative activities that will come a year or two later. At this time they are also learning their first lessons in how to put things together and how to take them apart. You will find they are very much interested in fitting objects to each other. For example, putting lids on containers is a common interest seen at this point; sliding one gadget into another is another activity of particular interest to them. These simple motor skills are interesting in and of themselves, but they are also preparing the child for later, more-complicated experiences.

Hinges and hinged objects

A curious related interest of this age is the interest in hinges and hinged objects. Rather early in our observations of Phase V children we noticed their fascination with swinging doors back and forth. The most common door we have seen used for this purpose is a lower kitchen cabinet door.

An interest in hinged objects is also revealed in the Phase V child's fascination with jack-in-the-box toys or other small boxlike devices with covers that can swing open and be closed, in spite of the fact that the typical jack-in-the-box cannot be properly operated by most children under three years of age. This is because they require the young child to perform two somewhat difficult acts at once. He must press down on the clown (or other object) then press down the cover onto the object; and, then while maintaining downward pressure with one hand he has to rotate a crank a few times to lock the cover in place. Such complicated motor coordinations are considerably beyond the capacities of the Phase V child. An exception is the Surprise Box, manufactured by the Kohner Company, which has five small jack-in-the-boxes lined up next to each other in a single plastic box. In order to get the lid to swing up, revealing a small animal figure, the child has to perform one of five simple motor activities, including pushing a lever one way or the other, rotating a telephone dial, or pushing a button, and so forth. Of the five activities the only one the child of this age can manage is pushing the lever one way or the other. We have found that most Phase V babies like this particular toy. I believe that one reason they like this toy, aside from the interest in activating simple mechanisms, is because they enjoy playing with hinged doors. Once they have caused the door to swing open, the next thing they usually do is to attempt to close it again. They repeat this behavior over and over again.*

An even more subtle manifestation of the apparently universal interest in hinged objects is the Phase V baby's interest in books. He is particularly intrigued with those that have stiff cardboard pages. His interest is based not on what is printed on the pages but on what is required to turn those pages to open the book, to turn it upside down, and so forth. In other words, this small cardboard-paged book is an object on which he can practice simple motor skills. One of the skills that he is particularly interested in involves treating any single page like one-half of a hinge and then swinging it back and forth.

---

* I might mention in passing, by the way, that the toy company has recommended this toy for children two to five years of age, for whom this toy has very little appeal. This is just another symptom of the lack of genuine professionalism in the toy industry. They do not often know the actual play value of their various toys for children at various stages of development.

It is relatively easy to see how some of the simple skills that are practiced by babies in Phase V will play a role later in more complicated activities. It is not quite that easy to see how an interest in swinging kitchen cabinet doors fits into the larger scheme of things, but whether or not we can understand the reason for this kind of interest, it is indeed there.

RECOMMENDED CHILD-REARING PRACTICES
AT THIS STAGE

The primary caretaker has three major functions during Phase V.* These are: architect or designer of the child's world and daily experiences; consultant, someone to provide advice and assistance to the child; and authority, or source of discipline and setting of limits. Let us examine each of these in turn.

THE PRIMARY CARETAKER AS THE DESIGNER
OF THE CHILD'S WORLD

In watching situations where children develop beautifully through Phases V and VI in particular, but also until three years of age, we have observed that their mothers have taken precautions to see to it, as soon as the child begins to crawl about the home, that the home is as safe a place as they can make it for the child.

Accident-proofing the kitchen and living area
Making a home safe for a Phase V child starts with making the kitchen safe, because the kitchen is where he will ordinarily spend more of his waking time than any other place in the home. The first order of business is to accident-proof all the low areas of the home. Kitchens are full of cleaning materials and sharp utensils and breakable objects that must somehow or other be treated so that they are not likely to cause the child any grief. All substances that might be hazardous to a baby if he

---

* These three functions continue to be the primary functions of a child-rearer throughout the remaining period covered by this book.

managed to put any into his mouth must be moved well out of his reach preferably before the baby is seven months old.

Relatively fragile glass or other breakable kitchen materials should be stored in hard-to-reach places. Objects that can cut or slice, such as sharp knives and chopping utensils, must be moved away.

Electrical cords and outlets must be attended to. Wherever there is an outlet not in use, you should purchase at your local hardware store the kind of blank plug that fits into the outlet. It is advisable to move all appliance cords out of reach of the baby. It is particularly important to see that all electric insulation is intact and in good condition. A less obvious, but important problem to cope with is that of unstable physical objects. If you have an ironing board that folds down from the wall, for example, you should see that it is very difficult for the child to inadvertently release it. If you have a chair that is fragile or tippable, see to it that it is removed. In addition, you should check any wood furniture for splinterable surface breaks. You will also want to make certain that all paints within reach of the child are lead-free. There are local agencies that can help you if you have any problem in determining whether or not you have lead-base paint in your home.

You should see that if there are areas such as steps from which the child can trip or fall, that the child is prevented from moving into those places until such time as you are sure he is going to be adequately careful. In the living room you should be sure that no part of any plant hangs so low that the child can reach it and pull the pot down on himself. You should be assured that if any television or stereo controls are within reach of the child that they constitute no shock hazard and that any knobs which might be removable do not come off easily and cannot easily be swallowed—i.e., that they are larger than an inch and one-half in breadth.

Accident-proofing the bathroom

The second important area to concern yourself with is the bathroom. Children have a universal interest in playing in water. They have a tendency to pull themselves over the edge of the tub and to fall in; and when they get to be about eleven months you are likely to see them climbing up onto diaper pails and other low objects, getting onto the sink, and occasionally climbing up to the medicine cabinet. Most of the families we have worked with have found that the only way to cope with this is to declare the bathroom off bounds and keep the door closed until the child gets to be old enough so that he is trustworthy and can understand instructions. Of particular importance is seeing to it that *all medicines* are kept totally unreachable to a child. For less than ten dollars you can get a small strongbox that can be kept locked—it is well worth the inconvenience and the modest expense to keep all medicines, even those as seemingly innocuous as baby aspirin, in such a container.

Coping with siblings and stairs

A more subtle source of danger should be dealt with at this time. If there is a sibling in the house who is less than three years older than the child, some of the hard feelings that this older sibling will occasionally have for his baby brother or sister can be intensified by the baby's intrusion into the older sibling's possessions and living area. At times it may be advisable to see to it that the older child's toy area and bedroom are off limits to the new baby (you might use a doorway gate).

The topic of stairs also deserves some consideration at this point. I have mentioned that babies seem to be fascinated by flights of stairs. The nine- or ten-month-old child inevitably wants to climb stairs. It is my recommendation that you give the child the opportunity to climb those stairs, but you should be there to supervise his first efforts and to assure yourself that there is no danger involved in his initial attempts. Even if you follow that practice, you will have two residual problems. First, you cannot always be around to supervise; and second, children do not learn to get down from stairs safely for at least a month or two after they learn to climb up them. Therefore, you may want to have a gate available for use with stairs. My recommendation is that you use the gate as little as possible, and try to resolve the situation by helping the child learn to negotiate stairs by himself, both up and down, as soon as he is physically able to do so. A useful procedure is to place a gate at the third or fourth step, rather than at the bottom.

Safety outdoors

You would probably be well advised not to leave a child of this age outdoors unsupervised for any length of time. Even if he is in the company of a slightly older child, I think you should keep an eye on your Phase V child whenever he is outdoors. You should, of course, be certain that there are no sharp objects around on which he can cut himself, and you should be especially careful of backyard pools. In general, common sense should get you through the business of accident-proofing an outdoor area. The cardinal rule is that it is unwise to expect a baby between eight and fourteen months of age to use *any* good sense when it comes to safety. You are going to have to be his good sense.

Protecting the home from the baby

Any fragile possessions that you treasure should be placed beyond the reach of the baby at this particular time. His capacity to understand instructions is very limited in Phase V. Even though by the end of this stage he will be able to understand a fair number of one-or-two-sentence instructions, you simply should not count on him to understand directions or to go along with them. Remember, there is good reason to believe his memory is poor. He may have the best of intentions, but not remember what you said. So get your breakable and precious belongings out of his way. Even possessions that are not precious but that you simply like having around, such as a plant that you may have spent three years to grow from a seed to four inches high, is clearly in jeopardy. Be forewarned.

Get that stuff out of the way.

Providing access to the home

Once the home has been made safe *for* the baby and *from* the baby, the next important step in designing a young child's world is to *give him maximum access to that living area*. The smallest, simplest home is an extremely rich environment for the Phase V baby. At this age everything is new and vital. What you do by providing the Phase V child with maximum access to his home is to nourish his curiosity in a natural and powerful way. I cannot overemphasize how important the freedom to explore is in the education of the young baby. It not only has its obvious primary utility of helping to deepen and broaden his curiosity, but will also facilitate his social development, another important goal of this period, by maintaining and deepening his interest in you.

By providing maximum access to a safe home, you have also gone a long way toward making possible the preservation of a *balance* of interest. Just think for a moment of the contrasting situation, where to avoid the danger, the extra work, the stress, and so forth, you routinely prevent your child from moving about the home by using a playpen. You may in the short run have an easier time of it, but in the long run the negative effects of such confinement on a child's curiosity and on the growth of his capacity to play alone far outweigh the short-term returns.

Supplying playthings

In addition to providing the kind of stimulation for a child offered by the run of the house, I recommend that you have available for special times, a certain number of toys and other physical materials. Occasionally children in Phase V appear bored, although boredom is not nearly as common in Phase V as it is later in life. More about this in the section on recommended materials.

THE PRIMARY CARETAKER'S ROLE AS CONSULTANT

You can be quite confident that if you have provided your Phase V child with a safe home and a few stimulating materials, he will explore and find things that interest and occasionally excite him. In addition, from time to time he will find himself in situations that frustrate him or cause him modest pain. Should any one of these occasions arise —excitement, frustration, or modest pain—you can be assured that in some fraction of those cases the child will turn to you for assistance, shared enthusiasm, or comfort. At this point, when the child approaches you, you have what I consider to be your second primary opportunity to really establish yourself as your child's educator.

What a baby is interested in during this stage of his life is relatively easy to see and see accurately most of the time. If you have a child who comes to you excited by something pleasurable or aroused by something in the way of a difficulty, you have a motivated child. If you know what he is focusing on, you have the ideal learning circumstance. *What we have seen effective mothers do in this regard is, first of all, be available for such experiences. If mothers take a full-time job, they are not even going to have a chance at these experiences.* Second, effective mothers pause and react to the baby as soon as they can, as often as they can. They do not keep the child waiting while they continue a conversation on the telephone. Now is the chance to give a child the sense that his mother is responsive to him, if only by saying, "You will have to wait a minute, I am busy now." That is better than not responding promptly.

Once the appropriate response is made, effective mothers pause to see what it is the child is interested in. They identify the subject, then usually provide whatever is needed by the child. They also provide a few words related to the topic in question, using language that is at or slightly above the child's apparent ability level; and they express a related idea or two. For example, if the child comes to you with what looks like a little animal figure with unusually large feet, you might suggest that, "Those feet are really large. Daddy has big feet, too, doesn't he, and you have small feet." The particular content of your words is not terribly important at this stage, provided that you refer both to the topic at hand and also to something else that the child is familiar with and has a chance of understanding in a concrete way. Once the assistance or the comforting and the language has been given (and of course, you do not *always* have to use language), the next part of the process is to let the child leave when he wants to. *Effective mothers do not bore their children.*

In this pattern of response I believe we have a beautiful mechanism for effective education of a young child. First of all, the child is learning to use another person as a resource in situations that he cannot handle for himself. That is a vital social skill, one which will serve him well in the years to come. Second, he is beginning to learn a little bit more about the nature of other people, and that will stand him in good stead when he begins to interact with people other than those of the nuclear family. Third, he is learning that someone values his excitement and the satisfaction of his curiosity. Fourth, he gets language tuition, because someone is providing language that is relevant and makes sense to him. Fifth, his intellectual world is being broadened by the content of the information. Sixth, in cases when he asks for assistance, he is learning about completing simple tasks. Seventh, on those occasions where he is attempting something that simply will not work, like wrapping a kitten's paw around its tail two or three times, he is being taught realistic task limitations as well. As you can see, the issue of how to respond to overtures from the Phase V child is a topic of central importance.

In the role of consultant you will find it both natural, easy, and generally enjoyable to nurture the emerging social competencies. Some of the Phase V child's overtures will be requests for assistance. Your natural inclination will be to help. Do so! But be careful as the child passes his first birthday not to let yourself become the child's all-purpose tool. Watch for the subtle differences between (A) use of you when a child has determined he can't handle a task himself versus (B) use of you as the easiest way to achieve a goal, or (C) use of you simply to monopolize your attention. (A) is fine, but (B) and (C) lead to an overindulged child.

Some of a child's overtures toward you as he turns thirteen or fourteen months will be attempts to gain praise or exclamations of delight for remarkable achievements like climbing down one step safely. Encouraging healthy growth in this area is a pleasure.

Another pleasure involves the child's first make-believe play. Often the behavior is hugely entertaining, especially when the child seems very serious in his grown-up involvement, for example, in nurturing dolls. Increasingly during the second year, you'll be called upon to participate in such episodes. By all means do so, it appears to be beneficial from an educational standpoint and it's often a good deal of fun!

THE PRIMARY CARETAKER'S ROLE AS AUTHORITY

In the homes we have studied where children are developing well, as contrasted with homes where children are developing poorly, we have always seen mothers run the home with a loving but firm hand. The babies in these home situations rarely have any question about who is the final authority. In homes where children are not doing very well, however, there is often ambiguity with respect to the setting of limits and the determination of who is going to have the final say on disagreements. You need not fear that if you are firm with your infant, if you deny him things from time to time on a realistic basis, or even occasionally on an unrealistic basis, that he will love you less than if you were lenient. Children in the first two years of life do not become detached from their primary caretakers very easily; even if you spank them regularly, you will find they keep coming back to you. This is very probably due to the absolutely vital need they have for close attachment to someone.

Be firm. You do your child no favor by yielding to him, especially if it is a first child, because that child is going to have to learn some of the harsh realities of life when the second child comes along, or when he leaves the home and enters into the non-nuclear-family world. A child who has not been dealt with firmly during late infancy is considerably less well prepared to cope with life situations than one who has.

Discipline

It is important to get a pattern of solid and effective discipline established during Phase V in order to prepare for the more difficult job when the child gets to be a bit older. We have very rarely seen the most effective mothers repeat anything more than once in the way of a restriction or a control sentence. If a child did not respond in the desired way after the message was repeated once, the mothers acted, either with a slight pat on the behind or arm, or more commonly with physical removal of the child from the situation that they wanted him to abandon. Distraction is also an effective tactic. But the main thing is to avoid such ambiguous kinds of discipline as, for example, when you insist that the child stop doing something, and then you do not follow up when he does not stop. Such behavior is extraordinarily common and only lays the foundation for later problems.

Coping with the next oldest child

In a sense this section deserves more prominence than as a subheading under the problem of discipline. It should be read carefully by concerned parents. One of the more interesting and more important pieces of the large puzzle of the educational development of a young child has to do with his relationships with other children in the family. We have all heard stories about how the nine-year-old older sister treats the baby with the kind of marvelous warmth that makes us all melt inside. However, we found over and over again, in families where there were widely spaced children, that the children six years old and older actually spend negligible amounts of time during the waking hours with the baby. I believe the major reasons for this are first, that older children are much more oriented toward children their own age than they were when they were much younger; and second, an infant is in many ways poor company for an eight-year-old.

The reason why this topic deserves serious attention is that it gives a great deal of difficulty to many a family in their attempts at rearing the baby well. Furthermore, in addition to the difficulty that it creates, I firmly believe that at times it can interfere, in a very negative fashion, with the growth and development of both the baby and the older child in question.

We have found over and over again that when the next older child is at least three years older than the baby, the quality of life in the home, particularly as it relates to their interaction, is by and large pleasant. We have seen genuine fondness again and again in interchanges between the older child and the baby. Bear in mind that a child at least three years older than the Phase V baby is nearly four years of age. A four-year-old child is a much more rational and mature being than the nine-month-old child—or even a two-year-old child. He is not only more rational and more mature than an infant, but as noted earlier he is also more attuned to activities outside the home, particularly in regard to other young children. From the time a child is two years of age he begins serious social relations with peers. Prior to that time most children really do not interact in a social manner with children their own age, but rather in a fashion closer to their interactions with physical objects. The social environment for most children under two years of age consists predominantly of the mother or other primary caretaker. The four-year-old, however, is already becoming peer-oriented, and has other interests beside the attentions of mother. It therefore becomes much easier for the four-year-old to cope with a baby's intrusion into the bosom of the family.

With the two- or two-and-one-half-year-old the situation is quite different. Indeed, the younger the older child is, the more aggravating and problematic such sibling relationships are. The sibling who is less than two and one-half years older is still predominantly oriented toward home and mother. The disturbance caused by the baby has a profound effect on his life. Not only is the disturbance greater and the dreamboat rocked even more powerfully than it would be if he were older, the resources he has to cope with that disturbance are more modest than they will be a couple of years later. Bear in mind that as a two or two and one-half-year-old, he has only recently moved away from the heart of the struggle with his mother to establish his own independence (more about that period of testing known as negativism in the discussion of Phase VI).

How do you cope with a child who is only a year or a year and one-half older than the baby, when the baby is nine months of age and starting to be a presence in the home in a manner that was not the case when he was crib-bound? We have had success with certain simple elements of advice. First of all, we feel that the older child is having at least as much trouble as the mother in coping with the situation and that this problem should be understood from the start. He needs very much to be reassured that he is still genuinely loved. This is very difficult when he has tangible evidence that he is no longer unique and at the same time is frequently being disciplined. The advice we have given to mothers in this difficult situation is as follows:

First, be very firm. The older child must understand that there are behaviors that are simply not acceptable no matter how grim he feels about reality. Behaviors such as self-inflicted punishment (banging one's head against the floor, the wall, or the furniture), and physical abuse of the younger child or of peers will simply not be tolerated. Often, in order to make this advice most useful, we have to explain very carefully to mothers that an overly verbal or overly rational style of discipline may not suffice. The language or other medium used in disciplining the child should be at a level that he is able to cope with at that point in time. If a two- or two and one-half-year-old is distraught and almost out of control, expecting that child to sit still while you explain something at great length, using impeccable logic, is simply unreasonable. Very often all that child wants is to be physically restrained, moved out of the situation, and cuddled or reassured that he is a good boy or girl but that he is simply not going to be allowed to do what he has been trying to do.

Second, give the older child some private time with you each and every day, free from distractions, and especially free from the younger sibling. We recommend that for at least one half-hour every day (perhaps while the younger child is napping), the older child be given your totally undivided attention to remind him that you can still treat him like you used to treat him.

Third, make a real effort to stimulate the older child's other interests. After all, he is at an age when he is naturally developing a true social interest in peers. Even though your efforts to interest him in play outside of the home may suggest to him that he is being pushed out of the bosom of the family, if he is buttressed by free private time with his mother every day, I believe the practice makes sense. Also, consider the possibility of using a young teen-ager for a few hours at a time to provide undivided attention to the older child.

In all honesty, however, I know of no way that this situation can be handled without some difficulty. It usually is a situation for which you have to pay the price. Quite simply, *it is better not to get into such a situation at all: It is better to space your children.*

Perhaps most interesting from a professional point of view, are the consequences for the young child of having this kind of a social scene in contrast to being the child in a family with a much older sibling or being a first child. The first child, or the child in a family with a much older sibling, is at nine to eleven months of age undergoing friendly social interchanges in just about all of his encounters. His mother is almost always loving and supportive, as are his father and any much older siblings. The vast majority of his experiences with people are warm, friendly, and loving. Such is not the case if the older child is not much older than the baby. Under such circumstances it is normal and predictable that a solid portion of experience day in and day out throughout the eight- to fourteen-month period is going to involve the older child behaving in a genuinely hostile manner toward the baby. I wonder seriously about what this sort of experience, as contrasted with the former kind, can do to the basic makeup of the baby. We have seen babies start off at eight months as benign, delightful creatures; then they are subjected to significant abuse from an older sibling, and by two years of age they become children whose social style is characterized by hostility and apprehension about interpersonal relations. This is sad to behold.

RECOMMENDED MATERIALS FOR THIS AGE

TOYS

As noted earlier, the Phase V baby may appear bored from time to time. We have seen effective mothers occasionally provide babies in this age group with a new toy or a new set of materials to rekindle their activity. This will not always work, but frequently it does. The number of important developments in a child's life in Phases V and VI is so great and their significance is so deep that commercial toys very rarely can compete successfully for the child's attention. I do not believe there are more than a very small number of commercial toys for this age range that are worth buying.

In an earlier section I described the basic interests of Phase V children. This information should be useful in helping you select toys for this age group. I might add, however, that the Kohner Company manufactures several toys that have substantial play value for children because they feed into the basic interests of the age. Earlier I described the Surprise Box, which contains simple jack-in-the-box devices. Kohner recommends it for the two- to five-year-old child, but it is of particular interest to the eight- to eighteen-month child.

Another useful toy for this age, again by Kohner, is the Busy Bath. Sears makes a similar bath toy. Phase V babies have a tremendous fascination with water, and of course water play is infinitely variable.

Another kind of commercially available toy from which children get a great deal of pleasure is balls of various sizes and shapes. In our research the ball was the single most popular toy in the one- to two-year age range. Earlier I recommended large, lightweight, inexpensive plastic beach balls. Any ball from eight to twenty-four inches in diameter makes a great toy for a child of this age. Phase V babies also like footballs, partly because of their unpredictable paths of motion; and you will find your child enjoying hugely any soft rubber ball of any size, provided that it is too large to be swallowed. Bear in mind that balls not only move in interesting fashion, but they move a great deal for a very little effort on the part of a child. They are somewhat unpredictable; in addition, they feed into his newly emerging motor skills, which he can practice endlessly, along with digital dexterity as he throws the ball and retrieves it. Finally, a ball can be used to engage an older person in a simple game of catch. All in all, a ball is a marvelous toy. Perhaps the most interesting and most elegant ball toy of them all is the Ping-Pong ball, which I recommend for children, but only after they reach thirteen or fourteen months of age (more about that in Chapter 7).

Another kind of commercial toy worthy of note is the small, detailed, schematic or real doll. Children are particularly interested in its small configured and articulated pieces. Make sure that for the Phase V child these pieces are too large to be swallowed.

You can also collect thirty or forty small objects of different sizes and shapes in some sort of large container, whether it is a simple, small suitcase or a one-gallon plastic ice cream container, and you will have a homemade toy that will keep a child occupied for long periods of time. They are fascinated by collections of small interesting objects.

BOOKS

As mentioned earlier, the storybooks available for children at this age are useful, provided you get editions with stiff pages rather than those with either cloth or paper pages. Phase V children will gum, tear, and crumple paper-paged books. Give them your old magazines instead.

CHILD-REARING PRACTICES I DO NOT RECOMMEND

FORCED TEACHING

In general, I do not believe in forced teaching at this age. I do not think the reading kits that are commercially available and claim to get children on the road to reading at eight and nine months of age should be used. I believe strong statements to the effect that you *must* read stories to your child, and that you *must* buy as many "educational" toys as you can are examples of exploitation of the insecurities of American families, and prey upon a widespread feeling of guilt and anxiety among parents about whether they are doing well by their children. Such statements also reflect an overemphasis on the value of a "bright" child, sometimes at the expense of whether or not he is a decent, likable child.

When somebody advocates an educational program for a baby, the only sensible way to evaluate it is to think in terms of *all* of the major processes that are developing in children. Earlier, I listed four educational foundations undergoing development during the eight- to twenty-four-months age range. You should examine the consequences for each of those processes of any proposed educational program. It is very possible that in attempting to teach a child something about reading at one or two years of age you may have to use procedures which are costly in time, energy, and money; or which bore the child and therefore may have a negative influence on his basic curiosity and interest in learning. We certainly do not have a great deal of general know-how about these issues, therefore you should be very conservative in beginning any forced teaching program.

RESTRICTIVE DEVICES

Another child-rearing practice which I discourage, as mentioned earlier, is the use of restrictive devices like playpens, jump seats, and gates. It is clear that such devices cut down on work, cut down on hostilities between siblings, cut down on breakage in the home, and cut down on danger to the baby; and these are four very good reasons to tempt the mother to prevent her child from moving about the home freely. Nevertheless, we have found that in families where children are developing very well, restrictive devices are rarely used. In families where children are developing rather poorly, restrictive devices play a relatively prominent role.

I have very rarely seen a situation where a nine- or ten-month-old has been in a playpen and has been actively engaged in any activity for more than a few minutes without lapsing into apparent boredom. When children get to be two and one-half or three years of age, and go to nursery schools, they spend a lot of time waiting for group activities to begin. This waiting is an inevitable consequence of being forced to live in a group. Waiting is a common experience in elementary schools as well, where the reward for being obedient and prompt is that you have to sit while other children are slowly getting into their seats and beginning to pay attention to the teacher. We call this sort of experience passing time. *There need be very little passing time in the life of a child in Phase V.* Somehow children seem to find a wide variety of interesting things to do at this point in time, given the chance. If, however, they are placed in a playpen or jump seat in front of the television set for long periods of time, or if they are given long naps morning and afternoon, they will end up passing a good deal of time.

BORING THE BABY

Ways of putting a one-year-old child into a psychologically boring condition include reading a story to him that he is not interested in, and trying to teach him something or otherwise force his attention when he is obviously not in a responsive frame of mind. Effective parents, we have observed, do not bore their children or force activities on them.

THE WORKING MOTHER: PROS AND CONS

Another point of likely importance at this stage of development has to do with whether or not a mother should work. I have described in some detail how children at this age are entering into complicated social learnings that I believe to be critical with respect to the basic social blueprint of a human being. As we have seen, during Phase V two basic social skills are being learned that we believe have long-term significance. One is getting and holding the mother's attention, and the second is using the mother as a resource when the child cannot do a job himself. In addition, there are several related learnings in the social realm having to do with a child's first perception of himself, his budding awareness of discipline and limits, and his learning the rules of living in his home. All these learnings are ordinarily guided by the mother.

If a woman takes a full-time job during Phase V of a child's life, she obviously has much less to do with this early learning process. If she leaves someone in the home whose primary job is to take care of the house, then the child is going to be shortchanged. If, on the other hand, she leaves someone whose job is defined so as to emphasize interactions with the child, the child has a better chance. But whether the child will profit as much from this kind of experience as he would from his own mother is an open question.

My feeling is that if a mother is aware of the importance of what is going on in a child's development at this point, she will be likely to stay home at least part of the day. Since most children of this age nap in the morning, I see relatively little lost to the child if a mother with employment aspirations works half time, arranging her work hours to overlap with the child's nap time as much as possible. This still gives the mother ample time to interact with the child regularly. Furthermore, there is no apparent reason why, in such a situation, a father cannot be called upon to help guide the social development of his child. We have seen fine social development both with mothers working part time and with active participation by fathers.

OVERINDULGENCE

Parents very frequently feel that the deepest love for a child is shown when they do everything they can for him. A corollary of this principle is the notion that giving in to a child's demands when he is being stubborn about something, even though it is against your best judgment, is advisable. Both for the child in question and for the younger siblings and other children he may deal with later, you are not doing a child any favors if you either do too much for him or if you give in to his unreasonable demands. He is, after all, going to have to live in a world with other people, and he might as well start getting used to the idea fairly early. At the very least, if you are firm in these regards, he will not have as much of an adjustment to make when he gets to be two or three years of age as he otherwise would have. The effective parents we have studied have always been loving but firm with their children from early infancy on.

OVERFEEDING

The Phase V baby rarely expresses himself clearly with words. While his needs of the moment are usually obvious, from time to time they are not. Furthermore, if you've not provided suitable conditions to keep the baby interested, he can get bored. In many homes we've studied, mothers have taken to offering the child snacks of juice, milk, or cookies, etc., throughout the day. Offering a small treat shows that you care, especially in some American subcultures. It also seems to be effective in reducing a child's mild discomforts and occasional badgering. In addition it's rather simple to do. But please don't do it very often. In our studies, Phase V children developing very well do nearly all of their eating and drinking at mealtimes. Frequent between meal snacks more often than not accompanies comparatively poor development. Furthermore, I have a hunch that certain cases of lifelong obesity have their roots in this rather common child-rearing practice.

BEHAVIORS THAT SIGNAL THE ONSET
OF PHASE VI

NEGATIVISM

Far and away the most significant behavior to signal the onset of Phase VI, which is roughly from fourteen to twenty-four months of age, is what we call negativism. Negativism is a perfectly normal stage in the second half of the second year of children. In the negativistic behavior of the second year the child seems to be providing his mother with a preview of the coming attractions of adolescence. For the first time the child is beginning to be aware of the fact that he is an independent entity. He will start to use his own name, he will start to be very possessive about his own toys and clothes, and he will start resisting simple directives from the mother. He will start testing his will against hers, and he will start finding that the word or concept *no* has a particular fascination for him. Negativism is the first and most compelling sign of the onset of Phase VI.

HOSTILITY TOWARD OLDER SIBLINGS

A second sign of the onset of Phase VI is only present when the infant has a slightly older sibling, but it deserves special attention as it is regularly associated with the onset of negativism. In such homes Phase VI ushers in a turning of the worm with respect to the older child. The first stage of relations with the slightly older child, as we have seen, features the older child "dumping on" the younger child—and the younger child taking it. There is an intermediate stage, between eleven and thirteen or fourteen months of age, where the baby adapts to the situation, learns how to complain a lot, and begins to use the mother as a defense. Starting at thirteen or fourteen months of age, however, the baby will begin to initiate hostile activities with the older child as part of his new individualism.

ONSET OF EXPRESSIVE LANGUAGE

A third sign of the new phase is the onset of expressive language in quantity. Talking is not as reliable a sign as some of the others we have spoken about. Although some children do not begin to speak much before their second birthday, they generally begin to speak their first words between twelve and fourteen months of age. This particular phenomenon seems to have a very powerful effect on adults in that it often is the stimulus for adults starting to treat their babies in a much more verbal fashion than they had in previous months. Even though it can easily be shown that babies understand some language when they are one year old, the fact that they do not say very much seems to keep even knowledgeable and perceptive parents from using language extensively with them. There are exceptions, of course. There are some parents who talk a lot regardless of whether or not anybody is listening. But by and large it is a common characteristic of effective parents that they begin to talk considerably more to their children once their children enter Phase VI and themselves become more talkative.

CHAPTER 7

Phase VI

FROM FOURTEEN to
TWENTY-FOUR MONTHS
of AGE

GENERAL REMARKS

IMPORTANCE OF THIS PERIOD OF LIFE

The fourteen- to twenty-four-month period (Phase VI), is, in my opinion, the second half of the most important period for educating a young baby. By two years of age the fundamental educational processes have developed so far that we researchers get the feeling that if we see a child for the first time at two years of age we are seeing him rather late in the game.

Let us refer for a moment to the four educational foundation processes that we feel are useful in understanding early development: language development, the development of curiosity, social development, and the nurturing of the foundations of intelligence. The two-year-old is a child whose language development can be rather remarkable and extensive, including the capacity to understand and express hundreds of words and all the major grammatical forms, or his language skills can be quite limited. With respect to curiosity, he can arrive at age two with a well-nourished, broad, and extremely healthy inquisitiveness, or he can have lost quite a bit of that spontaneous motivating force. In some cases his curiosity may have been constricted and channeled into a specialized area. Some two-year-olds are extraordinarily interested in physical materials and not much interested in people. Others are deeply involved with their primary caretaker, and show surprising little interest in the physical world in contrast to their behavior only one year earlier.

In the area of social development, a child's social style seems to have become very well established by the time he is two years of age. Almost every two-year-old child we have seen has been a complicated social creature in the sense that his behaviors are far more sensitive to the particularities of each situation than they were when he was eight

151

months of age. Along with the many nuances of emotional mood that he exhibits in his interactions with people, the two-year-old is far less abrupt than the younger child in his shifts of mood state from euphoria to darkest gloom or anger. He has a variety of social abilities and patterns; indeed, under the best of circumstances, he has by now acquired most of the social skills that he will exhibit at the age of six. These skills include getting the attention of adults and holding on to it, sometimes in very subtle ways. They include using the adult as a resource to help deal with problems; expressing affection and hostility toward adults in a variety of ways; a budding capacity to direct the adult in various activities; and exhibiting fantasy behavior on an interpersonal level. We will examine these abilities in greater detail later in this chapter. All in all, socially the child is a far more complicated creature at age two. You may recall that I have spoken about the creation of a social contract in the eight- to twenty-four-month period. This agreement is quite long and highly detailed. In it is contained what the child has learned through hundreds of interchanges with the primary caretaker. To the extent that another sibling has been regularly involved in his life, a whole set of behaviors has been assimilated with respect to interactions with other young people as well.

The fourth major educational goal, nurturing the roots of intelligence—the learning-to-learn skills—is another area where a child can have made tremendous progress by twenty-four months of age. He can have learned much about the physical world of objects, about the regularities in nature, and so forth. Indeed, during the months that immediately precede his second birthday the child will have entered into a qualitatively new and vitally important style of intellectual functioning which features the use of ideas and images in the head rather than overt physical actions. This growth of thinking ability, including the element of memory, interacts with his behaviors in the social realm.

It is apparent, then, that Phases V and VI cover a period when the basic shaping of a young human can be influenced in powerful ways by whoever is responsible for him. Again, I do not think it is possible to overemphasize the importance of these eighteen months of life.

DIFFICULT FEATURES OF PHASE VI

Not only is this period extraordinarily and almost uniquely important, but it can also be a very trying time for a young mother. This is the time when the child tends to oppose the will of his primary caretaker. All

Negativism

children we have observed go through this process, even those who are developing superbly well. Some families do better than others in coping with negativism. In general, families with well-developing children get through this period more easily than those with children who are developing poorly. Nevertheless, all parents should be prepared for some amount of friction during this phase.

Why a child has to become ornery and stay that way for a minimum of six or seven months is one of the mysteries that makes the study of early human development so rich and fascinating. Suffice it to say that somehow the young of the human has to go from total dependence to a stance from which he can face reality on his own. It looks like the second half of the second year represents a stage at which some major step in this process takes place. A second comparable step seems to occur at puberty, and takes the form of adolescent rebellion. I leave it for other researchers to figure out more about that fascinating problem.

REDEEMING FEATURES OF PHASE VI

As difficult and as serious as the business of development is at this age, it has its redeeming features. The new achievements of this particular period are especially rewarding to parents. This is the time when children begin holding real conversations with family members. This activity is usually extremely enjoyable for parents and of course for grandparents. Children are now moving from babyhood into the first forms of personhood. Their personalities are becoming clearer, more reliable, and more individualistic. Furthermore, they are very much interested in you, if you are the primary caretaker. These developments, along with the ease with which children can now walk about, contribute to a general feeling that you are living with a young, very interesting person rather than with a baby.

INVOLVEMENT WITH THE PRIMARY CARETAKER

A special interest in the primary caretaker is another dominant quality of this particular age range. More than at any other time in life most babies will focus on their mothers for substantial portions of the day during their second year. As mentioned earlier, the three kinds of overpowering general interests of this age range are the primary caretaker's actions, interest in exploration of the world, and interest in practicing new motor skills. In the best of circumstances, these three interests are pursued and developed throughout late infancy. None interferes with the others. In situations where children are developing nicely, a large portion of the child's interest is focused on the mother, as her role as someone to recur to for assistance, counseling, nurture, and simple pleasantries becomes well defined. During the second year of life the child will not usually spend long periods of time without checking on his mother's whereabouts. This orientation leads to the establishment of a social contract and the first reflected identity of the baby.

GENERAL BEHAVIOR DURING THIS PERIOD

PREDOMINANCE OF NONSOCIAL PURSUITS

In spite of the child's intense interest in his mother during Phase VI, if you actually watch a fourteen-month-old baby as he goes about his

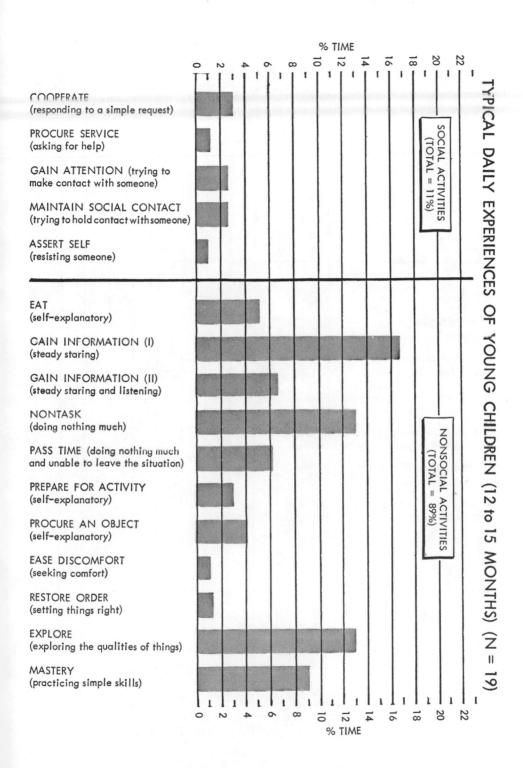

TYPICAL DAILY EXPERIENCES OF YOUNG CHILDREN (12 to 15 MONTHS) (N = 19)

% TIME

COOPERATE
(responding to a simple request)

PROCURE SERVICE
(asking for help)

GAIN ATTENTION (trying to
make contact with someone)

MAINTAIN SOCIAL CONTACT
(trying to hold contact with someone)

ASSERT SELF
(resisting someone)

SOCIAL ACTIVITIES
(TOTAL = 11%)

EAT
(self-explanatory)

GAIN INFORMATION (I)
(steady staring)

GAIN INFORMATION (II)
(steady staring and listening)

NONTASK
(doing nothing much)

PASS TIME (doing nothing much
and unable to leave the situation)

PREPARE FOR ACTIVITY
(self-explanatory)

PROCURE AN OBJECT
(self-explanatory)

EASE DISCOMFORT
(seeking comfort)

RESTORE ORDER
(setting things right)

EXPLORE
(exploring the qualities of things)

MASTERY
(practicing simple skills)

NONSOCIAL ACTIVITIES
(TOTAL = 89%)

% TIME

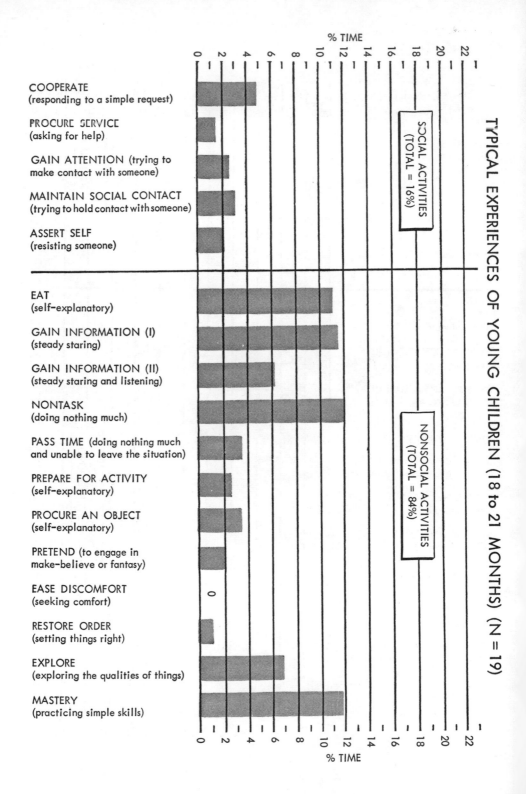

TYPICAL EXPERIENCES OF YOUNG CHILDREN (18 to 21 MONTHS) (N = 19)

% TIME

COOPERATE
(responding to a simple request)

PROCURE SERVICE
(asking for help)

GAIN ATTENTION (trying to
make contact with someone)

MAINTAIN SOCIAL CONTACT
(trying to hold contact with someone)

ASSERT SELF
(resisting someone)

SOCIAL ACTIVITIES
(TOTAL = 16%)

EAT
(self-explanatory)

GAIN INFORMATION (I)
(steady staring)

GAIN INFORMATION (II)
(steady staring and listening)

NONTASK
(doing nothing much)

PASS TIME (doing nothing much
and unable to leave the situation)

PREPARE FOR ACTIVITY
(self-explanatory)

PROCURE AN OBJECT
(self-explanatory)

PRETEND (to engage in
make-believe or fantasy)

EASE DISCOMFORT
(seeking comfort)

RESTORE ORDER
(setting things right)

EXPLORE
(exploring the qualities of things)

MASTERY
(practicing simple skills)

NONSOCIAL ACTIVITIES
(TOTAL = 84%)

% TIME

ordinary activities during the day you will find that he spends no more than ten to fifteen percent of his time in interchanges with his mother (or with any other person, for that matter). The remainder of his time is spent in nonsocial pursuits.

Staring behavior

The most common nonsocial behavior during Phase VI is simply staring at objects, people, or events. As we have seen, some twenty percent of all waking time is spent looking about in a steady fashion at one object, person, or scene. Why children spend so much time in steady staring is not clearly understood. It seems to be a simple form of exploration of the world.

Exploratory and mastery experiences

Two of the other major kinds of nonsocial experience, which should be discussed jointly, have to do with a more active exploration of physical objects, usually small portable ones. As noted earlier, we call these two types of experience *exploratory activities* and *mastery activities*. In the case of exploratory activities (which generally are more common at fourteen months than mastery experiences), the child spends a good deal of time examining the various qualities of as many objects as he can get to in the course of a day. Those objects range from toys to cellophane wrapping from a cigarette pack. They can, in short, be anything. Children try out a variety of standard action patterns on these objects, apparently trying to get to know as much about them as they can in a short space of time. They will strike objects against various surfaces, throw them, drop them, and look at and feel each of their surfaces. They will use objects to load and unload containers. They will mouth objects and chew on them, partly to relieve tenderness in the gums and partly to explore the object. They will do all sorts of things with these objects which can best be described as exploring their various qualities.

The second major active interaction with small physical objects is to practice simple skills on them. Some of those skills are: dropping and throwing objects, swinging hinged objects back and forth, opening and closing doors, opening and closing drawers, placing small relatively unstable objects into an upright position then knocking them down and replacing them, putting pieces together and taking them apart, putting objects through openings, pouring materials into and out of containers,

manipulating simple locking devices, and activating switches that produce light and darkness or other kinds of interesting consequences like
sounds or changing visual patterns. As noted earlier, together these two
types of activities take up twenty percent of the child's waking time at
this stage.

All sorts of simple, mostly digital finger skills are extremely popular
at this age. A peculiarly interesting activity is the spinning of various
sorts of wheels. Many times we have seen young children spinning
wheels and watching the consequences. Such wheels can be as small as
those of very small toy cars and trucks. They can be as large as the
wheels of a cart or a tipped-over bicycle. The pedals on a tricycle are
another object which children seem to be peculiarly interested in rotating. As mentioned before, the pages of books and magazines, particularly books with stiff pages, are objects on which children like to
practice finger skills. If you have a piece of furniture that is relatively
low but slightly difficult to climb, it is not uncommon for a toddler to
climb the object, then carefully come down and start all over again.
Toward the end of the fourteen- to twenty-four-month period you will
see more and more interest in gymnastics; for example, climbing and
descending small slides. You will also notice that most children are
quite a bit more careful than you might predict in performing most of
these activities.

By two years of age there has ordinarily been a reversal of the type of
play with objects, with a steady decrease in exploratory behavior and a
steady increase in mastery behavior. We have also noted that children
developing rather well have a steeper rate of increase of mastery versus
exploratory experiences in regard to small objects. I believe that what is
reflected here is the quality of sophistication of object play, and that this
finding will stand up as the years go by.

NONTASK BEHAVIOR

Another area of experience of the Phase VI child is that of nontask
behavior. By nontask behavior we mean behavior which is apparently
purposeless, where the child seems to be just hanging around or idling.
Such behavior is quite common in the lives of young children. Phase VI
children may spend anywhere from one to thirty percent of their time
idling.

In particular the *range* of the amount of nontask behavior grows rather rapidly during Phase VI. We have seen two-year-old children who spend a great deal of time doing nothing, standing in place. They may be thinking great thoughts; but high quantities of nontask behavior in two-year-olds have been so routinely associated with poor development in our studies that we are more inclined to think that they are indicative of blank states. If we see a two-year-old who engages four or five percent of his time in this fashion, we figure that he is clearly within the normal range. Variations up or down of a modest kind are perfectly common, but when a child begins to approach the fifteen-percent, twenty-percent, or twenty-five-percent area in regard to nontask behavior, we are dealing with a child who, at least for the cultures we have examined, may very well be showing signs of a considerably poorer pattern of experience than we would like to see.

PASSING TIME

A previously mentioned and related form of experience common in the lives of all young children is what we call passing time. In a pass-time experience the child is not doing much of anything; however, he is not free to the degree that he ordinarily is to get out of the situation and find something to do. A good example of a passing-time experience is when a mother says to a two-year-old, "You wait here, please, while I get you a new diaper," or "Wait while I get a car seat; we are going to go for a ride." If the child does wait dutifully and cannot find anything to occupy himself with for more than a few seconds, we label that kind of experience passing time. Perhaps the most common type of pass-time experience in the life of a fourteen-month-old is when he is placed into a restrictive situation such as a playpen, crib, jump seat, or highchair for long periods of time. Another common activity that usually produces pass-time experience is the automobile ride. If the child in one of these situations, where his movements are restricted psychologically or physically, finds something to really become engaged with, then we do not call it a pass-time experience. If, for example, a child in a playpen has a particularly fascinating toy or a small object, and plays with it for more than fifteen continuous seconds, we consider the experience a form of active play.

It is extremely difficult to keep a child engaged in any form of active play when he is a psychological or physical captive in a playpen, highchair, crib, small gated room, or even a car seat. You might have guessed that a Phase VI child in a car seat would spend a great deal of time drinking in the scenery on a trip through the streets or the country. Such is not the case. We do not know why, but from our extensive observations, children simply find themselves with nothing interesting to do for most of the time that they are in such restrictive situations.

LOOKING AND LISTENING

Another category of apparent educational significance, and one which takes up a substantial portion of a Phase VI child's day, is what we call looking and listening to relevant language. A typical example of such an experience is when a child is looking at his mother and older sibling, who are talking at a level that is within his capacity to understand. The two major classes of looking and listening experience in Phase VI are looking and listening to live language and looking and listening to mechanical language. By live language we mean spoken language the child may overhear, or spoken language directed toward the subject by another person. Mechanical language is usually delivered by a television set. We have found that how much experience children have in these categories is quite variable in Phase VI and we believe that the variations and the amounts are germane to educational development in this age range. Put briefly, as you might expect, *the more live language directed to the child, the better off he is in comparison to watching and listening to television.*

LIFE WITHOUT A SLIGHTLY OLDER SIBLING

I would now like to describe, in a more general way, what life can be like when dealing with the Phase VI child. First of all let us consider the case where there is no slightly older sibling in the home.

Exploration

When there is no slightly older sibling in the home, you will find that a Phase VI child will spend the bulk of the day, if allowed to, exploring the living area. This means that while you are working in the home (most commonly the kitchen), he will be moving in and out of various parts of the home, returning frequently to visit or consult with you. If you have made the kitchen an attractive place for him he will spend time exploring there as well. It is already most interesting to him because of your presence, but it can be even more interesting if you, for example, have accident-proofed the area and made available one or two of the lower kitchen cabinets or some section of the pantry or some other special area where he can explore. You will find that from time to time, as he moves through the other rooms, he will, if he can manage, climb something like an ottoman or a small chair in order to spend time looking out the window. This is a very common practice of children of this age. At fourteen months, if there are stairs in your living area that are not gated, he will spend a fair amount of time getting to them and practicing climbing. Stair climbing is of universal appeal to fourteen-month-old children.

Another focus of universal appeal is the toilet bowl. Unless you prevent him, he will make regular visits to the bathroom, stand next to the bowl, and splash the water around. If available, he will use small utensils to pour water and occasionally even drink it.

One place where he will ordinarily spend relatively *little* time is in his own room with his own toys, at least during the beginning of Phase VI. He has too much else to see and do.

In regard to the topic of opening doors, you will find that babies are peculiarly handicapped with respect to rotational hand motions at this stage. We have never found a baby of fourteen to twenty-four months of age that could unscrew anything beyond one turn. Phase VI babies manage a quarter turn or so and then cannot seem to continuously move the item to be unscrewed much further. They seem to forget which direction they should continue to turn, or there is a drag such that the objects get refastened by as much as they have been unfastened. It is a manual skill that is beyond them.

Television viewing

There exists a good deal of mythology with respect to the television viewing habits of young children. There is only one reliable way to know just how much television very young children watch. That way is expensive and laborious and involves a professional observer spending a good deal of time in the homes of large numbers of children, recording where they are looking and what they are apparently listening to. As far as I know, nobody has done this sort of research extensively except our Preschool Project at Harvard.

After watching several hundred children in eastern Massachusetts during the day, in their own homes, we have found that they watch very little television before they are two years of age and not very much during the third year of life. A rare child, one who is relatively well developed and whose intelligence level is precociously high, may toward the end of the second year of life begin to spend a fair amount of time watching *Sesame Street* (indeed, one out of four precocious children during our observations have at times spent a full hour staring at *Sesame Street*). However, our data shows that the average is approximately two minutes an hour for the waking hours. During the second year of life television viewing is only a momentary and sporadic affair for most children.

Outdoor activities

Weather permitting, children usually spend a fair amount of time outdoors during Phase VI, and they ordinarily enjoy this activity very much. Given the opportunity, they will show that same profound curiosity about exploring a grassy yard, plants, dirt, picnic tables, and so forth, that they show indoors.

Occasionally you will find rather unusual and hard-to-understand behaviors being shown by children of this age in their first encounters with the outdoors. You will find, for example, that one child in twenty will resist being put down on the grass, and will neither want to crawl on it nor walk on it. Others tend to avoid asphalt surfaces. These are typical, passing quirks, and nothing to worry about. A favorite activity of children of this age is swinging through the air. If you have a safe infant seat arranged on an outdoor gym set, you will find your child enjoys it hugely. Another favorite outdoor activity is water play. Miniature pools are inexpensive and readily available.

LIFE WITH A SLIGHTLY OLDER SIBLING

A baby's life is significantly different when there is a slightly older sibling in the house, although the overall pattern of experiences remains much the same. The most common experience will be steady looking at people or objects, and much time will be spent in small-object play. *The differences of consequence will be in the everyday social experiences of the baby.* From eight months on through the second year the baby will be involved in thousands of interchanges with a slightly older human with whom he shares the home and the primary caretaker.

Since the older child may be less than three years of age for much of this period, he usually finds the presence of the baby quite difficult to deal with. We discussed the reasons for this in Chapter VI. Perhaps the greatest irony involved here is the fact that if the older child vents his wrath on the baby he is likely to be scolded by the very person he is feeling rejected by.

Within the baby's social experiences the effects of the slightly older sibling will be seen in two types of situations. Most commonly they will be seen in the presence of many more child-to-child encounters than otherwise would be the case. Furthermore, as noted earlier, these encounters in marked contrast to most of the child's other social experiences will feature rejection, hard feelings, and outright abuse at times. I do not mean to say that a kind word will never pass from the older sibling to the baby. I *do* mean to say, however, that the baby will almost certainly get a good dose of unpleasant social interaction over a period that may last for longer than a year. The second situation worth noting is when both children interact simultaneously with the primary caretaker. Given such a situation, the baby at times must share his mother's attentions, while at other times he has to compete for it. Associated with such experiences, the baby will at times be present when his mother is scolding the older child. Over a period of many months it is likely that these types of experiences have lasting effects on the development of the baby. Just what those effects are is not yet known, but again what I have seen has led me to recommend that parents space their children at least three years apart. Closer spacing not only makes for extra difficulty for the baby, it is also tough on parents and *most of all* on the slightly older child.

THE APPARENT INTERESTS OF THIS AGE

The three dominating interests of the Phase V child carry over into Phase VI.

INTEREST IN THE PRIMARY CARETAKER

The Phase VI baby's interest in his mother takes the form of a general orientation toward her location and regular overtures to her. These overtures can be for several basic purposes. One is simply to socialize, to reestablish contact. Another common purpose is to ask for assistance of some sort. Less commonly, a Phase VI child may come to his mother simply to express affection or to seek approval for something he is proud of.

When children are out of sorts because of fatigue or minor illness they are likely to be even more clingy, even more oriented toward the primary caretaker than under ordinary circumstances. It is relatively easy for a mother to indulge her child's interest in her to the disadvantage of the other two major interests of the child during Phase VI. After all, babies of this age are extremely attractive creatures, and holding them close is very rewarding to most parents. Sometimes a mother finds it easier to indulge a child's interest in her rather than finding him something to do or suggesting that he play by himself; especially if the latter suggestion leads to displeasure and hurt feelings. I would like to stress the fact that this interest of the young child in relating to the primary caretaker is at once both an important, healthy sign, and also one that can be misdeveloped in ways that are not in the child's best interests. More about that topic in the section on recommended child-rearing practices.

INTEREST IN EXPLORATION OF THE WORLD

Interest in objects

The second interest area is in exploring the world at large. Phase VI children show a continuing interest in small objects, marked by a gradual shift in emphasis from exploring their qualities to practicing simple skills upon them. Toward the end of Phase VI, and especially as the third year of life begins, children begin to synthesize what they have learned in the first two phases of small-object play, and start to use objects for imaginative play, constructing scenes with dolls and animal figures, and using objects to build towers, fortresses, ranches, and so forth.

Interest in changeable factors

Beyond physical objects which, of course, will include toys and many common household objects, the physical surroundings continue to intrigue the child, but less and less so as he approaches his second birthday. It is as if he is gradually coming to be so knowledgeable about what the living area looks like, feels like, and contains that the newness is wearing off. He now is becoming more interested in new events that transpire within and outside of the walls of the living area. He will spend more and more time looking out the window at the new events of each day. He will spend a little more time watching people and their actions in the home. He will begin to spend a little more time looking at things on a television screen. His focus is shifting with respect to explorations into directions which are more changeable, more likely to be different from day to day, than the more static qualities of the living area which had occupied him during his first explorations of the home.

Water play

Water play continues to be great fun for the Phase VI child. It seems to have more lasting capacities than many other kinds of play. Unlike most commercial toys whose actions are restricted by their design and physical limitations, water can be used in an infinite number of ways.

Balls

In repeated observations of the utilization of toys and other physical materials, we have found the ball ranking right at the top of the list in terms of frequency of use. This is especially true in the first half of Phase VI. One of the best ways in which to engage the attention of a fourteen- or fifteen-month-old child is with a plain, inexpensive Ping-Pong ball. Particularly when used on a hardwood floor, a Ping-Pong ball has everything. To begin with, by simply dropping it, you create a lot of movement, which lasts for quite some time. In addition, that movement has a kind of antic quality to it in that the bouncing is crisp and orderly in contrast, for example, to a dead tennis ball or a piece of Silly Putty. Second, the bouncing is accompanied by interesting sound patterns. Third, the Ping-Pong ball is small enough so that the child can manage it much better than he can manage balls of five or six inches or more in diameter. Fourth, it is light enough so that it can be thrown some distance by the child. Fifth, although of less significance, is the notion that a throw of the Ping-Pong ball is not likely to incur scolding from the parent in the same sense that throwing a baseball might. In addition, playing with a Ping-Pong ball can feed a child's growing ability to chase and retrieve thrown items. This latter attribute feeds into the child's third major interest, the mastery of the newly found motor skills.

A cautionary note: Ping-Pong balls are going to be put into the mouth. They are a bit too large for comfortable swallowing, but I would be inclined to wait until a child is at least fourteen months of age and can understand simple instructions before I made these balls available to him. Also, check once in a while to see that the Ping-Pong ball is still intact, because the hard edges of a crushed Ping-Pong ball can constitute a hazard.

Oral exploration

Throughout Phase VI the mouth continues to be used as an exploratory organ. In recent studies that I performed for a major United States manufacturer, we found that the child in Phase VI is very likely to put *any* material to his mouth, whether it be solid or liquid. His next act is to gum the substance in question, and then swallow some, if possible. It is not surprising that this is the time of life when many accidental poisonings take place. You are advised to be doubly cautious about such matters in Phase VI. The research that we did on the topic revealed the impulsivity of children of this age. They did not pause to test the odor, to taste, or for any other reason. The poison-control centers of this country report that children swallow all sorts of foul-tasting substances such as gasoline and cleaning fluids. Indeed, the research we did indicated that there was absolutely no effect of odor on the tendency of a child to swallow a fluid. We used odors ranging from pleasant foodlike odors such as chocolate, to floral odors, to extraordinarily unpleasant noxious ones like rotten eggs. The amount of swallowing was totally independent of the associated odor. Here is one place where the powerful curiosity of a child can have harsh consequences indeed.

INTEREST IN PRACTICING NEW MOTOR SKILLS

The third major area of interest in Phase VI is in motor development. The fourteen-month-old child generally is a fairly good walker, although slightly unstable and still inhibited by a good deal of body fat. He is also, at this point, reasonably skillful at climbing and, as noted earlier, loves to do so. I would encourage you to let him climb, but always under close supervision until you are thoroughly assured that he can handle the situation well. On the other hand, if you do not want him to climb one or another object for any reason I would urge you to prevent him from doing so. Many parents find early climbing too anxiety-provoking to deal with.

Beyond walking and climbing, the emerging activities of Phase VI include skillful running, a typical activity of the age, and operating four-wheeled carts and wagons by straddling them and walking them along. Although the Phase VI child will enjoy practicing his new ability to move four-wheeled objects, he is not yet likely to be able to do much with even the smallest of tricycles. I recommend that in order to avoid frustration and minor accidents, you hold off on the purchase of tricycles until after a child's second birthday.

EDUCATIONAL DEVELOPMENTS DURING PHASE VI

In my discussion of the Phase V child I cited four relatively indisputable educational foundations that undergo important development from eight months of age on. They are: language development, the development of curiosity, social development, and nurturing the roots of intelligence. These foundation processes are still undergoing vital structuring during Phase VI. It may be useful at this point to add the two other ways in which we frame our discussions of educational development.

IMPORTANCE OF KEEPING INTERESTS IN BALANCE

I have already alluded to an additional way of evaluating educational development in describing the desirability of *maintaining a balance* among the growing major interests of a child, *i.e.,* interest in the primary caretaker, interest in exploration of the world, and interest in practicing new motor skills. I have stressed the fact that if this balance is lost the child's educational progress can suffer, and that such imbalance is chiefly caused by an overconcentration on the primary caretaker. Less frequently, the child's interests in exploration and motor mastery are adequately supported by the environment, but the normal growth of his interest in his mother is interfered with—usually inadvertently—by parental behaviors. The saddest of all situations is when *none* of the three major interests are nurtured by a child's environment.

EMPHASIS ON SELECTED ABILITIES

A third way of dealing with what is going on educationally in Phase VI stems directly from our research on well-developing young children. In that research an early goal was to come to know, in some detail, what it was about a well-developing three- to six-year-old child that we could identify as special. We came to an understanding of good development in three- to six-year-old children through extensive observations of such children in their homes, at nursery schools, and in day-care centers. The following list of characteristics or dimensions of competence are the distinguishing behaviors of very well-developed children as far as we could tell. The well-developed three-year-old child shows the following abilities in greater and more impressive ways than the average or below-average three-year-old:

Social abilities
- getting and holding the attention of adults
- using adults as resources after first determining that a job is too difficult
- expressing affection to adults
- expressing mild annoyance to adults
- leading peers
- following peers
- expressing affection to peers
- expressing mild annoyance to peers
- competing with peers
- showing pride in personal accomplishment
- engaging in role play or make-believe activities

Nonsocial abilities
- good language development
- the ability to notice small details or discrepancies
- the ability to anticipate consequences
- the ability to deal with abstractions
- the ability to put oneself in the place of another person
- the ability to make interesting associations
- the ability to plan and carry out complicated activities
- the ability to use resources effectively
- the ability to maintain concentration on a task while simultaneously keeping track of what is going on around one in a fairly busy situation (dual focusing)

This list of abilities can serve as a guide to child-rearers in their activities with a child during the second year of his life. Although some of the above behaviors will not be observable until the child's third year, it may be useful to be aware of them in advance of their emergence. Later in this chapter we will examine them more closely and see how some of them can be reinforced as early as Phase VI by proper child-rearing practices.

RECOMMENDED CHILD-REARING PRACTICES
AT THIS STAGE

INTRODUCTORY REMARKS

A good introductory focus for this section is the basic question of how balanced a child's development is at *any* point during the eight- to twenty-four-month period. You will recall that in the discussion of Phase V, I pointed out that the eight-month-old baby starts out with a strong interest in each of three major directions: in the primary care-taker, in exploring the world, and in mastering the use of his body, particularly in regard to emerging gross motor skills. *I want to reemphasize my belief that maintaining a balance across all three, while simultaneously nurturing their solid development, seems at the heart of good early education.* I believe most families have the resources to do that job well. But once again I doubt that many currently do as well as they could.

The second way of thinking about the goals for this period is to think in terms of the four fundamental educational processes that we have talked about; language development, the development of curiosity, social development, and nurturing the roots of intelligence. The third way of considering Phase VI goals is in terms of the above-listed special abilities of a well-developed three-year-old child. I think each way of looking at educational goals has its own usefulness.

COPING WITH NEGATIVISM

We have already examined the intensification of negative behavior that ushers in Phase VI. This behavior takes several forms, none of which are terribly pleasant to live with. The child may or may not say the word *no* to you, but he certainly will express the concept *no* in his behavior.

The emergence of negativism is extremely regular with children. Whether it first appears at thirteen, fourteen, or as late as sixteen or seventeen months, you should expect to see it sooner or later during the second year of life. Once negativism begins to take hold, it—along with other factors in the child's life, such as his continued tendencies to explore and to bring things to the mouth—produces more pressure on the primary caretaker. With this increase in pressure, the issue of discipline becomes more salient. As we have seen, distraction is often a very useful and effective mechanism in dealing with a one-year-old baby. If the baby has begun to play with the trash bag, the skillful caretaker may very well seduce the child into other more acceptable kinds of play by offering the child a new toy or access to a previously unexplored household item or area. Distraction, unfortunately, does not work quite so well with a baby in the middle of negativism. It is at this point that sustained stubbornness rears its head for the first time with most children. They want their own way. At times they will not be dissuaded from something they are doing, especially if it is something that they see their mother disapproves of. This quality of personally directed orneriness can be hard to live with, but there are two consolations for you. One is that it happens with just about every child, so it is not because you are an inadequate mother or disagreeable person that the baby is behaving this way. The other is that it will probably eventually go away.

Unfortunately, negativism does not go away with every child. Some children have such a difficult time in this stage of life that I do not believe they *ever* really thoroughly outgrow their orneriness. Under optimum conditions, by the time the baby reaches twenty-one or twenty-two months of age, the pressures toward this kind of behavior subside, the clouds break, the sun comes out, and living with the child becomes pleasant again. However, I do not think you should expect a perfect outcome. It is more realistic to expect that contentious behavior will continue at least until the second birthday.

Firm discipline is still strongly advised, but because it is clear that there are very great pressures on the Phase VI child (especially during the fourteen- to twenty-one-months period) occasionally to contest and to win over authority, *I believe wise parents are well advised to yield occasionally to the child in areas where the stakes are not particularly high (from the parents' point of view).* This does not mean that I advocate a general permissiveness or a general abdication of responsibility for controlling the home. The parents we have watched doing an apparently effective job with their children *never* abdicate their control in this regard; but they are wise enough and personally secure enough to occasionally let the child win a minor struggle at this particular stage of life when it seems especially important for the child to flex his muscles a little bit, interpersonally.

LANGUAGE DEVELOPMENT

Effective language encouragement

In the preceding chapter we talked about what I conceive to be the most probable means by which children learn language effectively in this age range. I pointed out that at about eleven months, children begin to make overtures more frequently to the primary caretaker. When they make an approach it is usually for one of a very small number of purposes. Usually the need is easy to identify, and if an adult responds according to the ways we have seen apparently effective mothers respond, we believe that good language learning will result. I have also tried to be specific about the language learning during Phases V and VI. The recommendations for how to react to a child's overtures, plus the information about the particular level he is at with respect to language development, underlie effective language encouragement. The list of first words on pages 84–85 contains information about the specific linguistic acquisitions during Phase VI.

Both in Phase V and Phase VI, I believe that talking to a child is most effective if it is at or slightly beyond his apparent level of understanding. Language that is too simple for him or considerably beyond his capacity to understand seems less useful for sponsoring linguistic development.

Language development like any learning, occurs best when a child is paying attention. That is why I emphasize the desirability of doing your language teaching when the child comes to you with a particular interest in mind. If you correctly identify that interest, speak to it, and act to it, you will be assured of the child's attention. Otherwise, getting an infant to pay attention to what you are saying is rather difficult.

Reading aloud

Also, as in Phases IV and V, reading simple, entertaining stories to your child, particularly at night before he goes to bed, seems to be a good idea. On the other hand, if you insist on story reading during the waking hours when the child wants to be doing something else, out of some sort of notion that it is an absolute essential or very desirable, I think both you and your child will pay for it.

The role of television

Toward the end of Phase VI you can expect to see your child paying more and more attention to television. Exposure to programs like *Sesame Street* probably will, in a modest way, have an impact on the child's level of language development, but rest assured if he never sees a single television program he still can learn language through you in an absolutely magnificent manner.

Grammar and comprehension

During the fourteen- to twenty-four-month age range, language ability develops at a very rapid pace. Even though the child less than one and one-half years of age still is not likely to speak very much, the rate at which he is learning to understand new words and new grammatical arrangements like prepositions, negatives, and plurals is dramatically high. The receptive vocabulary of a child in the second year of life, for example, is likely to go from perhaps a dozen words at his first birthday on up to several hundred by the time he is two years of age. Indeed, by the time he is two he knows a substantial percentage of the grammatical structures that are the bases of communication in simple language. The fourteen- or fifteen-month-old child can understand a fair number of simple instructions, including prohibitions and warnings. This means that if a mother is beleaguered and wants very much to leave a child alone for awhile to get him out of her hair, she is now for the first time able to say I do not want you to do *A*, *B*, or *C* and have some confidence that he may toe the mark.

In spite of the fact that the Phase VI baby has come a long way linguistically, it is clear that he still has a long way to go. For example, you should not use instructions and admonitions that involve threats of punishment that might come several hours later or a day or two later. If you tell the fourteen-month-old baby he will be spanked when daddy comes home unless he does *X* or *Y*, you will be misreading his capacities. Babies of this age are still living in the here and now. They are still responsive primarily to things that they can see in front of them rather than things that might happen sometime in the future. Therefore, while you should take advantage of the new levels of ability, you also run the risk of expecting too much from the child. Expecting too much from an infant is a relatively common phenomenon in our experience.

First attempts at speech

On the positive side of the ledger, during the fourteen- to twenty-four-month age range, most babies gradually begin to speak. This is, of course, a slow process. It is a rather unusual child who says nothing for several months and then opens up with full sentences and complicated phrases. What is more likely is that your baby will use a few words, singly or in telescoped fashion, like the word "some," intended to mean, "I want some," or the word "more," meaning "I want more." Soon after the onset of these brief expressions, the child will begin to expand into the use of phrases, and it is quite possible that shortly before his second birthday he will be speaking in fairly complete sentences. Another phenomenon that is interesting and fun is when the Phase VI child uses long collections of sounds arranged in sentencelike form, with inflections and emphases, but with no recognizable word meaning. I have no notion as to the significance of this gibberish.

The importance of conversation

Once the child begins to speak fairly regularly during the day, the potential for conversation comes into existence. This potential has many dividends. First of all, it is another sign of increasing personhood. Adults are not very used to creatures who cannot speak. The only living nonverbal creatures that are typically in the home are household pets. An infant is obviously a considerably more complicated and important being than a goldfish, but at the same time, until he can speak he is different from older children and adults. This picture starts to change during the second year of life, and perhaps the most conspicuous sign of change is the use of language.

One of the characteristics of the well-developed three-year-old is a tendency to hold conversations with adults as if they were peers. *I believe this peerlike quality to the conversations of three-year-olds has its roots in the earliest conversations of the Phase VI baby.* In a good rearing situation the baby naturally interacts conversationally, sometimes for very serious purposes, at other times just for fun, and at other times primarily to maintain social contact. Comfortable, effective parents move naturally into responding to such language and into the carrying on of modest trains of conversation. Once this phenomenon surfaces, experiences with children are that much richer, and the possibilities of encouraging growth in several dimensions of competence become considerably greater. For example, a talking child is considerably easier to encourage in his role play, his fantasies, and his make-believe experiences than a child who says nothing.

THE EMERGENCE OF THINKING ABILITY

Sensorimotor intelligence

In the classical work of Piaget there are elaborate descriptions of what he calls sensorimotor intelligence in the first two years of a child's life. By "sensorimotor intelligence" Piaget is referring to a set of abilities different from "higher" intelligence. Most of us think about the concept of intelligence in terms of mental activity, of what is going on in the head, in the brain, in the gray matter. We admire someone like Albert Einstein, who has done magnificent work by manipulating ideas rather than, for example, by adjusting the clutch on a Volkswagen. And yet Piaget and many others recognize the fact that to the degree that intelligence is broadly defined, there are many forms of intelligence within the human capacity.

First signs of intelligence

In Piaget's description of intelligence (which involves the capacity to adapt flexibly to problems that one faces) there is room for much behavior shown by a child in the first one and one-half years of life, well before he is capable of very much internal thinking. As noted earlier, in Piaget's system the first signs of intelligence are often seen in connection with the reaching behavior of a six- or seven-month-old child. When a child pushes an obstacle aside in order to grasp an object, he is solving his first simple problem and is therefore showing practical or sensorimotor intelligence. Piaget does not describe the act of reaching itself as an act of intelligence. But when a child does action *A* (pushing an obstacle aside), obviously in a manner intended to make action *B* (grasping an object) possible, there is a means-ends relationship between the two behaviors. Piaget considers the use of a behavior to overcome difficulty in the way of a goal as a form of problem solving, and therefore of intelligence. It is Piaget's claim that children begin to become thinkers toward the end of their second year.*

Initial indications of thoughtfulness

Children under one and one-half years do not reflect upon ideas in any extensive way. The image of a thoughtful person is incompatible with the kind of intelligence shown by a child in the first eighteen months of life. In Piaget's system, at least, it is not fair to call the child under eighteen months a thoughtful creature, although something "mental" may be going on in the mind. Beyond approximately eighteen months it is increasingly appropriate to talk about degree of thoughtfulness in the behavior of children. You can actually begin to see the mind working and the "wheels turning" in the behavior of the child toward the end of Phase VI. There are interesting and pregnant delays in his behavior; and you can often predict his next act on the basis of the circumstances and his facial expression. His next behaviors often seem to confirm that he had actually been thinking out alternatives and options, or at least had been dwelling on a particular move that he was going to make.

Children under eighteen months of age are much more impulsive than two-year-olds. They try possible solutions in the open rather than in their heads. In Piaget's original writings on the growth of intelligence in his own three children, he described in great detail how his twelve- and thirteen-month-old children actively experimented in situations by trying out different ways of getting something that was out of reach, for example, when they were confined to a crib. However, when the same sort of problem was provided to these children when they were closer to two years of age, there would be a pause where they were apparently thinking through alternatives, and then the first act that followed the pause would be a correct or near-correct solution to the problem.

More elaborate descriptions of the rather dramatic and exciting changes in the quality of intelligent behavior are beyond the scope of this book. The best and indeed virtually only place to find such material, is in the work of Piaget himself, which you will find listed in the recommended readings section at the end of the book. Suffice it to say at this

---

* You must remember that these ideas are not fully established. They represent the best we have to offer at this point in time and in my opinion they are likely to someday be proven largely true.

point that the possibilities in dealing with a child expand directly with the growth of his mental abilities. During Phase VI the child's capacity to understand explanations is growing. His capacity to deal with phenomena that extend in time is growing because of his increased grasp of reality. His capacity for memory is moving ahead rather rapidly. He still, however, exhibits clear signs of being far from mature mentally.

Phase VI and the random event

One interesting example of the mental immaturity of the Phase VI child, which we will talk more about in the next phase but which starts toward the end of this one, is the absence in the mind of the child of the possibility of a random event. One of the most common ways in which this is clearly evident is in misunderstandings between siblings. Your two-year-old child who is accidentally hurt by his older sibling is apparently totally unable to understand the concept of an accident. He assumes that if he was hurt, someone *intended* to hurt him. It is as simple as that. You can argue the point with him or explain it until you are quite fatigued, and it is not going to make a bit of difference. In the work of Piaget there are some fascinating explanations of why children develop this way.

THE DEVELOPMENT OF CURIOSITY

With respect to curiosity the same general guidelines set down for Phase V continue to apply. Make certain that the child has maximum access to the living area. Try to make the kitchen as interesting, as accessible, and as attractive as possible to the child. Get him outdoors as much as you can. Have available a special supply of materials that he cannot have access to regularly, with which to stimulate him when he seems bored or at a loss for something to do. Try not to create boredom for him by misguided attempts at insisting he attend to something. Try to build upon his natural enthusiasm for learning by responding as warmly and as supportively as you can when he does make an overture to you and wants to share an enthusiasm. Try to build on his interests by introducing related information and ideas when he makes an overture. If, for example, he brings you a big piece of Play-Doh and mumbles something about what a wonderful car he has made, you can suggest that he try to make a boat like Daddy's or like his own toy, or you can suggest that if he made a truck and another car he would have several cars. It is not terribly important that you come up with a brilliant observation; the major requirement is to support and broaden his curiosity. Implicitly, such behavior on your part makes it clear to the child that to be curious, to be learning, to be exploring, is something that you strongly approve of. And what you approve of means a great deal to your child, especially at this particular point in his life.

SOCIAL DEVELOPMENT

During Phase VI social development becomes a relatively delicate matter. This is a time when things might well go wrong. The preceding discussion of the topics of curiosity and language is important not merely because of the intrinsic value of curiosity and language, but also because if the child is not developing well in those areas it becomes nearly impossible to do a good job with his social development. Once again, the important thing is to maintain a solid and balanced course of development. If you encourage a child's natural tendencies to gravitate around you during much of this period, you are likely to find nurturing good, all-around development to be a hopeless task.

It is very difficult to live with a two and one-half-year-old clinging vine. We have seen a fair number of women get themselves into this situation and sorely regret it. In addition, such a situation, in my opinion, can lay the groundwork for further grief if you are dealing with a first child and are soon to produce a second. As we have seen, the child who is excessively wrapped up in his primary caretaker, and is relatively poorly developed in terms of his interests in the rest of the world, is the child who is less likely to succeed in overcoming the difficulties brought about by the introduction of a second child into the family. He is also the child who is likely to have difficulty moving into the world of the nursery school.

You really should not, at this point in time, prolong unrealistically the child's initial conception that the world was made exclusively for him and revolves solely around him. This prolongation is relatively easy to do, especially in the case of a first child, but I do not believe you are doing the child a service if you fall into such a pattern. Therefore my first message in regard to the Phase VI child and social development is,

*look upon Phase VI as a transitional period between early infancy and
that first point where the child is going to begin to move out of the home,*
whether it be out to a playground, the backyard, or into a nursery school.
Now is the time to start preparing him to cope with the outside world.

Independence training is particularly important in the case of a first
child. If you are dealing with a second child you will have to spend a
good deal of additional time dealing with the interaction between the
two children, particularly if the gap is less than three years. What we
find is that the child of fourteen or fifteen months of age with a slightly
older sibling finds the combination of the onset of negativism and
self-awareness, plus the consequences of having been occasionally
abused by his older brother and sister, plus the immaturity of his control
of his own emotions and ideas, too much to handle at times. Remember
too that if your older child is still less than three years of age, he too is
still mentally quite immature and emotionally even less mature. Given
such circumstances, you may find yourself in one of the more painful
kinds of child-rearing situations.

Should you find yourself in the above bind, remember: Continue to be
firm but loving with the older child; reassure him that you still love him
by spending a small amount of time alone with him daily in loving
interaction; and encourage his outside-of-the-home interests, so that if
he has an unhappy time in the home from time to time it will not destroy
his world.

NURTURING THE ROOTS OF INTELLIGENCE

The emergence of thinking ability during Phase VI is a remarkable
phenomenon. It is one of the mysteries of the ages, and one of the most
dramatic and exciting experiences parents can have, particularly with
their first children. I cannot count the number of times that young
parents, friends, and colleagues have reported to me how bowled over
they were by the new mental capacities of their one and one-half- to
two-year-old children. You can only understand this point thoroughly,
in my opinion, if you have gone through it on a personal level. No
amount of book learning will have quite the impact in this area that the
firsthand experience provides.

I do not believe that it takes great resources for families to do a good job of fostering a child's thinking ability at this stage.* In the second year of life, many facts about the world, and collections of ideas, are beyond the child's comprehension. What we are dealing with here is a core level of intelligence, and any normal adult possesses all that it takes to facilitate such development.

This brings us to the interesting question of whether a parent should attempt to develop his child's intelligence in special ways. I have always felt that the only way to respond to this question is to remind parents that a child is more than a possessor of intelligence. He is also a person who has his own pattern of social skills, and his own set of attitudes about people and life. He is, in short, a complicated creature who is at least as much heart as he is mind. My way of describing what a child is—in more technical detail—is contained, *in part,* in the list of abilities characterizing well-developed children which we will examine in the next section. I stress the words *in part* because that list does not include any reference to a child's sense of humor or his motor skills, yet such attributes are also important. The reason you do not find them listed is that we did not find that our well-developed children were unique in any way in regard to these qualities. It does not follow, however, that we, as parents, should neglect the development of humor or motor abilities in young children. I think any educator of a young child (especially his parents) should keep in mind *the full array of developmental goals:* the social, intellectual, and linguistic skills referred to throughout the text, plus the general goals of a sound body and a humanistic value system. I evaluate each suggested set of activities in regard to child-rearing in the light of its likely consequences for the entire array of desirable outcomes.

If teaching a child to recognize letters and numbers two years before most children do so, can be accomplished without in any way jeopardizing any other developmental goals, then I would consider doing it. If, on the other hand, such teaching incurs the risk of unbalancing a child's development by, for example, focusing so much of his time on intellectual and verbal tasks that he tends to have little time left over for motor

---

* Once the child gets to be three or four years of age, I think people with good educational backgrounds may have something of an advantage. Specific information and ideas become increasingly important to mental growth, and, generally, the more extensive your education, the richer the reservoir of ideas and information of a specific kind you have available to pass on to the child.

exercise or for interactions with other children, then I believe that it would be a disservice to the child. At the same time, you can see how one could overemphasize motor-skill development or social development to the point where some of the other developmental outcomes are in jeopardy. In sum, then, I think that one should consider the possibility of any special ideas about early education, but always in the light of the likely effects on the full range of developmental processes and outcomes.

FOSTERING THE DIMENSIONS OF COMPETENCE DURING PHASE VI

Social abilities

Getting and holding the attention of adults. This is the earliest acquired social skill of babies. Because of his ability to cry, the infant begins to get used to capturing the attention of adults very early in the game. The Phase VI child is still very much involved with getting attention, and may come up with a variety of tactics for doing so. This is natural, but parents should nevertheless try to deal with it as intelligently as possible. I think some parents do a disservice to their children by being around them too much and paying too much attention to them. This can prevent children from learning very much about different ways of getting and holding someone else's attention. I believe a second or third child is probably better off in this respect because his mother will simply not have the capacity to spend as much time hovering over him.

Using adults as resources after first determining that a job is too difficult. Although a child does not deliberately use adults as resources until he is at least nine or ten months of age, by the time he is four or five months of age he will have experienced many a reduction in discomfort after the appearance of an adult. And he will have noted that the appearance of the adult often follows his crying.

During Phase VI the handling of a child's appeal for help becomes particularly delicate. It is closely tied to the question of how strong the child's interest in the mother should be. You should help the Phase VI child to understand that by and large you can be counted on for help. But if the child is really not asking for help in accomplishing a particular task, but rather is using such overtures to monopolize your time, then his efforts are not appropriate and should not be encouraged.

Expressing affection and mild annoyance to adults. This capacity re-flects a feeling of comfort and confidence in interpersonal relations. It is extremely germane to the day-to-day living of the Phase VI child, whose tendencies toward expressing modest annoyance increase as he flowers as an individual. A balance needs to be maintained at this stage between overindulging the child's tendencies toward testiness (the con-sequences of which can be temper tantrums and bratty behavior), and suppressing such tendencies in such a way that you stifle his capacity to relate naturally to people.

The parent's own deeply rooted feelings about the expression of positive and negative emotions will probably influence a young child's capacities in this domaine. I suggest that you try to help your children acquire as much spontaneity of emotional expression as your own behavior patterns will allow.

Leading and following peers. These behaviors do not begin to become visible until the third year, since social behavior with peers is not commonly seen before the second birthday. Presumably, however, the behavior of a parent or other sibling has an influence on the later behavior of the child in this regard. Your child should be given the chance to offer you suggestions during shared activity in the first years of life. There will be many occasions during this early period when he will be asked to do what you say.

Expressing affection and mild annoyance to peers. The easy expression of feelings with peers is related to the same ability with respect to adults or older siblings. Like the preceding peer-oriented behaviors, these abilities begin to undergo rapid development during the third year of life, as true social interest in peers emerges and grows.

Competing with peers. The tendency to compete is one of the more debatable dimensions of competence on our list, at least from a value standpoint. It is nevertheless found regularly in the behavior of the well-developed three- to six-year-old children we have studied. Since the value of competitiveness is viewed differently by different families, I would not try to argue anyone into encouraging this behavior in his child. Whether you do or do not wish to encourage this tendency, during Phase VI you should be on the alert for the first signs of this behavior. It is most likely to occur in connection with rivalry with an older sibling.

Showing pride in personal accomplishment. This particular behavior, which can be so rewarding for parents, begins to develop substantially during the second year as the child begins to achieve skills that he can crow about. Phase VI skills are mostly manifested in activities rather than in the creation of such products as paintings. The child very often shows a delight in his first successes at walking and is a pushover for praise. Likewise, when he manages to move a four-wheeled toy about with some success he may often look to you with a light in his eyes that suggests that he is quite proud of what he has done. I strongly urge you to support these feelings of pride and achievement.

Engaging in role play or make-believe activities. It is desirable to enter into a child's natural tendencies to fantasize and to pretend, particularly as he looks forward to being grown up. Do not, however, expect to see much elaborate behavior of this type during Phase VI.

Nonsocial abilities

Good language development. How to assist language development at this stage has been discussed adequately elsewhere. This is not an especially difficult task and is well within the capacity of most people. Beginning at about fourteen months of age and continuing thereafter, children begin to show genuine interest in picture books. Within a few months, interest in stories emerges and begins a steady growth. Magazines and books are therefore very useful accessories for language learning from Phase VI on.

The ability to notice small details or discrepancies. This ability deserves a comment or two at this point. We have found that very well-developed three- and four-year-old children are very accurate observers. They notice things in the way of small differences and anomalies faster than most children. This talent is not only apparent when somebody makes an error in a drawing or when somebody sets the wrong things on a table, but it is also present in areas of logic. These talented children quickly notice when somebody telling a story or explaining something makes an error in logic. They are also better able to keep track of the sequence of events in a story than most children, and they quickly notice when somebody goes out of turn in a game. Keep this sort of talent in mind in your interchanges with Phase VI children, and try routinely to bring similarities, differences, small details, and interesting peculiarities to their attention.

The ability to anticipate consequences. A baby as young as nine or ten months of age, when noticing his mother go toward the front door with her coat on during cool weather, may begin to complain. This is a primitive form of being able to anticipate consequences, a skill that in later life is reflected in such important areas as effective driving. By three years of age stable differences in this ability among children are already visible.

I discussed how to coach your child to anticipate consequences in Chapter VI. This ability can be encouraged in the ordinary course of the day's activities. Again, it is easier to do so when the child brings a topic to your attention than when his attention is directed elsewhere.

The ability to deal with abstractions. Probably the two most common kind of abstractions that children learn to deal with during Phase VI are words and numbers. This does not mean that they can count, nor does it mean that they can write words or even use them particularly well. However, especially with respect to nouns, Phase VI children learn that certain words apply to classes of objects rather than merely to individual items. To an eight-month-old child the word "bottle" may refer only to *his* bottle. "Bottle" to the two-year-old can refer to any number of objects that have bottle characteristics. In that sense the two-year-old has learned an abstraction. Toward the end of the phase when children learn that "two cookies" means one cookie and one more cookie, they have learned an abstraction to the extent that they can apply the concept of two to other things as well.

In dealing with the Phase VI child, remember that he is a concrete thinker. He can communicate about objects that he can see, feel, and touch, but he is not particularly good at thinking or talking about objects that are not present. Stay with the here and now. If you want to talk about a particular subject or event that is not on the immediate scene, take care to relate it to something in the current situation.

The ability to put oneself in the place of another person. This is a particularly interesting dimension of competence, and one that is difficult to foster in a young child. Piaget points out that the capacity to put yourself in someone else's shoes and see things from his viewpoint is generally not seen much before the seventh or eighth year of a child's life.* We find that in children who are developing very well, this ability is pronounced by age six; in some cases, primitive forms of it are fairly well established as early as age three.

The ability to make interesting associations. We have often seen this behavior in talented three- to six-year-old children. It seems to be indicative of an agility and creativity of mind. To the extent that your

---

* Piaget's research on this topic was done during the 1920s with Swiss children. In general, his discoveries have been shown to be true, but the modern American child has often been found to reach new mental stages earlier than Piaget's subjects did.

natural style with the child features related ideas, and to the extent that you occasionally develop these ideas in storytelling, you will provide a model for your child in this valuable area.

The ability to plan and carry out complicated activities. This is an additional characteristic that distinguishes more competent children from others. In nursery-school situations, only a few children can bring several others together and manage to organize proceedings. This function can be taught by example. You can also assist the child in taking on and executing tasks which are a little more complex than the one- or two-step tasks of the first year of life.

The ability to use resources effectively. Closely allied to managerial ability, this skill is also relatable to the uses of adults as resources. It can be taught in a natural style, if you show imagination in the ways in which items are used. For example, if in order to reach something on a high shelf, you use a chair to stand on one time and a stepladder at another, or if you use several different objects to stir food, you may teach the child a bit about the multiple uses of materials. If, without overdoing it, you show a capacity to use resources effectively, and occasionally point out how you are doing it to the child, it will probably affect him beneficially.

Dual focusing. The capacity to maintain concentration on nearby work and simultaneously monitor or be aware of what is going on around you in a busy place is a fascinating behavior to observe. If you visit a nursery school or day-care center where groups of children are engaged in such activities as doing puzzles or drawing pictures, you will note that a small number of the children will be able to resist distractions better than others. This select group will frequently look around as if to keep track of what is happening. This ability is something that we really do not know how to teach. You can encourage a child's involvement in more than one task at a time, but if you attempt this too soon, you will only interfere with his capacity to do either task well.

RECOMMENDED MATERIALS FOR THIS AGE

The following chart is a summary of selected recommended materials for the Phase VI child. It has been compiled on the basis of his special interest in exploring appropriate objects, in practicing simple skills with them, in practicing gross motor skills (especially climbing), and in certain standard action patterns as present in rotating wheels and hinged materials. Commercial toys are not particularly *necessary* to the child's

LARGE TOYS		SMALL TOYS	
Especially Recommended	Of Moderate Use	Especially Recommended	Of Moderate Use
Small wagons and other stable, four-wheeled devices on which the child can sit and move himself about (Fisher-Price makes one or two good ones) Doll carriages Swings (make sure they are safe) Small slides and related junior-sized gym equipment	Pull toys	Kohner's Surprise Box Busy Bath (or Sears version) Books with stiff pages Balls of all sizes and shapes, especially large, light, plastic balls, Ping-Pong balls, and footballs Dolls and toys that feature relatively small human and animal figures such as toy buses and airplanes Pails suitable for pouring Carriages	Toy cars and trucks, *but* no small cars with thin metal axles such as Matchbox cars or Hot Wheels Crayons and scrap paper Stuffed animals The simplest puzzles Plastic pop beads Three-dimensional puzzles, like the standard mailbox with triangular, circular, and rectangular openings and pieces Stacking toys like the Fisher-Price doughnuts with base Toy telephones

LARGER MATERIALS
Especially Recommended

Empty boxes of all sizes and shapes
Small children's chairs
Full-length door mirrors
Adult furniture such as ottomans
Low cocktail tables
Small cushions
Living room furniture in general
Stairs (with caution)

SMALL PORTABLE ITEMS
Especially Recommended

Pots and pans of all sizes and shapes
Plastic refrigerator containers of all sizes and shapes, with lids if possible
Canned goods (you must monitor play with these)
Plastic jars with covers and other expendable, safe household items

OTHER ITEMS
Especially Recommended

Water
(a cheap medium with endless fascination)
Paper
(a cheap medium with endless fascination)

educational development at this stage. Phase VI children are too interested in social events (particularly those involving their mothers), in practicing the skills that help them master their own bodies, and in exploration of the living area and all its elements to limit themselves to one specific object. Besides, toy companies rarely know much about what really interests a child at this particular age. You will have to be your own judge and censor with respect to selling pressures.

CHILD-REARING PRACTICES I DO NOT RECOMMEND

PERMITTING TANTRUMS

Do not allow tantrums. Banging one's head against the floor, throwing objects, and so forth have never, in the history of our observations of children, been associated with good development. In my opinion, when children first engage in such activities they usually are earnestly seeking a limit, asking you to stop them. Tantrums can become common during the second year of life. I strongly advise you not to let them develop.

CONTESTS OF WILL

As mentioned before, during the middle of the second year your baby will probably start testing wills with you. Do not try to win all of the disagreements you have with him.

PREMATURE TOILET TRAINING

Do not try to force toilet training. Once a child gets to be about two, he will train himself in a relatively short space of time. Trying to toilet train a child much before two years of age is generally very difficult. If you attempt training when he is between fourteen and twenty-four months of age, you will run headlong into the rise of negativism. That is the worst possible time to try.

OVERFEEDING

My comments about between meal snacks in Phase V continue to apply to Phase VI. Whereas in Phase V the primary apparent causes of this practice are a desire to show that you care along with inadequate knowledge of how to keep a child happily engaged, in Phase VI, the normal negativistic behavior of the child may be the root cause. The Phase VI child can become a chronic nuisance at times, and almost anything that will give you some peace is likely to be considered. My hope is that by following the suggestions of this book, you'll be in less trouble on this score. If for any reason, however, you find yourself feeding snacks or drinks to the Phase VI child several times between meals, pause and review the situation. Something has probably gone awry.

MATERIALS NOT RECOMMENDED FOR THIS AGE

WIND-UP TOYS

At this point in a child's life, I would advise you to stay away from a fair number of materials whose sales are substantial. These include jack-in-the-box toys (with the exception of the Kohner Surprise Box mentioned earlier). The manual skills necessary to make such toys function are beyond virtually all children under two years of age. The same principle applies to wind-up musical toys. If you are willing to do all the winding, and it gives you and the child pleasure, go right ahead. I should warn you, however, that we have found that Phase VI children tire rather quickly with the simple sounds of music such toys produce. The common plastic nut-and-bolt toy is also inappropriate for Phase VI. Infants cannot screw the nuts on or off the bolts.

TRICYCLES AND XYLOPHONES

Tricycles are often introduced into a child's life before his second birthday. Once in a while you will find a precocious child and a properly designed tricycle; but, as mentioned earlier, I think it is preferable to reserve these until the child is slightly older. Another much-purchased toy for infants is the xylophone, especially in pull-toy form. In fact, few children that we have seen have ever seemed to get any enjoyment out of such a xylophone beyond the fifteen minutes that every child in this age range devotes to any new item introduced by his parents.

POTENTIALLY DANGEROUS ITEMS

Be on guard against items that are small enough to be swallowed, sharp enough in any of their edges or surfaces to be a hazard, or small and heavy enough to be used as dangerous missiles.

An example of the first category would be marbles, checkers, or anything else under one and one-half inches in any of its major dimensions.

An example of the second group would be Matchbox or Hot Wheels cars because once the wheels are pulled off (which is not too difficult to do), the axle that is left exposed is capable of inflicting significant damage on young children.

An example of a small item that can become a dangerous missile is a toy soldier. Toy soldiers made of lead are small enough to be thrown well by children of this age range, yet heavy enough to inflict damage on people and things.

BEHAVIORS THAT SIGNAL THE ONSET
OF PHASE VII

Phase VII, the third year of life, is the final one to be covered in this book. Several interesting processes are appearing at this point in a child's development.

A DECLINE IN NEGATIVISM

If all has gone well, you will find a general decline in negativism sometime around the second birthday. Not only will the child become less contentious, but you can expect an increase in general sociability.

EMERGENCE OF TRUE SOCIAL INTEREST IN PEERS

From this point on, interest in play with other children—often outside of the home—will gradually and consistently grow, and the exclusive concentration on the nuclear family and the home will decline.

INCREASING MENTAL POWER AND EMOTIONAL CONTROL

With the emergence of Phase VII you will begin to notice a rather dramatic increase in your child's sheer mental power and in his ability to control his emotions. You will find that you are living with a much more mature human being than you were six months ago. This rather impressive maturity is, of course, not going to appear suddenly, but I think you will be struck by the rate with which the child substitutes reasoning and impulse control for impulse-determined action.

AN INCREASE IN CONVERSATION

Closely associated with the preceding phenomena is a general rise in sheer talking and especially in conversational language. Phase VII children usually can deal with sentences and with streams of thought to an extent which makes it possible for them to carry on simple, pleasant conversations.

CHAPTER 8

Phase VII _____

FROM TWENTY-FOUR to
THIRTY-SIX MONTHS
of AGE

GENERAL REMARKS

The two-year-old is a fairly stabilized personality. He has constructed with great effort, over long periods of time and through many interchanges, an elaborate social contract with his primary caretaker. He has become truly familiar and involved with the object world. He has achieved substantial control of his own body. He is in a condition which perhaps still can be best characterized as babyhood, but by a child's third birthday, to call him a baby can in some respects be misleading.

In that third year we see a substantial and steady rise in interest in other children and true social peer interaction with them. We usually see a steady rise in activities outside of the home, along with a lessening in intensity of the exclusive focus on the nuclear family and on mother. We find a substantial increase in sheer maturity in the common-sense meaning of that term. The child's mental powers are growing at a really remarkable rate. He seems more aware of things, particularly in the social realm. Whereas the one-and-one-half-year-old can be overwhelmed rather easily by feelings of anger or hurt, the three-year-old is far more in control of his emotions.

Along with these dramatic developments comes the flowering of speech and the resultant inclination toward conversation. In addition, the newly developed ability to use the body with skill for walking, climbing, sitting, and running adds to the feeling that we are now dealing with a relatively complete junior human being. Babyhood is over. The distance already traveled by a three-year-old in terms of human development is staggering.

191

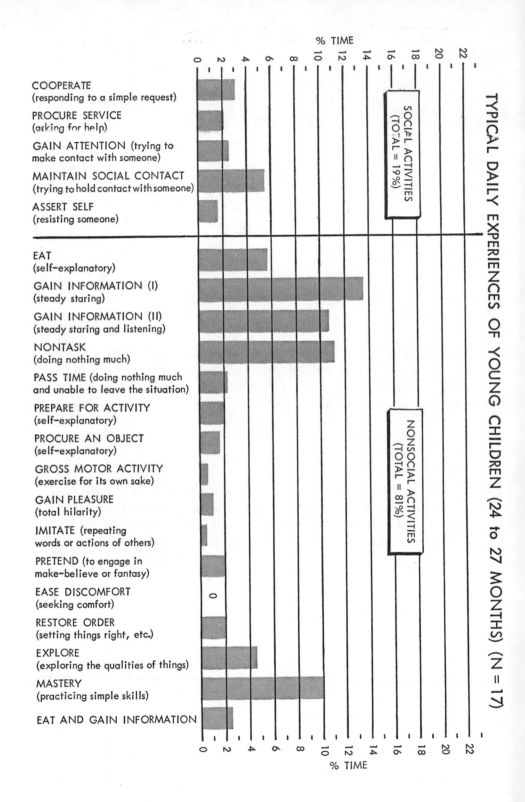

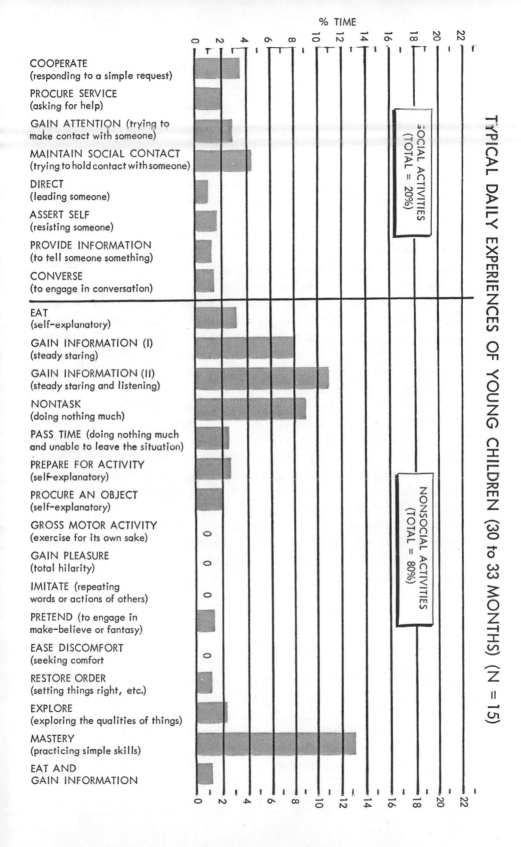

% TIME

COOPERATE
(responding to a simple request)

PROCURE SERVICE
(asking for help)

GAIN ATTENTION (trying to
make contact with someone)

MAINTAIN SOCIAL CONTACT
(trying to hold contact with someone)

DIRECT
(leading someone)

ASSERT SELF
(resisting someone)

PROVIDE INFORMATION
(to tell someone something)

CONVERSE
(to engage in conversation)

SOCIAL ACTIVITIES
(TOTAL = 20%)

EAT
(self-explanatory)

GAIN INFORMATION (I)
(steady staring)

GAIN INFORMATION (II)
(steady staring and listening)

NONTASK
(doing nothing much)

PASS TIME (doing nothing much
and unable to leave the situation)

PREPARE FOR ACTIVITY
(self-explanatory)

PROCURE AN OBJECT
(self-explanatory)

GROSS MOTOR ACTIVITY
(exercise for its own sake)

GAIN PLEASURE
(total hilarity)

IMITATE (repeating
words or actions of others)

PRETEND (to engage in
make-believe or fantasy)

EASE DISCOMFORT
(seeking comfort

RESTORE ORDER
(setting things right, etc.)

EXPLORE
(exploring the qualities of things)

MASTERY
(practicing simple skills)

EAT AND
GAIN INFORMATION

NONSOCIAL ACTIVITIES
(TOTAL = 80%)

TYPICAL DAILY EXPERIENCES OF YOUNG CHILDREN (30 to 33 MONTHS) (N = 15)

GENERAL BEHAVIOR DURING THIS PERIOD

THE DECLINE OF NONSOCIAL EXPERIENCE

Starting with a child's first birthday, experiences oriented toward people begin to increase at the expense of experiences not oriented toward people. Near the first birthday about ten percent of all experience is people oriented. For some six minutes out of the average hour, the child tries to create an effect in another person by trying to get his attention or trying to get him to perform a certain action. At about two years of age the balance is about twenty percent social to eighty percent nonsocial experiences. By the time the child reaches three years of age that figure is closer to thirty percent for social experiences, and nonsocial experiences have dropped correspondingly.

The major nonsocial experiences of the Phase VII child are similar to those he was engaged in during Phase VI. Thus *exploration of object qualities* and *practicing simple skills on objects* remain a prominent part of a child's waking life, but their relative importance is lessening. Whereas at eighteen to twenty-one months of age our research indicates that children engage in these two major types of activities with small objects about eighteen percent of their waking time, by two and one-half years that figure has decreased to about fourteen percent. As the years go by the child will move beyond these simple kinds of interactions with objects to more complicated ones, often involving social interaction with other children. But active play with small objects still occupies a substantial amount of the time in Phase VII.

The third year of life is also marked by a decrease in *staring behavior*. As we have seen, at one year of age we routinely find such looking behavior accounting for slightly under *twenty percent* of all real time, whereas at two years of age our figures are somewhere in the vicinity of fourteen percent, and at three years of age they have dropped to six or seven percent. As simple, steady staring decreases, a related kind of activity increases. That activity is gaining information by both *looking and listening* to relevant language. It occupies a little over six percent of a child's waking time at one year of age, and as much as eleven percent of that time at two and one-half years.

Since Phase VII is a time of tremendous growth in language ability, it is no surprise that children in this age group are very much interested in attending to language of one sort or another. Incidentally, there are several sources of language that children can attend to at this point in time. Language can come from a human being speaking in their presence, or from a television set or record player. Language from a live human being can be language a child listens to as his mother talks with an older brother or sister, or language directed to the child himself. We believe that the latter is the most important with respect to education.

The next nonsocial experience of consequence is what we call *nontask experience,* or *empty time.* Such behavior generally declines during the third year of life, dropping from ten to twelve percent during the second year of life to seven or eight percent during the third year. Its companion category of *passing time* is also on the decline during this period. I think this trend reflects the fact that children are less prone to accidents after infancy.

Eating accounts for another five percent of the child's time during the third year of life, so you can see that relatively few types of nonsocial experiences account for the bulk of a child's activities during the typical day. In fact, the seven types of experiences discussed above account for about fifty-three percent of a three-year-old's waking hours. At two and one-half years of age the same seven account for about forty-seven percent of his time. This difference is significant in that with each passing month experience becomes richer. More and more types of experience are engaged in by children.

SOCIAL EXPERIENCE

Turning to social experience, we find that the two-year-old engages in very few kinds of social experience for any appreciable length of time. In addition, the amount of time he devotes to this pursuit is considerably smaller than that given over to nonsocial experience. The most common social experience we find in Phase VII is the child attempting to hold on to another person's attention; that is, *maintaining social contact.* As might be expected, his mother is the person most involved (about ninety percent of the time). At about two years of age *maintaining social contact* accounts for about six percent of all waking time. The two-and-one-half-year-old is considerably less "clingy," with this type of experience accounting for only four percent of his time.

The second most common social experience is complying with simple requests that mothers make (about three percent for both ages).

The third most common social experience is *attempting to get somebody's attention*, again usually the mother (from two and one-half to three percent throughout the third year of life).

Two additional categories of social experience of probable consequence are *attempting to get some help from an adult* (about two percent of the time) and *resisting suggestions by either mother or another child* (between one and one and one-half percent of the time). All five of these social experiences combined take less daily time than, for example, *active exploration and practicing of skills on small objects*.

You will notice that the picture I have drawn of what is going on in the life of a three-year-old, does not project a morning-until-night, sitting-by-his-mother's-feet image. The older literature on early child development was so concentrated on the importance of the mother-child relationship that people tended to get the impression that all the child was doing all day long was relating to his mother. The fact of the matter is that for the vast majority of a child's waking hours during his first three years of life he will be exploring the nonsocial world and practicing motor skills.

THE APPARENT INTERESTS OF THIS AGE

CONTINUING INTERESTS

The three major interests I cited for Phases V and VI—interest in the primary caretaker, interest in exploration of the world, and interest in practicing new motor skills—continue as the dominating interests during the third year of life, but with some important changes. For example, in the area of social development, as we have seen, a child's almost total concentration of social interest on mother's behaviors, especially mother's reactions to his own acts, lessens, and during Phase VII the new and important element of true social interaction with peers emerges. With respect to exploration of the world at large, you will find that the child in his third year has major interests on which you can capitalize. Especially noteworthy are the increasing interest in language (especially if that language is directed toward them), and in the practicing of simple skills on small objects.

As concerns the practicing of new motor skills and the mastery of the body, the child is now adept at most of the elementary gross motor skills that emerged during infancy. All children over two years of age can generally handle walking, running, and climbing with ease, and immensely enjoy the two latter activities; although, of course, they are not as skillful at climbing as they will become. There are new motor skills emerging, but nothing dramatic at this point. You can teach a Phase VII child to ride a small tricycle during the third year of his life, and he will very much enjoy doing so. Children continue to enjoy swing sets in the third year of life every bit as much as they did in the second year of life.

EMERGING INTERESTS

Creative activities

Toward the end of the third year of life children begin to put together the various prerequisite skills and information they have been gathering so busily for the preceding couple of years, into what we call consummatory or creative activities. During Phase VII you see the first drawings by young children, especially if you encourage them or if there are older siblings around. You will also find the first "constructions." Block play may now include the creation of forts, or at least towers; again, especially if encouraged by others. This newly emerging interest will grow quite steadily in the years to come.

Pretend activities

Looking to another emerging activity of particular interest and apparent importance, you will find children with the new-found capacity to speak well entering into imaginative fantasy situations, either alone or more commonly with the primary caretaker. The meaning of the earliest pretend activities is not really clear to anybody. However, such behavior, as we have seen, is a distinguishing characteristic of well-developed children.

Interest in television

Another emerging interest of the third year is a genuine interest in television viewing. This interest seems to begin with responses to commercials, particularly those with the loud, fast-paced music. Do not expect your two-and-one-half-year-old to watch somebody deliver a lecture on how to sew an apron, but you can expect him to follow the moving forms on children's cartoons. Also he is likely to show a good deal of interest in programs like *Sesame Street* or other televised material which is specifically designed to capture and hold the attention of the very young child.

EDUCATIONAL DEVELOPMENTS DURING PHASE VII

The four educational goals set forward earlier—language development, the development of curiosity, social development, and nurturing the roots of intelligence—continue as objectives throughout the child's third year of life. The three major interests of the eight- to twenty-four-month period—interest in the primary caretaker, interest in exploration of the physical world, and interest in practicing new motor skills—also continue to prevail during Phase VII. Again it is important not only to encourage these interests but to keep them in good balance.

LANGUAGE DEVELOPMENT

If development has proceeded well, your two-year-old should understand the majority of simple words and sentences that you address to him. He should be speaking, although he may not be saying very much as yet. Some two-year-olds use small sentences and carry on simple conversations. Others are only using a few simple words or sentence fragments. Again, you need not worry about a two-year-old's language development as long as his understanding of language is moving along well.

DEVELOPMENT OF CURIOSITY

In the area of curiosity, the hope is that you have a two-year-old who can play alone well; who is genuinely interested in new circumstances, new physical objects, new people, and indeed in anything new.

SOCIAL DEVELOPMENT

The third area, social development, is considerably more complicated. We want a two-year-old child to have acquired an initial set of
social skills, the details of which I will discuss later in this chapter. We
want him to be a pleasure to live with most—if not all—of the time. We
want him to have left negativism behind, for the most part. We want him
to like himself, to have come to feel that he is valued by others. We want
him to get along reasonably well with everyone in the family, not just the
primary caretaker.

NURTURING THE ROOTS OF INTELLIGENCE

In the area of intelligence we hope that the two-year-old will have
entered a new level of intellectual function which increasingly features
the use of ideas in the mind as well as problem solving with his hands
and eyes on a trial-and-error basis. Most of the intelligence that was
manifested in the first two years of life, as we have seen, was of the latter
kind; what Piaget calls sensorimotor intelligence. An infant trying to get
an object that is hard to reach will actually attempt various procedures to
reach the object, whereas the child over two years of age will very often
consider alternatives in his head, choose the one most likely to succeed,
and then act. *It is this shift from working problems out with actions to
thinking them through that takes place in late infancy.* Your child is now
much more able to reflect upon events and situations than he was at age
one, for example. He is a thinker.

The Phase VII child is a considerably more mature mental creature
than he was in the second year of life. He knows much more than
previously about the world of objects and about their permanent existence, even when he is not in the room. He knows much more about the
paths of motion of moving things. He knows a good deal about simple
cause-and-effect sequences. He knows enough about chains of events to
anticipate consequences in many situations. He is what Piaget has called
egocentric in his thinking. By *egocentric,* Piaget means he tends to see
things exclusively from his own point of view. For example, as noted
earlier, it is very difficult to convince a two- or three-year-old who has
been bumped into by an older sibling that the bump was unintentional.

The concept of an accidental occurrence is foreign to the mind of such a child.

Piaget describes other peculiar mental qualities of the Phase VII child as well. One of particular interest has to do with the concept of life. At this point in time anything that moves is alive. It is therefore not safe to assume that a child will view a leaf being blown about a street by the wind the way you will. One way of illustrating this point is through the use of an item a two- or three-year-old is afraid of. I used an intact lobster shell to explore my three-year-old daughter's ideas about the concept of life. Her first view of the empty shell produced a small but real fear reaction, until I assured her that the shell could not hurt her because the lobster was not alive. She did not fully believe me at first, but she was intrigued enough to make a cautious approach. Suddenly the shell, which was on a step, slipped slightly. This made her jump back two feet through space—and considerably further psychologically —because for her that movement meant that the object was alive. In dealing with a two- to three-year-old it is important to remember that his mind is still very immature. For more details on what goes on in the mind of a very young child, I again recommend some of the earlier works of Piaget, which you will find cited in the recommended reading section of this book.

A final way to think about educational goals for the Phase VII child is in terms of the dimensions of competence discussed in Chapter 6. Our evaluation of the competent three- to-six-year-old becomes increasingly relevant to this book as the child moves through Phase VII and ap-proaches three years of age. During the third year of life, if things go well, you can expect to see all of the dimensions of competence become functional. We will examine how parents can foster the development of these competencies during Phase VII in the following section.

RECOMMENDED CHILD-REARING PRACTICES
AT THIS STAGE

FOSTERING THE DIMENSIONS OF COMPETENCE

Social abilities

Getting and holding the attention of adults. This early-developing ability was discussed in detail on page 180. The child's techniques for

getting and holding adult attention become increasingly sophisticated
during Phase VII. It is important at this stage to be sure that the skills
children use in holding your attention are socially acceptable and
reasonable, as well as effective, and that the child knows when to stop.
Earlier I pointed out the natural tendency of infants to concentrate on
their primary caretaker at the expense of other kinds of useful experiences. Suffice it to say that if you will be alert to how and how much the
child is trying to hold on to your attention, it will help you to shape a
solid ability in this particular area.

*Using adults as resources after having first determined that a job is too
difficult.* There are two ways in which children can determine that a task
is too difficult for them. The more obvious is to try it out for themselves.
This is especially common in conjunction with the predominance of
practical intelligence in the child less than two years of age. During the
third year of life, as children increasingly develop more thinking ability,
they resort to the second method of determining the difficulty of a
task—trying things out in their minds. A decline in efforts at actually
trying to physically solve a problem prior to a request for your assistance
does not necessarily mean that the child has not thought it through and
concluded that he could not handle the problem. This shift in problem-
solving style may lead you to the erroneous conclusion that a child is
making less effort than previously to work things out for himself before
asking for your help.

In cases where a Phase VII child is seeking your assistance solely for
the purpose of monopolizing your time, his motives are usually obvious. As in Phase VI, my recommendation is to show a certain amount of
indulgence regarding appeals for aid, but not to encourage the masking
of true purposes and overconcentration on close contact to you.

Expressing affection and moderate annoyance to adults. We spoke, in
reference to the Phase VI child, of the importance of spontaneous
emotional expression. Again my advice is to try to encourage a Phase
VII child to express his feelings toward you whenever he is so inclined.
By that I do not mean that you should continually ask him whether he
loves you or dislikes you. What I do mean is that when a child spontaneously shows affection you should relax and enjoy it. Correspondingly, if
he registers mild displeasure at you or someone else, pause to think
about whether he is justified in the behavior and if so, give him some
leeway. (This does *not* mean condoning seriously hostile behavior or
temper tantrums, which require understanding but very firm handling.)

It is not uncommon for parents to find it difficult to accept expressions of dislike of one or another of their behaviors by a very young child. But you should be prepared to deal maturely with such situations if they arise by reminding yourself that the expression of negative feelings is a natural part of growing up. Simply be firm about setting limits and be careful to explore possible causes for this behavior.

Leading and following peers. You should be sensitive to the emergence of these abilities in the third year of life. As mentioned earlier, one way you can facilitate their development is by giving your child the chance to exercise simple leadership skills in interactions with you. Although we do not know to what degree skills, attitudes, and behaviors that have to do with leading and following an adult or older sibling will transfer over to interactions with peers, some transfer most probably does occur.

There is, of course, no proving ground for these abilities like play with peers themselves. Thus a second way to help a child develop leading and following skills with other children is to arrange for regular experiences with peers in pleasant and supervised circumstances. Such experiences can be arranged in many ways—play groups, nursery schools, and even day-care centers from the time the child is two and one-half years of age are examples.

During the third year of life a child's natural peer group size is two; therefore, I do not believe that there is a need for large numbers of other children in the very young child's life. If there is another child or two living nearby with whom he or she can play regularly, the child may have the opportunity for peer play at no real cost to the family. The problem here is that with only one or two other playmates the opportunities for diverse kinds of group experience are, of course, strictly limited; and unfortunately, Phase VII children can quickly form relationships with each other where one child is dominant. As a result, the opportunity for practicing both leading and following skills is considerably less available than it might be when several peers are available. A good reason for having experience with several peers during Phase VII is to provide for a diversity of learning opportunities. Such considerations are also relevant to decisions about the advisability of play groups and nursery schools.

Expressing affection and mild annoyance to peers. This ability is parallel to the previously mentioned ability, *expressing affection and mild annoyance to adults,* and advice in regard to this dimension of competence follows my advice in regard to the earlier item on *leading and following peers.* The capacity to express your feelings—both positive and negative—to other people, is probably developed in the first three years of life, partly through nuclear family experience and partly through poor experience. It is a valuable capacity and should be encouraged intelligently in both the home and the nursery school.

Competing with peers. As previously mentioned, the notion of fostering a competitive spirit in their children is distressing to some people. For those of you who have no strong objections to this behavior, let me urge you to encourage a reasonable spirit of competition in your child —competition in the healthiest sense of the term. For years a Harvard psychologist named David McClelland has been doing research on what he calls "the achievement motive." Particularly in this country, with its orientation toward individual excellence, independence, and personal responsibility, a child who is reluctant to compete is probably at a disadvantage. Furthermore, many connotations of the word "competitive" are generally accepted as desirable. Implicit or implied in the concept of competitive behavior is some perception of when a job is well done, some understanding of a beginning and an end to a task, and some interest in how to find and use resources to do a job. Competition is occasionally, in my opinion, misinterpreted when it comes to child-rearing practices. In the best sense of the term, a competitive person is very much interested in achieving, in doing things well, and in having his output compare favorably with others. It is in that healthy sense that the children we have studied have been competitive, and it is in that healthy spirit that I urge you to encourage your child in that regard. This encouragement is easily provided through attention to the child's achievements, and appropriate expressions of pride as well as the provision of assistance that might enable him to develop his skills better, produce better products, and in general become a more capable person.

Showing pride in personal accomplishment. Along with the growth of the child's sound sophistication and awareness in the third year of life comes an ever-increasing tendency to seek approval for activities or products successfully achieved. This tendency can be relatively well established by three years of age. Phase VII children will from time to time comment proudly on a new skill or on a creation of their own. New abilities in the third year of life may include riding a tricycle, making a simple construction out of blocks, or producing some sort of drawing or writing which crudely resembles an older child's work. In these and in numerous other ways a child will show an interest in achievement, and pleasure in being praised for that achievement. Of particular importance here, I think, is the reminder that you do the child no good if you praise him for things that are not really worthy of praise. This does not mean that you should set unrealistically high standards. But if a child is praised for an accomplishment considerably below his real ability level, he may begin to develop invalid standards or inappropriate levels of aspiration. Keep your praise tied realistically to the level of achievement, remembering that achievement should be generously rated in the light of the child's relatively simple level of development, even in the third year of life.

Engaging in role play or make-believe activities. In Lois Murphy's pioneering work, called *Personality in Young Children*, one of the interesting qualities of behavior of her central figure, a well-developing boy, was that he frequently would come into the nursery school dressed up as one or another character, and spend a good deal of the day acting as if he were indeed that character. The role selected generally was an adult role. Role play is engaged in to some extent by virtually all two-, three-, and four-year-old children. However, in our study of well-developed three- to six-year-old children, their role play differed both in amounts and in type from that of children not developing nearly so well. In general, the roles selected by the former group, as in the case cited above, were adult roles. These children routinely acted out such parts as doctor, lawyer, nurse, actress, truck driver, and pet-store owner. In addition, these children would occasionally make believe they were fictional hero-figures like Batman or Superman. Children not developing particularly well are more inclined to include role play that looks backward or involves more modest aspirations. The two most common forms of such role play are acting like a baby or an animal.

In addition to role play, other types of behavior included in this dimension have to do with make-believe fantasizing, such as baking cakes or interacting with imaginary playmates.

Here is one of the more enjoyable areas in which child-rearers have an opportunity to interact constructively with their Phase VII children. Some parents may feel that somehow or other the child's grasp on reality will be loosened if he is encouraged in unreal kinds of talk and play. Our observations suggest otherwise. Most well-developed children seem to have received a good deal of encouragement from their primary caretakers to indulge in fantasy play. You would probably do well to give your Phase VII child similar encouragement.

Nonsocial abilities

Good language development. We have repeatedly noted that well-developed three- to six-year-old children speak especially clearly, use a great deal of expressive language, and are in general strikingly advanced in all language skills. By the time a child reaches his third birthday, he should be able to understand the majority of all language he will use for the rest of his life in ordinary conversation. The more you use language effectively with him, the better off he will be in this regard. Remember the particular description of the ways in which apparently effective child-rearers respond to overtures from their children. By now you will have had many thousands of opportunities to respond to overtures from your child, and hopefully by now you should have adopted a comfortable and effective style of interacting with him. *Identifying what the child is really interested in at the moment* is probably the key to good language teaching. Once you know this, you can then talk to that topic, thus maximizing your effectiveness. As noted earlier, this "reactive" style is the easiest way to get a very young child to attend to what you say to him. In contrast, chasing him across a room and saying, "Look at this, look at the pretty picture," can be both tiring and ineffective.

If you do not underestimate the child's language understanding level, nor on the other hand speak at a level that is way beyond his capacity to understand, you will be providing the most effective raw materials from which the child can extract maximum benefits.

The ability to notice small details or discrepancies. As noted earlier, very well-developed three- and four-year-old children are extremely accurate observers, quick to pick up differences and anomalies in a variety of areas.

Helping your Phase VII child to refine his observational capacities is a relatively simple and pleasurable job. If, for example, a child comes to you (at two and one-half years of age) and shows you something in a picture book, this is a natural opportunity to feed language development, heighten curiosity, and sharpen observational skills. Assume that he has come to you with a picture of a train. Rather than simply remarking, "Oh, a choo-choo," you can take another moment or two to say something like, "Oh, yes, isn't that an interesting-looking train, notice it's got three wheels on this side and probably three on the other side. Daddy's car has only two wheels on each side."

The number of subjects that can serve as a basis for pointing out similarities and differences is infinite, and most of them are interesting to the Phase VII child. Let me remind you not to overextend such interchanges with your child. Keep them short and sweet unless the child wants to prolong the event. You will find that the child's interest in these kinds of topics is real but usually limited.

The ability to anticipate consequences. When, for example, a child thinks ahead to the events that are likely to follow the failure to turn off the water when someone is filling the tub, the child is anticipating consequences. Thus a child with this talent, when watching another child trying to carry more than he can handle, is likely to point out that the other child is going to drop or break something.

It is relatively easy for you to help your child move into the habit of thinking ahead by pointing out from time to time what is about to happen next. You will be doing this in a natural way whenever a child is hungry and you point out to him that he must wait while you prepare his meal. There may be times when the child will be more receptive to learning than when he is feeling the discomfort of hunger, but a moderate degree of hunger is probably good for a learning situation in the sense that the child is likely to be paying attention to what you are saying.

The ability to deal with abstractions. This is a very broad cognitive ability. A child who can count, one who can use words well and understands the names of classes of objects, one who knows letters and colors, is a child who is dealing effectively with simple abstractions. A child who can easily hold a conversation about things that are not physically present, or events that took place earlier, is a child who deals well with abstractions. Usually conversations between three- to six-year-old children depend very heavily for their success on the actual physical presence of a person, toy, or other object around which the conversations revolve. They must be linked directly to concrete points.

Here is an area in which you have to work within certain limits in child-rearing practices, due to the mental immaturity of a child. For example, you can demonstrate to a Phase VII child how a key works, using several keys and locks in the home. You can then talk about keys as they relate to locks in general so that an abstract conception of a key and its unlocking function may be learned (to some extent). But if you raise the stakes and introduce topics like truth, morality, or random events, you will find that you quickly exceed the capacity of the child. I therefore recommend that you be modest in your attempts to heighten the child's capacity to deal with abstractions, since such teaching will happen naturally in your spontaneous conversations together.

The ability to put oneself in the place of another. Piaget has an interesting little test for this ability. He uses a model of a mountain range, onto which he puts doll figures at different points. He then asks the child what it is that the dolls can see from the different spots where they are standing. The child who has not yet achieved much talent in this area can only describe what he himself sees. The child who is well-developed in this area can tell you, with a fair degree of accuracy, what it is each doll sees from its own perspective. We have found a substantial degree of development of this ability in well-developed three- and four-year-olds even though, as noted earlier, this is considerably younger than the average age at which Piaget pointed out emergence of this behavior.

The ability to put oneself in another's place is a relatively difficult kind of competency to encourage in the young child. Such behavior, during the third year of a child's life, is contrary to a very powerful tendency *not* to take the perspective of another. The Phase VII child tends to see the world exclusively from the point of view of his own needs. The name for this style of thinking, as mentioned before is

Test case: The chocolate child

egocentrism, a phenomenon extensively discussed and studied by Piaget.

What egocentrism means is revealed reasonably well in an example I like to cite about different responses in mothers. If a two-year-old child approaches his mother wearing a bright, excited look on his face and a substantial amount of chocolate frosting on his clothes and hands, the response he will get varies with the woman involved. The mother may perceive both elements of the situation—that is, the frosting and what it may mean plus the bright, excited look on the child's face—to an equal degree; or she may concentrate on the child's bright look, be pleased by it and wonder why he is pleased; or she may barely notice the expression on his face in her concern for the chocolate frosting and what it signifies. The mother who focuses on the chocolate frosting is probably experiencing the situation from an egocentric point of view, in other words, with her own interests and needs uppermost in her mind; the mother who concentrates on the child's excitement is probably more oriented toward the child's perspective.

Egocentricity is not solely a characteristic of the thinking of the young child. We all engage in it throughout our lives. Ordinarily whether or not we are egocentric or the degree to which we are varies as a function of a given situation and its emotional impact on us.

Given a child's tendencies at this stage, I suggest you be modest in your aspirations in regard to this mental ability. Whenever you get a chance to do so, point out to the child what the world looks like to someone else. You will find that your child will occasionally show some interest in such instruction if he is not under pressure at the time. Do not, however, try such teaching when he is feeling a good deal of anger or displeasure. If the Phase VII child comes to you furious because his older brother has taken back a favorite toy, this is not the moment to attempt to teach taking the perspective of another. You will naturally want to point out that the toy is one of his older brother's favorites. You probably will ask, "How would you feel if someone kept a toy of yours?" But do not be surprised if your remarks make surprisingly little impact on a Phase VII child. According another person his rights at the expense of your own is a very difficult notion at this stage.

A good person to use in pointing out to a child what the world looks like from another viewpoint is yourself. It is relatively easy for most people to explain to children, even as young as two or two and one-half years of age, how they feel about something, particularly when there are

concrete clues present to facilitate such explanations. If you are talking about a pair of shoes that you are having trouble squeezing your feet into, you can use that situation as an example by pointing out that although the shoes seem too small for you and hurt your feet, they would not hurt the child's feet because they are obviously not too small for him.
The ability to make interesting associations. In our observations in nursery schools and kindergartens we often watch teachers in story-telling sessions with children. Such stories sometimes deal with exotic topics like prehistoric monsters or fairy tales. We find our especially well-developed children introducing interesting and apparently original associations and trains of thought to story sessions often enough so that our group agreed that this is a regular distinguishing characteristic. Such creative imagination can be seen by the third birthday.

Listening to stories, whether they originate from better-quality television like *Sesame Street*, or some adult or older sibling, helps spark the imagination of a very young child. If you provide encouragement for any reasonable effort at original thinking, modest though it may be, you will be helping to stimulate the growth of a considerable talent.
The ability to plan and carry out complicated activities. We have characterized this as an executive ability. The three-year-old who is developing very well can bring together two or three children and a collection of materials and introduce, organize, and carry out complicated activities like playing store or house, or capturing a lion.

Here again is a talent which takes a certain degree of living and mental maturing to develop. In the first three years of life, it can only be helped along modestly. You can draw a child's attention to the ways in which you organize activities. Without overdoing it, you can describe some of the steps you use when baking a cake or putting together a meal. You can encourage the child to look over his father's shoulders while a toy is being assembled, with some attempt to explain the steps in the process to the child. Getting into the habit of talking out loud as you are doing things, when a child is paying attention, is probably the simplest way to be effective in this domain.
The ability to use resources effectively. Real lions are in ordinarily short supply for children of this age, along with cages to put them in and nets in which to trap them. The ability to take big cardboard boxes and use them as cages effectively enough to hold the interest of other children is an example of a capacity to use resources effectively.

This is another area in which talking out loud can be helpful. If you do so as you decide on how to organize a task, you can teach the idea of multiple uses for resources to the child. Tell him, for example, that if something needs a little force and a hammer is not present, force can be exerted by using substitute measures. Point out that using a heavy rock to pound in a stake is a form of effective use of a resource, and that getting three or four people to help lift something rather than straining yourself is another way in which resources can be used flexibly to get jobs done.

Dual focusing. This ability of the child in a busy situation to maintain his focus on an immediate task while at the same time keeping track of what is going on around him can be observed in a roomful of busy three- to six-year-olds. As noted earlier, the well-developed three- to six-year-olds we have studied are particularly able in this area. In a group situation the average child, in the face of an overture by another child, is likely either to yield to that overture and drop what he is doing, or at the very least lose his train of thought or his concentration. Some children in the three- to six-year-old range can never do concentrated close work in a busy situation. They just cannot focus their attention, given the distractions typically present. Again, we do not know how to foster this ability.

In summary, each of the above dimensions of competence can be used as a guide to effective child-rearing practices. It is not necessary, however, to think about all of them all of the time. The families that we have watched do a fine job with their children do not put a tremendous amount of work into the process during the third year of a child's life; nor do they give up all their other interests, pleasures, and activities at any point during the child's first years of life in order that the child acquire a fine early education. It is not unduly time-consuming to do the job extremely well, and I would be misleading you if I suggested or implied that it was. On the whole, we find our parents actively interacting with their children in Phase VII no more than ten percent of the time during the average day. Most of the time the women we have watched, have been busy with housework or their other children, and have been doing many other things during the day rather than concentrating on the educational development of their children. The reason for all this detail is so you may become better informed about what I consider reasonably reliable new information about the process. Once you are comfortable with the ideas, I recommend that you use those that feel right, that strike you as being reasonable. At the very least I hope you will find that your child is considerably more interesting, and more fun to live with as a result of this detailed description. If such is the result then the book will have been well worth the writing.

CHILD-REARING PRACTICES I DO NOT RECOMMEND

AN OVEREMPHASIS ON INTELLECTUAL GROWTH

Perhaps the most common problem I see with respect to education during the third year of life among caring families is a tendency to worry too much about the intellectual growth of their children. Because of inadequate information on early education, many people have come to the conclusion that it is extremely important for their two- or three-year-olds to be in an "educationally powerful" nursery school. *I know of no good reason why this should be so.* This does not mean that I do not recommend nursery schools. There are many reasons why nursery school might be a useful experience for a child of this age (and a help to his mother). But in terms of solid intellectual growth, I do not believe that nursery schools are essential. A child is a complicated creature with many processes moving forward at the same time. To elevate his intellectual growth to a position where it becomes the primary concern is, in my opinion, potentially harmful to a child. In extensive observations of three- to six-year-old children, we have found many children who are intellectually quite precocious, able to converse fluently, able to do simple arithmetic, equipped with all sorts of information far in excess of what most children of their age have, and yet are quite unhappy and uncomfortable in dealing with children and adults other than those of the nuclear family. It is possible to help a child move ahead in all areas (intellectual, social, motor, etc.) at once. It may be that a child who is moving ahead in a balanced way will not be able to achieve a degree of precocity in any single direction that a child especially taught might. If you are working very hard to produce a musical prodigy, for example, the numbers of hours spent in teaching, in learning, and in practice, may very well produce a child with extraordinary musical skills. On the other hand, such a child may experience very few interactions with children outside of the home; may not master general motor skills of the sort that most children master at that time in life, and so forth. My message is, beware of equating brightness with good development. Intellectual superiority is very frequently obtained at the expense of progress in other areas of equal or even greater importance.

EXPENSIVE EDUCATIONAL TOYS

Everything I have said about overvaluing the importance of nursery school experience and intellectual ability is equally applicable to the question of how much of the family's resources you should devote to educational materials for children in the third year of life. No matter what you receive in the mail, no matter what you read in the newspapers, I cannot think of a single proven educational product for the third year of life without which a child would experience a meaningful delay or inferiority in any area of educational development. Do not worry that the child next door who has every "educationally relevant" toy ever manufactured has any advantage over your child. It just is not so.

UNSUPERVISED PLAY GROUPS

Particularly in the early stages of the third year of life I would advise you to be very careful about play-group experience for your child, or for that matter day-care experience or nursery-school experience. The child of three is already pretty much of a little person with a fair degree of mental maturity and control over his emotions. As we have seen, however, the child of two is a far cry from this condition. He is still capable of succumbing to primitive, destructive emotions. It is painful to watch two children who play together regularly form a relationship where the submissive child gets used to being intimidated by the other on a week-to-week basis. This form of psychological pressure may not be as obvious as the occasional physical abuse that is often evident in such situations, but I believe it is probably of even greater long-term significance. I am not opposed to group experiences for children two to two and one-half years of age, but you should know that your child can undergo experiences of a relatively painful kind if supervision is not adequate and effective.

OVERINDULGENCE

Phase VII, the third year of life, is a period when children are often overindulged. Some children are very tough to handle during the third year of life, particularly if there is a mobile baby in the home. Yet this is a time when discipline must be firm. You do your child no service by routinely giving in to him or allowing him to engage in temper tantrums and other undesirable behaviors. You do him no service by loosening up on limit-setting and on control in general. Do yourself and the child a favor—maintain a loving but very firm hold on the life of your child in his third year.

CHAPTER 9

AN OVERVIEW of
EDUCATIONAL DEVELOPMENTS
DURING the FIRST
THREE YEARS of LIFE

GENERAL REMARKS

This section is devoted to summing up the many aspects of early educational development that have been examined in these pages. It features nine charts, designed to provide the reader with concise overviews of the topics in question and to serve as simple points of reference.

The charts are divided into three groups. The first of these is labeled prerequisite information, by which I mean the information about the growth and development of a young human during the first three years that is needed in order to approach the task of education sensibly. The second section is called educational foundations, and deals with the development of the four major educational processes that have been referred to throughout the text. The third section is labeled the growth of special abilities (competencies), and concerns itself with the characteristics seen in well-developed children in the three- to six-year age range. I use the term *special abilities* because I do not deal with *all* the abilities that develop in the first three years of life, but only those that I think require special encouragement on the part of the caretaker. Others are not included in the list because as far as we can tell no special tuition or circumstances are necessary for their solid development. In our research we did not find that children developing poorly were usually less competent in the areas of perceptual or motor development. That statement will be considered a controversial one by people with special interests in those processes. As you probably know there are books available which purport to give you guidance on how to develop your child's motor abilities in the first years of life. There are other books that try to persuade you that it is very important that you guide a child's sensorimotor development (especially his visual motor development) in the first three years of life. If you choose to follow the advice of such authors, that is your own decision.

One of the key problems facing child-rearers is the confusion that is rooted in inadequate dependable knowledge about early development. If you will follow the recommendations of this book, I am confident that your child will be well educated. But if you want him to be able to play the violin, do push-ups, or swim at two or three years of age, you will have to look elsewhere for guidance.

These charts are organized around a scale going from birth to three years of age, subdivided into quarter-year units. The age at which you should expect the typical child to exhibit the behavior in question is indicated by the point at which a short vertical line bisects the horizontal line. The horizontal line in turn is meant to convey to you some sense of how variable the date of onset of that behavior or process is. It also, in some instances, is meant to indicate that the process is ongoing from the beginning of the time indicated through to the end of that time as represented by the horizontal line.

In most instances the length of time a process is undergoing development will be self-evident. In Chart A-1, on motor development, you will see that the first entry is *head control*—the vertical and horizontal lines indicate that on the average you can expect children to acquire head control, the ability to hold their head steady when in an upright posture, at about three months of age. There is also the information from the horizontal line that this ability may first be seen at any point from two to four months of age. In contrast, if you look ahead to Chart C-1, social abilities, in the section on the growth of special abilities, you will find that there is no vertical mark across the top line of the graph, labeled *getting and maintaining the attention of adults*, which stretches horizontally all the way from birth to two years of age. This suggests that there is no particular point at which these particular abilities come into a child's repertoire, but that these abilities are emerging more or less continuously from the time he is born until he is at least two years of age.

Even though the horizontal line representing attention-getting abilities ends at age two, this does not mean that children do not do any further learning in regard to such abilities after their second birthday, but rather that the bulk of the learning process transpires in the time span represented by the horizontal line. Furthermore, the fact that in Chart A-1 I show a central tendency and a range under *head control*, does not mean that a child who acquires head control earlier or later is necessarily atypical. These charts are meant to describe how most children develop. Three quarters or more of all children will probably fall within the ranges indicated.

PREREQUISITE INFORMATION

CHART A-1—MOTOR DEVELOPMENT

Chart A-1 portrays the major motor developments as they appear during the first three years of life. There are additional motor developments that are not included. These include the eye blink to the sight of a rapidly approaching target during the first three months, and focusing ability of the eyes appears during that same period give or take a week or two. Both behaviors are important, but Chart A-1 is intended to include only those motor achievements which have major educational implications. I have suggested throughout this book that problems in motor development are not nearly as likely as in the areas of language, intelligence, and social skills. Given the average expectable environment, most children develop normal motor abilities. I therefore have not given the topic emphasis in this book.

CHART A-2—TYPICAL EXPERIENCES

In order to educate a baby and in order to enjoy him to the fullest, I believe you should know what he is likely to be doing from day to day. This chart, and the material it deals with, is complex. For more detail I suggest that you refer back to relevant sections in the preceding chapters.

CHART A-3—SHEDDING LIMITATIONS

This chart is one that deserves a few special remarks because the conception of shedding limitations as such has not been focused on in the preceding chapters.

It seems to me that a knowledge of what a child's natural limitations are as he goes from a state of utter helplessness (at birth) to a state of rather miraculous accomplishment at age three can be useful. For example, a child under three months of age is a crib-bound creature with modest sensorimotor capacities. Looking at mobiles is one of the few activities he can engage in during those limited periods when he is awake. In this regard it is useful to know about the role of the tonic neck reflex, which predisposes the normal child under two months of age to look to his far left or far right rather than directly overhead. The result of this specific limitation is that if you are inclined to design a mobile for him you had better not place it directly overhead.

Similarly, the fact that all children require some degree of control and guidance by older people in their first years of life, and that most grown-ups tend to make some use of language in controlling and guiding them, means that basic information about the language young children cannot cope with is a prerequisite to effective activity

A. PREREQUISITE INFORMATION   1.   MOTOR DEVELOPMENT

Birth · 3 mos. · 6 mos. · 9 mos. · 1 Year · 3 mos. · 6 mos. · 9 mos. · 2 Years · 3 mos. · 6 mos. · 9 mos. · 3 Years

Head control
Turning over
Reaching
Unaided sitting
Crawling, scooting, etc.
Climbing six-inch units (including stairs)
Climbing twelve-inch units (including furniture and appliances)
Climbing down stairs
Cruising (walking while holding on to a support)
Unaided walking
"Riding" small four-wheeled wagons
Riding simplest tricycles

A. PREREQUISITE INFORMATION   2. TYPICAL EXPERIENCES

Timeline markers: Birth · 3 mos. · 6 mos. · 9 mos. · 1 Year · 3 mos. · 6 mos. · 9 mos. · 2 Years · 3 mos. · 6 mos. · 9 mos. · 3 Years

- Sleep/Sucking and gumming the fists/Brief visual interest/Arm and leg motions

- Extensive visual interest (own hands and faces of others)/Batting with hands/Arm, leg, and head motions/Sucking and gumming anything handy/Socializing with anyone

- Extensive visual interest/Hand-eye activities (batting, feeling, reaching, and grasping/Arm, leg, and torso exercises (including turning over)/Sucking and gumming anything handy/Play with own sounds/Socializing, especially with primary caretaker

- Extensive visual interest/Simple manual activities with small objects/Practice in sitting up/Leg exercises/Sucking and gumming anything handy/Play with own sounds and attending to words/Socializing, especially with primary caretaker

- Extensive visual interest/Practice in emerging gross motor skills (crawling, climbing, cruising, walking)/Attending to words/Gumming anything handy/

- Socializing with, and getting to know, primary caretaker/Exploring the qualities of objects, especially small portable ones/Gumming anything handy/Attending to words/Practicing simple skills, e.g., closing and opening doors and covers, filling and emptying containers, standing objects up, etc./Learning about simple causes and effects, e.g., light switches, pushing balls, jack-in-the-boxes, TV switches, etc./Coping with a slightly older sibling (reactively)

- Extensive visual interest/Listening to language/Practicing simple skills, gross motor skills (running, "riding" wagons, etc.)/Exploring objects/Doing very little (idling)/Procuring objects/Getting and holding the attention of the primary caretaker/Going along with simple requests (cooperating)/Asserting himself and testing wills/Coping with a slightly older sibling (reactively and proactively)/Seeking assistance when needed

- Extensive visual interest/Using and listening to language/Practicing motor skills, gross and fine (including tricycle riding and scribbling)/Exploring new objects/Engaging in fantasy activities (make-believe)/Creating products (simple drawings and puzzles, buildings, etc.)/Getting and holding the attention of the primary caretaker and peers/Practicing leading and following peers/Going along with simple requests/Conversing/Seeking assistance when needed

A. PREREQUISITE INFORMATION   3. SHEDDING LIMITATIONS

Timeline axis: Birth — 3 mos. — 6 mos. — 9 mos. — 1 Year — 3 mos. — 6 mos. — 9 mos. — 2 Years — 3 mos. — 6 mos. — 9 mos. — 3 Years

- Capacity to remain awake for many hours each day/First simple ability to control hands
- Freedom from tonic neck reflex control (full head mobility)/Freedom from grasp reflex (fingers unclenched)/Visual convergence of the eyes (three-dimensional sight)
- Head control (when torso upright)
- Torso control (turning to the side)
- Torso control (turning over)/Vision—mature focusing ability
- Visually directed reaching
- Unaided sitting
- Locomobility/First language (understands a few words)/Intelligence (first use of means to achieve ends)
- Vision—fully mature/Climbs very low objects (six inches)
- Stands, with support/Climbs chairs and furniture to several feet/First deliberate use of an adult for assistance
- Walks alone/Understands a few dozen words and a few phrases
- Basic control of the body complete/First spoken words—several dozen understood and many grammatical structures used
- Freedom from negativism/First capacity for basic mental intelligence (problem solving through manipulation of ideas in advance of motor action)

EDUCATIONAL FOUNDATIONS

CHART B 1   LANGUAGE DEVELOPMENT

Do not be confused by the fact that the first few entries on this chart do not, strictly speaking, have to do with language per se. Since they do involve the child's earliest responses to sounds, I feel that they should be included here. Note in particular the wide ranges in onset of the various language capacities. These can be observed in preceding charts as well, but language seems to be an area in which wide variability is particularly evident. Parents often become needlessly concerned by insignificant delays in the acquisition of speech.

CHART B-2—CURIOSITY

As noted earlier, there is very little material available in this area. I am particularly pleased to be able to provide the information included here, and again stress my certainty that nothing is more fundamental for a child's educational development than a well-developed sense of curiosity.

CHART B-3—SOCIAL DEVELOPMENT

The only potentially confusing thing about this chart has to do with special entries about a child's development in regard to older siblings (if an older sibling is less than three years older). No information is presented as to relationships with siblings considerably older than the baby.

CHART B-4—ROOTS OF INTELLIGENCE

This chart leans very heavily on the work of Piaget. For more information on this fascinating topic, I urge that you take a look at the reference readings, particularly J. McVicker Hunt's *Intelligence and Experience*.

B. EDUCATIONAL FOUNDATIONS   1. LANGUAGE DEVELOPMENT

B. EDUCATIONAL FOUNDATIONS   2. CURIOSITY

Birth | 3 mos. | 6 mos. | 9 mos. | 1 Year | 3 mos. | 6 mos. | 9 mos. | 2 Years | 3 mos. | 6 mos. | 9 mos. | 3 Years

Sustained hand regard/Some interest in faces/First interest in objects (batting, feeling, and gumming)

Own hand as a tool/Faces and voices/Sounds (including own with saliva)/Socializing (primitive interchanges with people)/Own feet

Effects of actions on objects (dropping and throwing)/Small particles/Faces and voices/Sounds/Socializing

*

Exploring entire living area/Causes and effects (simple mechanisms, consequences of actions, etc)/The primary caretaker (all behavior, but especially reactions to subject)

Same as previous period, but with more interest in effects of motor actions (re mechanisms and objects) than simple exploration/Special emphasis on language and on interpersonal experiences

Intellectual curiosity with considerable reflection/Continuation of themes of eight- to twenty-four-month periods with peer focus emerging

A period of life virtually dominated by pure curiosity

B. EDUCATIONAL FOUNDATIONS   3. SOCIAL DEVELOPMENT

| Birth | 3 mos. | 6 mos. | 9 mos. | 1 Year | 3 mos. | 6 mos. | 9 mos. | 2 Years | 3 mos. | 6 mos. | 9 mos. | 3 Years |

No sociability, but crying can force adults to act

First social smiles (indiscriminate)

First preference shown for primary caretaker/Endearing behavior typical

Gradual narrowing of focus to nuclear family members/Possible onset of wariness with others

Establishing a social pact with primary caretaker—Part I/On receiving end of occasional hostility from sibling (if sibling less than three years older)

Establishing social pact—Part II/Equilibrium with sometimes hostile sibling

Onset and working through of negativism/Dawning of self-awareness/Completion of basic social contract/Worm turns re occasionally hostile sibling (subject now may give as much as he takes)

The clouds lift—a return to civility/The primary caretaker as a friend, partner in conversation, haven in times of stress, source of power, etc.

B. EDUCATIONAL FOUNDATIONS 4. ROOTS OF INTELLIGENCE

Timeline from Birth to 3 Years (markers at 3 mos., 6 mos., 9 mos., 1 Year, 3 mos., 6 mos., 9 mos., 2 Years, 3 mos., 6 mos., 9 mos., 3 Years):

- Exercising crude reflexes
- Refining simple reflexes/Discovers hands/Beginning of object interest/Gathering information through visual exploration
- Achieves reaching ability/Sharpens sensorimotor skills (vision, localizing and identifying sounds)/Gathering information through visual exploration
- First signs of intelligence (problem solving)—moves obstacles aside in order to grasp desired object/Shift of interest from mastering hand-eye skills to their effects on objects/Continued visual exploration/First language learning
- Burst of active exploration (with locomobility)—special targets for learning: small objects and their physics, language, causes and effects, social phenomena
- Growth of practical (sensorimotor) intelligence culminates in emergence of mental abilities of reflection manipulation of ideas, etc./Dramatic language learning/Dramatic social learning, emergence of fantasy behavior, role play
- Growth of capacity of mind to control impulses, emotions/Majority of basic language acquired/First creations (scribbled drawings, constructions, etc.)/Continued expansion of imaginative role play

THE GROWTH OF SPECIAL ABILITIES
(COMPETENCIES)

CHART C-1—SOCIAL ABILITIES

The two charts in this section point to what I consider particularly important educational abilities that can emerge during the first three years of life. As we have seen, these abilities, develop over many months. Note for example that the long and steady evolutionary process surrounding getting and holding the attention of adults spans two full years.

A word about expressing affection and annoyance when appropriate to adults and to peers. Some people do not like the idea that a child should be able to express hostility in any form to other people. The point I make is that most of the well-developed children we studied were capable of expressing mild displeasure or annoyance. They did not act this way very commonly or very frequently. They were also able to express affection easily, and this they did more frequently. In contrast, children who were developing relatively poorly seemed to be constricted in the expression of their emotions to adults and to other children.

CHART C-2—NONSOCIAL ABILITIES

Like the social abilities shown in the preceding charts, these abilities typically are acquired over a long period of time. In particular, see that the ability to notice small details and discrepancies is shown as developing throughout the entire three-year age range. The moment the three-week-old child learns to discriminate between a nipple which contains milk and the adjacent parts of the human body, he has begun the long-term acquisition of the ability to notice differences. When he is two and one-half years of age he may catch an adult making an error in logic. I think these two instances of noticing differences have something in common.

It is interesting to note that the majority of these nonsocial abilities begin to develop substantially sometime after the child's second birthday.

C. THE GROWTH OF SPECIAL ABILITIES (Competencies)   1. SOCIAL ABILITIES

Timeline: Birth — 3 mos. — 6 mos. — 9 mos. — 1 Year — 3 mos. — 6 mos. — 9 mos. — 2 Years — 3 mos. — 6 mos. — 9 mos. — 3 Years

Getting and holding the attention of adults (in socially acceptable ways)

Expressing affection and annoyance (when appropriate) to adults

Using adults as resources after first determining a job is too difficult to handle alone

Showing pride in personal accomplishment

Engaging in role play or make-believe activities

Leading and following peers *

Expressing affection and mild annoyance (when appropriate) to peers *

Competing with peers *

*Major development of this ability continues beyond 36 months of age.

C. THE GROWTH OF SPECIAL ABILITIES (Competencies)   2.   NONSOCIAL ABILITIES

Birth	3 mos.	6 mos.	9 mos.	1 Year	3 mos.	6 mos.	9 mos.	2 Years	3 mos.	6 mos.	9 mos.	3 Years

The ability to notice small details or discrepancies *

Anticipating consequences *

Good language development *

Dealing with abstractions *

Making interesting associations *

Planning and carrying out complicated activities *

Using resources effectively *

Dual focusing—maintaining concentration on a near task, and simultaneously keeping track of what is going on nearby *

Putting oneself in the place of another person *

*Major development of this ability continues beyond 36 months of age.

Section II

TOPICS RELATED to CHILD-REARING DURING the FIRST THREE YEARS of LIFE

VARIATIONS IN THE ONSET
OF EARLY BEHAVIORS

Many interested and devoted parents become anxious about the developmental progress of their preschool-aged children. Over the last few decades, such concern has become almost typical among child-rearers. I believe that some of this anxiety is reasonable and indeed healthy to the degree that it indicates an awareness of responsibility. But much of the existing concern is based on a lack of understanding of early development. One of the purposes of this book is to do as much as possible to reduce such anxiety by contributing to a general understanding of early child development.

One of the most common sources of concern is whether or not a child is doing "well enough." This is a very difficult question to judge if you are the parent of that child. The question is emotionally loaded, and even if it were not, it is difficult to answer because of the scarcity of detailed and reliable knowledge about children. Almost everyone who has studied young children agrees that one hallmark of early human development is variability. After all, children are not production-line products. You can expect just about every Ford Pinto to look and to perform pretty much like every other Ford Pinto. You can expect that after ten minutes into the final assembly line a certain percentage of that automobile will have been assembled. Such is not the case with a young human.

A particularly good example of variability is the age of walking. Children in various parts of the world have been reliably reported to be able to walk as early as seven or eight months of age. Yet a substantial percentage of perfectly normal children do not walk before they are one and one-half years old. The average parent may be aware of a dozen other family situations with children just beginning to walk. The amount of anxiety a parent feels varies from none at all to a fairly significant quantity, depending on the developmental rates of these other children as compared to his own. The fact of the matter is that enough is known about children from all over the world to conclude that the date at which walking comes into a child's repertoire varies widely among children, and for the most part that variation means absolutely nothing in terms of the child's educational future or physical well-being. (I do not mean to say that you never need worry about when your child starts to walk. If a child is one and one-half years of age and not walking I would want to check out the child's physical health and make certain that I received professional guidance as to his welfare, but I would not be alarmed. If at the age of two years he still did not walk, then I think there would be some reason for serious concern.)

Among people responsible for rearing children there is a need for widespread understanding about the normal range in the date of onset of certain landmark abilities and capacities. There is no reason why such information should not be common knowledge. People who have good medical care for their young children are in fact inevitably exposed to this kind of support by physicians. It is my contention, however, that *everyone* who has the responsibility for rearing a young child should have this information. Unfortunately, some physicians lose credibility with parents by overusing an all-purpose answer to questions in this general area. Many parents have complained to me that their pediatricians say that the child will "grow out of" just about anything they are worried about, provided the child is not running a fever. Such an answer is at times appropriate because it is true or because a parent may be needlessly anxious. To the extent that it is used indiscriminately, however, it can be a substitute for a knowledgeable and useful response.

In summary, then, you should expect significant variation in the date of onset of a wide variety of abilities and other phenomena in the first three years of life. The charts in the preceding section illustrate how consistently these variations are seen in development.

SPACING CHILDREN

Over the last three or four years I have become especially interested in and concerned with the topic of spacing children. On the basis of recent, extensive work with young families, I have come to certain conclusions.

Let me begin by repeating the advice that I have given so frequently throughout this book. *Try not to have your children closer than three years apart.* In earlier chapters we discussed the dramatic difference siblings or their absence make in the life of the infant. We have found over and over again that a first child has a particular kind of family environment, which differs radically from that of a second child with a sibling less than three years older than he, and differs yet again (although not as much) from that of a child with one or more siblings more than three years older. Let us review these three alternative situations.

SITUATION OF A FIRST (ONLY) CHILD UNDER THREE YEARS OF AGE

The first child of less than three years of age is surrounded in his day-to-day activities by an environment that is predominantly adult. I say predominantly adult because it is a rare child, even if he is a first child, who has no exposure whatsoever to children his own age or slightly older children. There are, after all, visitors to the home. There are related family members. The child does move out of the home at times, accompanying his parents on shopping trips and other visits, perhaps to the beach or the playground. But certainly for well over ninety percent of his waking experience the infant who is a first child has a social environment consisting predominantly of his nuclear family. (I am setting aside for the moment the infant who is in day care or some other special arrangement.)

A first child living as he does is very likely to be treated extraordinarily well in most of his social interchanges. Since the figure he interacts with most commonly is his own mother, he is very likely to be surrounded by love, support, and encouragement, particularly if he is under fifteen or sixteen months of age. Of course he will also be exposed to occasional disciplinary action, to the setting of limits, and to an occasional cross word. But by and large he lives in a benign, warm, supportive social environment.

Another significant factor in the life of a first child is tied in with the fact that he lives in an environment where the models are adults. The child spends a good deal of time watching adults in operation, particularly his mother. As she goes about her tasks, she provides a model of a wide variety of adult behaviors. We do not know how much a child learns from this exposure, but we do know he spends a great deal of time closely observing maternal behavior.

Another important factor in the development of a first child is that when there is interaction between mother and child involving language, the language that the child hears is adult language. Hence he will profit from a variety, range, and richness of ideas, words, and grammatical structures. This can have profound consequences in terms of daily experience.

SITUATION OF A NINE-MONTH-OLD WITH A TWENTY-ONE-MONTH-OLD SIBLING

Move now to the child at the other extreme, the infant who is nine months of age and has a sibling one year older. The day-to-day environment of such an infant will be dramatically different from the previously described situation of a firstborn child. First of all, in terms of the quality of the social environment, the twenty-one-month-old child will inevitably resent and dislike the nine-month-old baby at times. What this means concretely is that he will occasionally act toward the nine-month-old in a hostile and aggressive fashion. The baby will be exposed to a quality of behavior on the part of the twenty-one-month-old that has virtually no parallel in the experience of a firstborn child. Let me enlarge on this point. We have seen twenty-one-month-olds striking their nine-month-old sibling, throwing objects at them, picking them up and deliberately dropping them, or pushing them about. We have seen repeated snatching of toys, food, and other materials from the nine-month-old. Think for a minute about what these experiences mean to an infant. I maintain that anger, even hatred, from a two-year-old toward his younger sibling is *normal*. This does not mean that such ugliness is not counterbalanced at times by genuinely pleasant interchanges between the two. It does not mean that in every case closely spaced children behave this way. What it does mean is that such behavior is the rule rather than the exception.

It is difficult to believe that exposure to hostile behavior does not affect the shaping of a nine-month-old. Indeed, as we have watched these situations evolve, we have found that the social behaviors and attitudes of the nine-month-old toward the twenty-one-month-old, toward his mother, and toward other children begin to resemble those of his sibling toward him. What seems to happen is that once the child of nine months learns how to cope with abuses, he begins to adopt some of the behaviors himself. This kind of antisocial behavior tends to emerge toward the middle of the second year of life.

There are those who say that all of these negative factors are counterbalanced by the fact that closely spaced children can be companions for each other, both at an early age and as they get older. You may, in fact, be fortunate and pay a relatively small price for such potential companionship. I find it hard to see, however, how an abusive early social experience can be helpful to a nine-month-old developing human, and it seems relatively easy to see how it can be harmful.

SITUATION OF A NINE-MONTH-OLD WITH A SIBLING MORE THAN THREE YEARS OLDER

In this case, we are dealing with a forty-five-month-old sibling at the very least, a child who is nearly four years of age. As pointed out in earlier sections of this book devoted to the development of intelligence and to emotional control, what we are talking about here is a rather advanced human being. Not only is the four-year-old much more able than a younger child to cope with emotions of resentment that emerge when he has to share his parents with a newcomer, but in addition, he has spent at least a year in developing interests outside of the home. He is well on his way with respect to peer interest and general outside-the-home activities. The cost to him of displacement within the home is considerably less than the cost to the twenty-one-month-old whose whole life still revolves around the home situation and the primary caretaker. For the four-year-old, the problem posed by an infant sibling is smaller and his capacity to deal with the problem is greater.

In conclusion, it is very difficult on both young children when they are spaced closely. The closer the spacing the greater the difficulty. Correspondingly, the wider the gap the more delightful the experience. The five- or six-year-old is much more inclined to genuinely enjoy the new baby. Bear in mind that grief or delight between young children plays a large role in determining how much pleasure a mother gets each day. In turn, how happy or distressed a mother is plays a large role in determining how rewarding a marriage will be. Once again, take my advice and space your children.

PROFESSIONAL TESTING OF YOUNG CHILDREN

LACK OF INFORMATION AND PROCEDURES

The testing of young children is another area which is adversely affected by the dearth of useful information. So much is still unknown about the details of growth and development in the first three years of life that the problem of assessing educational status becomes much more difficult than it need be. For example, I have emphasized repeatedly in this book the role of curiosity in early educational development, yet to this day we have next to no scientific knowledge about the day-to-day development of curiosity. We do not even have a way of assessing how well a child is doing in this critical area. I have provided what basic information *is* available in these pages, but this comprises only the simplest kind of information that any scientific process develops in its very first stages. What is needed is considerable research by a number of capable people over a number of years.

IMPORTANCE OF GESELL'S WORK

To date there has been a reliance on very old information and procedures in the area of testing for early educational development. Dr. Arnold Gesell did extremely important foundation work on the behavioral development of young children back in the 1930s. From his research, which was done on the children of 109 middle-class families in the New Haven, Connecticut, area, he was able to describe the general shape of early development. On the basis of that early research, Gesell produced a test which could be used by any pediatrician to screen children for gross normality. His test has been in widespread use ever since. It has proved extremely valuable in research studies and in private practice all over the world.

Shortly after Gesell's test came into general use, new and supposedly improved tests of a similar nature began to be produced, and we now have a fair number of them. They include the Bayley Test of Infant Development, the Cattell Test, and the Denver Developmental Test. Significantly, *all* of these tests depend largely on the work of Gesell, with each of them using test items that very much resemble those of the original Gesell schedules.

None of the people who followed Gesell did original item creation for their own tests in any extensive way, although some of them made significant technical improvements in their tests. For example, the Griffiths scale from England, created by Ruth Griffiths, is technically considerably better than the Gesell test, but its items very much resemble those of the Gesell. The last five to ten years have seen some progress in early assessment and general developmental testing, but it will be some time before more sophisticated procedures become available.

NECESSITY FOR VARYING EVALUATION SYSTEMS

Another consideration to be kept in mind in any discussion of early testing is the fact that at about two and one-half years of age a child changes from one kind of testee to another. The child over two and one-half years of age generally is assumed to have enough skill in language so that language can be used rather extensively in instructing him during the testing process. The child under two and one-half years of age, on the other hand, is considered to be largely unreliable concerning language skills, and is therefore generally tested as if he knew no language. In this respect testing the very young child most closely resembles evaluation of the abilities of other animal species. Testing of children over two and one-half years of age, on the other hand, more closely resembles the kind of testing that you may remember from your school days.

Testing of infants has traditionally employed both the mother's reports of what a child can do, and the use of machinery. A good example of machinery for testing the intactness of a baby is the electroencephalograph. This machine produces records of brain activity, which can be examined for signs of abnormal developmental status. Other tests of infant behavior and abilities involve the use of optical instruments like the retinoscope or ophthalmoscope to check visual

function. It is interesting to note that it has been repeatedly found that
mothers' reports of the capabilities of their children, particularly in the
educational achievement realm, are not nearly as reliable as those
generated by less partial observers.

PROBLEM OF FALSE POSITIVES

A final concern that complicates the problem of testing young children is the problem of false positives during the first year of life. Put
simply, false positive is a symptom or a behavior that suggests that there
is something wrong with the baby but that eventually proves not to have
been meaningful. Babies often behave in ways that worry pediatricians
and families but later turn out to have no particular prognostic value.
This is so common that pediatricians and other child-development
testers have adopted a very conservative attitude toward the significance
of occasional symptoms during the child's first year.

The problem of false positives puts the professional into a dilemma.
If, on the one hand, he conscientiously reports every little anomaly or
unusual element of behavior to the baby's parents, he can cause parents
much needless anxiety. On the other hand, if he ignores such signs, he
runs the risk of paying insufficient attention to the earliest points at
which a real problem begins to develop. Parents should therefore be
patient and understanding with their physician or psychological or
educational tester when it comes to the evaluation of behavior in the first
two years of life.

GENERAL DEVELOPMENT TESTS

By far the most common testing done that could be called educational
testing is the testing of general development. As we have seen, the
Gesell test is widely used for this purpose, as are some of the newer
tests. In our own work, for example, we use the Bayley Scales routinely
to test all of our children under two years of age. Such scales generally
produce at least two, sometimes as many as four, scores. From the
Bayley the tester calculates a mental and a physical score. The Gesell
generates four subscores and a fifth overall score called the Develop-

mental Quotient (DQ), so-called to distinguish it from the Intelligence Quotient or IQ. For many years professionals have acknowledged that children under two years of age do not show the same sort of intellectual capacity that older children and adults do, to any extensive degree. Nevertheless, the Bayley Scale does have a mental index. What kind of "mentality" it measures is unclear. The Gesell scale enables the tester to gauge a child's overall DQ; the tester also calculates a motor score, a personal-social score, a language score, and an adaptive score. The testing on these general developmental tests, particularly for the child under two, is predominantly a matter of eliciting a performance by the baby through the use of attractive materials, or by asking the mother to report on the child's behavior at home. In the Gesell test, the examiner may present the baby with one or more one-inch, red, wooden cubes. The examiner then moves aside and watches the baby's behavior with these cubes. The behavior can range from ignoring the cubes to building towers with them.

On the basis of the typical behaviors of the 109 middle-class children in his original sample, Gesell created a framework within which the behavior of other children might be placed and compared. Other items on such tests involve eliciting reflex behaviors. You can determine how much head control a baby has by placing him on his stomach and waiting a while. He generally will produce the behavior you are interested in. Often in the thirty minutes he sees a baby, an examiner will not hear many of the words that a baby of a year and one-half of age might occasionally use at home. Even if he hears them he might not recognize what they refer to. Therefore, many tests rely on the mother's knowledge of her child's vocabulary.

These general developmental tests are in widespread use. They are used by some people to test the overall development of children right up through entry into kindergarten. Generally speaking, scores on these tests with children under one year of age do not have any predictive value, with one important exception: If a child scores very low repeatedly, you probably have something to worry about. By very low I mean somewhere below 85 or so on tests where the average score is 100. But curiously, a child who scores 95 at one year of age on one of these general developmental tests is no more likely to score under 100 at three years of age on a Stanford-Binet Intelligence Test (perhaps the most popular of all IQ tests) than the child who scored 115 at one year of age on a general developmental test. The major uses of such tests are, first of all, to find the child who is doing very poorly (although very frequently any practiced pediatrician can spot such a child without the test); or, for research purposes, to roughly describe particular groups of children and individuals for the purpose of comparing samples.

TESTING THE FOUNDATIONS OF INTELLIGENCE

Let us turn now to the testing of the four educational foundations of the first years of life as described in this book.

Testing language development

In the area of language development we find that in a crude sense the general developmental scales, particularly the Gesell-type scales, can be used to generate information about a child's language development. There is indeed a language subscale within the Gesell. But again, such tests are very crude devices. They are neither powerful nor very reliable. The language subscale serves as a crude screening index, which is all it was designed to do.

The Preschool Project has developed a very good scale for assessing language development, starting when the child is seven or eight months of age until his third birthday. It depends very heavily on what the child *does* in response to situations and verbal instructions. That particular scale is, though experimental, very useful, and I expect others like it will soon be developed. There are a variety of other language scales around; but for the child under two they are not terribly impressive, largely because, as we have seen, most language ability for the very young child is receptive language ability. Although his understanding of language is reasonably well developed, his production is often very modest; and it is much easier to make up a test for spoken language than it is to make up a test of understood language. Furthermore, it is not all that easy for professionals to test children under two years of age. It is particularly difficult to test children between one and one-half and two years of age, since they are in the midst of negativism and hence often uncooperative in test situations. It is interesting to note that a child of three years of age is easier to test than a child of a year and three-quarters, and that a one-year-old child is also easier to test than a child of one and three-quarter years.

Testing social development

Social development is assessed in the same generally crude manner by the general developmental tests. Social development is also assessable using experimental instruments that our Preschool Project has produced. Otherwise, early social development is not usually assessed except informally. By that I mean no one else has explored the problem extensively to date. Until now, intelligence and perception have been much more popular than social development in infancy. I am sure, however, that this situation will change as time passes. There are some very promising ways of assessing the type of attachment that the baby has formed to an older person during the first two years of life; this is a sign of things to come.

Testing curiosity

In the area of curiosity we draw just about a total blank. Difficult though it may be to believe, we have neither the basic research nor the standardized instruments for assessment nor even any fairly well-developed experimental instruments in this area.

Measuring the roots of intelligence

The development of intelligence is tested in a rather crude way by certain portions of the general developmental tests. The Bayley mental index is related in some sense to the growth of intelligence, as are the language and adaptive scales of the Gesell. How they are related is not known. By far the most sophisticated treatment of the development of intelligence from a testing standpoint comes from the work of Piaget. There are now three or four new tests available where the items were selected directly from Piaget's basic research on the growth of intelligence. Although these particular tests are nowhere near as well developed (technically) as some of the older general developmental tests, they are the most promising with respect to monitoring intellectual growth in the first years of life. These tests that I refer to are tests of sensorimotor intelligence, and they are applicable during the first two years or so of life. In addition, once the child gets to be two and one-half years of age, one can use the Stanford-Binet. However, the Stanford-Binet is not as powerful an instrument when the child is two and one-half years of age as it will be when he is a bit older.

There are some experimental testing procedures currently undergoing development; but none of these tests is as yet well developed. I predict that sooner or later, however, this particular gap in our knowledge base will be filled.

TESTING PREREQUISITE TYPES OF DEVELOPMENT

Moving on from educational achievement per se, we now turn to prerequisite types of development, which are sometimes assessed during the first three years of life.

Assessing neurological damage

The central nervous system (the brain and the spinal cord) is the physical basis of all educational achievement; and traditionally its condition is the province of the physician. At birth and soon after the birth process most babies are examined closely to determine whether or not there is any significant damage to the central nervous system. If the damage is severe, it is generally observable in the first week of life, sometimes even at the time of birth. However, children who appear to be seriously damaged during the first year of life may later prove to be normal. Nevertheless, some babies begin their postnatal life under a serious and continuing physical handicap.

For quite some time now people have been working on ways of assessing less severe but real (borderline) and prognostically significant neurological damage. To date not much progress seems to have been made. In some of our research (particularly the Brookline Early Education Project), when the children are about two weeks of age, we use a neurological examination developed by a European pediatric neurologist named Heinz Prechtl. Prechtl claims that over many years of research his tests have identified borderline or moderate neurological damage. A fair number of leading physicians in this country, however, do not accept his views. These very early neurological examinations usually consist largely of the eliciting of reflex behaviors from the baby. These involve the fanning of the toes by a certain kind of stimulation of the soles of the feet (Babinski reflex), the eliciting of a head-righting reflex, a sucking or pupillary reflex, and so forth. As such, they overlap with the general developmental tests, whose motor-scale items often are identical.

Assessing vision and hearing

Vision and hearing are two especially important prerequisite capacities underlying educational development, and as such should be tested in the first years of life. Unfortunately, they are only tested adequately in rare cases. There has been a classic disagreement over the years between ophthalmologists and optometrists about visual function and early development. The ophthalmologist, I remind you, is a physician who specializes in diseases of the eye. The optometrist is not a physician. The optometrist's role is supposed to be measurement of eye function. The territories of these professionals overlap and instead of cooperating, they tend to squabble.

All physicians who have responsibilities for health care do some sort of visual examination of children beginning shortly after birth. These examinations are generally cursory, although some highly trained and outstanding pediatricians do considerably more than the average physician in this area. Some go so far as to check visual abilities in three-, four-, and five-month-olds, for example, looking to see whether their eyes focus well on nearby objects, whether they track moving objects well, and so forth. In most cases, however, even that degree of sophistication is not represented in early visual screening.

The first time the majority of children get sophisticated visual assessment is when they enter school. I consider this to be a serious problem for early educational activities, and I hope that it will soon be remedied. Ophthalmologists who do more-sophisticated examinations of the eye are more inclined to focus on the state of health of the eye than they are on the various visual activities, such as focusing, that are of visual consequence. The ophthalmologist characteristically uses drugs to put the eye into a state where the focusing mechanism is not working. He then examines the characteristics of the eyeball to see whether it looks healthy, whether its size and comparative dimensions look within normal range, and so forth. A small minority of leading optometrists do considerably more, even in the first months of life, in that they are particularly interested in the functioning of the eyes in their natural undrugged state. They attempt to measure the infant's capacities in such areas as three-dimensional vision, accurate visual convergence, and tracking in one or another major direction. Unfortunately, these sophisticated and talented people are relatively few in number, and the whole idea of doing detailed early visual testing is an idea whose time has not yet come.

As bad as it is to have children with undetected but significant visual deficits, it is considerably worse educationally for a child to have an undetected hearing deficit. Hearing is crudely tested at birth and at every regular pediatric examination. But the typical test does not amount to much more than determining whether or not a child is stone deaf. Obviously this is not enough. Children can accurately localize sounds at three, four, and five months of age, while at the same time having very significant (for educational purposes) deficits in discriminative power. It is now clearly within our capacity to do sophisticated hearing screening from the time a child is three and one-half months of age. Since language development begins at about six or seven months of age and moves forward very swiftly in the following year or two, it seems obvious that any child who has a correctable hearing deficit should be assisted *before* he gets to be six or seven months of age. Unfortunately, this is not being done routinely in this country; although I predict that it will be a routine part of educational practice in another decade or two. In the meantime, I would advise you to look for the most sophisticated hearing specialists in your community, and to use them with your child as early as possible.

A GUIDE TO VARIOUS PROFESSIONALS AND SERVICES

There are many different kinds of professionals who work in the area of early childhood education. I am going to restrict my comments to those who work with children under three years of age.

NEED FOR PARENT-EDUCATORS

I believe that we will see tremendous change in the next decade or two in respect to professional treatment of young children. The first people you might think of in regard to early educational development are educators themselves. You will find rather quickly, however, that there is no profession of infant-educators or parent-educators for infant development. Perhaps the most crucial need in this area is for professional educators who can teach parents how to educate their own children, rather than for professional educators to educate infants directly. You cannot, however, have extensive numbers of people trained adequately to educate parents without institutional support. Without large numbers of paying jobs available in one field, you will not have large numbers of people available for those jobs, nor will there be opportunities for training them. In this country the idea of the importance of education during infancy is quite new. As a result, we are only now beginning to see institutional support for this particular kind of professional role. Again, in the Brookline Early Education Project we have an extremely rare example of a situation where the professional task of several staff members is to help prepare and assist parents in their role as the initial educators of their new child. Each year that goes by will see more and more of such activity.

ROLE OF THE PHYSICIAN

Many people involved in parent education are inadequately trained for the task. Perhaps the most common kind of professional in parent education is a physician. Pediatricians nowadays are not as worried about rickets and malnutrition and other infant diseases as they were twenty or thirty years ago. Instead, their time seems to be increasingly spent in coping with the management problems of young mothers. Very commonly they are asked for guidance in areas that overlap significantly with the educational topics we have been discussing. Unfortunately, except for the fact that they have a brief exposure to child development during their medical school training and they have been exposed to many children and parents, the background of such persons is not adequate for this particular task. Nevertheless, the need for information is so great that parents will seek it from anybody who might be able to help. I believe that pediatrics will gradually become stronger in the area of early education. There are signs of growth in this regard in many places in this country, including within the Brookline Early Education Project.

ROLE OF THE SOCIAL WORKER AND RELATED PROFESSIONALS

In addition to physicians, I have found that there are people in social work who pride themselves on providing professional assistance in the area of rearing young children. Social workers become intimately involved in the problems of large numbers of families; as such, the opportunity is there to respond to a request for help by young parents. Public-health nurses provide a similar function, as do visiting nurses, homemakers, and child-study association people. All of these people from time to time offer guidance in this area. It is unfortunate that none of the professions involved provide very high-caliber training in parent education. But even if someone had attempted to prepare professionals as parent-educators, he would have been operating from the same fragile scientific base that everyone else has had to operate from until the last few years. In other words, even if someone in one professional capacity or another claims to have had an exposure to all that was available about the early educational development of children, if that exposure took place more than five years ago the chances are high that he still does not have a particularly substantial background in this topic.

ROLE OF DEVELOPMENTAL DAY CARE

A new kind of professional has been surfacing in recent years along with the growth of the day-care system. Although day care is not restricted to children under three years of age, increasingly such young children are being served by day care. Day care has long been designed primarily to serve the purposes of the parents rather than the child. Until fairly recently, as long as the child was safe and reasonably happy, the day-care experience was considered adequate, provided that it meshed with the needs of the parents, their work hours, and so forth. In the last five to ten years, with the growth of interest in and awareness of educational developments during the first years of life, such requirements are no longer considered adequate in many parts of the country.

Now we have what is called developmental day care. The definition of developmental day care not only includes but, as its highest priority, focuses on the educational development of the child, with the needs of the adults in the family considered to be secondary. There are increasing numbers of talented professional people in developmental day care, but by and large I would say that the caliber of training that they have received still suffers from the general immaturity of the field. I believe that you are well advised to be cautious to the degree that a person claims to have special knowledge about early education. More often than not, an overly confident attitude has masked inadequacies in knowledge.

ROLE OF THE CHILD PSYCHIATRIST

Child psychiatrists do not often work with children under three years of age, although from time to time you come across one who does. Occasionally you will find a program for early treatment of emotional handicaps or potential emotional handicaps. These are, unfortunately, areas where we have next to nothing to offer parents beyond a sympathetic shoulder to lean on and some general supportive advice. A two-year-old child with a significant behavior disturbance is a difficult case for any professional, whether he is a child psychiatrist, child psychoanalyst, clinical child psychologist, or psychiatric social worker. If you have a child with a behavior disturbance that is or may be significant, you should attempt to deal with the problem first with your physician or another health professional. But do not expect the same kind of "cure" in the area of behavior disturbance that you might expect in the area of orthopedics or infectious disease. We are unfortunately nowhere nearly as well developed in coping with the former area. If you find a professional who seems overconfident of positive results, beware. I would urge you to be very conservative when seeking help, to speak to a number of people, and to be slow in coming to a judgment as to how to proceed. I would even suggest that if you are lucky enough to know a wise woman who has raised three or four or more children, and if you are on good enough terms with that person to be able to get the benefit of her advice, you will more often than not find that she will be better able to help you deal with educational concerns in the first years of your child's life than a professional can.

A GUIDE TO INFORMATION ABOUT CHILDREN

Where can you go to get high-quality information about children? Those who have participated in the Brookline Early Education Project have found this an easy problem to cope with. You would be able to drop in at your pleasure at our local resource center, where you would find the best information available in written or filmed or personal form. You would find a lending library from which you could borrow books on just about any subject on young children, and from which you could borrow pamphlets and recent reports not yet in book form. You could even get information about the pros and cons of different toys. Indeed, if you could not afford it, you would be loaned one toy or another that you might want to use for a while with your child. Furthermore, you would find videotapes available dealing with such subjects as the testing of young children, sibling rivalry, and language development. In addition, if you wanted to talk to a professional in public health, medicine, or early education, you could make arrangements to do so. Finally, and by no means least important, you could compare notes with other parents like yourself. Hopefully more facilities of this kind will be available to parents in the future. In the meantime, what can child-rearers do to get the information they need?

First of all, you can utilize the material found in this book. You can also make use of the experience of capable and warm human beings who are not professionals, as noted at the end of the last section. In addition, you can resort to a huge number of books, both technical and nontechnical; droves of magazine articles; various government publications from the U.S. Printing Office; an occasional television program; and films that can be rented. You can also seek advice from various professionals of the sort mentioned in the previous section.

I do feel, however, that you should stick to the principle of safety in numbers in using these sources. Try to get the best-quality materials, and do not depend on only one of them. The more information you can get, the better.

BOOKS

My office contains several hundred books on early child development, yet if you had mastered all of them, I do not believe you would be particularly well advanced with respect to parenting your young child. A few books do, however, deserve special mention. Joan Beck, who used to write a syndicated column for the Chicago *Herald Tribune*, recently wrote a book called *How to Raise a Brighter Child*. In it Ms. Beck does a fine job of translating into practical and understandable terms some of the better work that has been done in studying the growth of the young child. Another outstanding book is *Revolution in Learning* by Maya Pines, a free-lance writer. These and other recommended books are cited in the recommended reading section of this book. The fact that so many books are available, particularly popular books, is a symptom of the widespread need on the part of parents in particular to know more about young children, and of the failure of our educational system to provide the needed help.

Perhaps the most relevant and valuable technical books I can recommend would be the aforementioned works of J. McVicker Hunt and, of course, Jean Piaget. Hunt, in his book *Intelligence and Experience*, does a magnificent job of discussing that topic and introduces you to Piaget's studies of early sensorimotor development. Piaget is far and away the outstanding authority in the area of the growth of intelligence, and you will find some of his less difficult works listed in the reference list. I also recommend Stone and Church's introductory text, called *Childhood and Adolescence*, a solid, easy-to-read book that will give you a general introduction to childhood. Among the many popular books available to help you educate your young child, the only one I can honestly recommend is Benjamin Spock's book on child care, which is excellent, particularly in the areas of the child's physical well-being.

FILMS

You can rent good films on child development from rental libraries around the country. Yeshiva University, Boston University, and Pennsylvania State University all have film libraries, and there are a handful of others that will send you films for private or group showing at very moderate rates. Joseph Stone of Vassar College has some particularly fine films on early childhood development, and also on some outstanding kibbutzim in Israel. There are older films of uneven quality available from Gesell's work.

MAGAZINES

Magazines have for years specialized in this field. In fact there are magazines devoted entirely to the topic of early development. Occasionally you will find a genuinely helpful article, but many are misleading, inaccurate, or simply a waste of time. I hope as a result of reading this book, you will be in a better position to judge such material.

GOVERNMENT PAMPHLETS

The U.S. Government Printing Office has produced a series of relatively unsophisticated pamphlets on raising young children over the decades. *Infant Care* is the best known of these pamphlets. It is available for under one dollar, and along with the Bible and Dr. Spock's books is one of the best-selling four or five written publications of any kind in this country. Such pamphlets are adequate beginner's texts, but you will want to look elsewhere for further details.

I would like to stress my belief that early education is basically a responsibility of government, and that the Office of Education and your local school system should provide the child-rearing information you need. Indeed, I predict that in ten to twenty years, this will be the case.

EXPERIENCE VS. HEREDITY:
THE NATURE-VS.-NURTURE CONTROVERSY

The theme that has dominated early childhood research throughout its history has been the relative contributions to achievement of experience versus heredity. From time to time this topic is temporarily resolved (at least in a superficial sense), only to resurface a decade later just as vigorously as before. During the late nineteenth century it was assumed that whatever was inherited was of the greatest importance with respect to achievement levels. The child's "nature" was considered to be pretty well brought into the world with him. The influence of Freud and his followers, and of people in learning theory, starting with Ivan Pavlov, the Russian physiologist, somewhat turned the tide. During the second and third decades of this century people became increasingly impressed with the importance of early experiences (particularly those of the first five years of life). A reaction began during the 1930s, with Gesell among its leaders. The result was a host of research experiments designed to show that there were limits to what early learning and early teaching could achieve for a child. These studies were designed to remind researchers and the public alike that extreme environmentalism did not make any sense. There were interesting studies in which identical twins were used to show the effects of the limitations of immaturity. In one case a twin was taught to roller skate earlier than he might ordinarily have learned the skill. The other twin was prevented from learning to roller skate; yet when the latter twin took up the activity at a more appropriate (later) age, he caught up rather quickly. Similar experiments were done in the use of scissors and stair climbing. The tide in the Thirties turned away from emphasis on the power of early experiences and back toward the importance of maturation and inherited traits.

We saw a reversal yet again in the Fifties and Sixties, as the work of Piaget became more influential and as the civil-rights movement gathered power. The undying optimism that we seem to have about the potential of children pushed again to the forefront. This resulted in more and more research and practical activity based on the notion that early experience was important. The 1960s saw the establishment of such programs as Project Head Start, designed to help young children obtain a better set of early educational experiences.

The controversy is far from over. Once again, more and more people are voicing the importance of heredity, but we still do not have enough dependable evidence to make reliable judgments as to how much achievement can be ascribed to experiences and how much to competence. Perhaps the most succinct way to express my judgment in this matter is as follows. What a child brings into the world sets an upper limit to the achievement level that he can attain. However, it provides no guarantee whatsoever of reaching any level of achievement. A child with serious brain damage simply cannot reach the achievement levels of a child with an intact central nervous system, no matter how good his experiences may be. On the other hand, a child with the best possible central nervous system and physical apparatus at birth may not achieve even average levels of competence unless the experiential requirements are there. For example, the most beautifully endowed baby can be prevented from ever learning language simply by being prevented from ever hearing any. Such a child will never reach his intellectual potential, nor will he be a particularly effective social animal.

The responsibility of those of us who rear children is to provide the best possible set of experiences that we can, particularly in the first years of life, *regardless* of the amount of inherited potential of the child.

DAY CARE: SHOULD YOU OR SHOULDN'T YOU?

In the last year or two I have done a good deal of traveling in this country and participated in many discussions about services for young children. Increasingly the topic of day care emerges as one of great interest to many people. Day care is often discussed in emotionally charged terms. Since the welfare of children and ambivalence about the roles of parents are involved, this is not surprising.

Many people are very distressed by the difficulties involved in obtaining first-rate day care. My own feelings on the subject stem from my special interest in the quality of early childhood experiences, hence my remarks will be confined to day care for children under three years of age.

One of my primary goals in writing this book has been to help those responsible for young children to maximize the potential each child brings with him into the world. If a child is born into a well-put-together family, his chances of achieving a fairly solid early education within that family are good. His chances of receiving a superb early experience are less good due to present inadequacies in preparing and assisting families to do the job.

Some families are better equipped to educate young children than others. But assuming the most common situation of a loving, reasonably well-put-together family, and a child under three years of age, what about day care? It is my considered opinion that attending just about any day-care installation *full time*, is unlikely to be as beneficial to the child's early educational development as his own home during these first three years. Notice that I say *full time*, because in the case of half-time day care or less, I think the likelihood of the child's early education being adversely affected is limited. Indeed, I think for certain kinds of families such an arrangement is preferable to one where no day care is involved. This is because there are benefits to be had when the full-time responsibility for rearing a child is periodically relieved by the opportunity for a woman to pursue a career interest or to simply be away from responsibility for a baby for several hours at a time. I personally believe that a person can be a better child-rearer if he or she has regular time off from the job. In most cases, then, for middle- and upper-income families where there are no serious problems such as an extremely weak marriage or borderline alcoholism, I think that full-time day care is inadvisable, but that part-time day care may very well be better than none whatsoever.

As mentioned before, until recently day care has concentrated more on the needs of the parents than the child. It has been seen primarily as a means by which parents, particularly women, could be freed from the time-consuming responsibilities of child-rearing in order to do other things with their lives. Most notably these other activities have included paid work or some kind of advanced training. Within the last five to ten years, the tendency has grown to talk about the child's developmental needs on an equal—if not superior—level with those of the adults in the family. As we have seen, we now have what is known as developmental day care, which focuses primarily on the developmental needs of the young child. Do not be misled by the label. While day-care operations certainly are variable in quality—and some of them are of very good quality—the whole institution of developmental day care is an extremely weak one. It suffers along with all efforts in child care from the problems of an inadequate knowledge base.

In my opinion, the best of the day-care centers are those that have personnel with extensive experience and natural talent, and who operate on a practical intuitive rather than a theoretical level. Day-care centers that advertise that their curriculum and program is inspired by or based on the works of Piaget, Erik Erikson, or other well-known psychologists, should be looked upon with great suspicion, because there is no such thing as a collection of ideas within our research literature (with the exception of the ideas contained in this book) which can serve adequately as a detailed basis for an educational program for children under three years of age. Therefore you cannot comfortably place your faith in a day-care center to provide a first-rate educational service and experience for your child.

On balance, I would say that your own family is definitely likely to do a better job acting naturally with your child than any day-care center you can put him in. The only place where you are likely to get a better set of early experiences for your child is in a family day-care operation run by a woman in her own home, provided that the woman has been one of the minority of people who has done an unusually good job with her own children in the past. Under such circumstances I think you might stand a chance of getting an even better early educational experience for your child than in your own home. Whether or not you find a superior home-run day-care operation is a matter of luck. The odds are against you.

There are some situations where day care seems to make sense. If, for example, for one reason or another the family simply does not have the resources and/or the inclination to do a good job with their very young child, then perhaps it might be in the best interests of the child to place him in a first-rate professional setup where the personnel are not only competent but also very affectionate and devoted. Parenthetically, I would remark that within the last couple of years we have seen a few legal cases where children have been removed from their own homes by judges who believed that the child's chances of a decent set of early experiences were poor. We are talking now about exceptional cases.

It is my hope that we will soon get to a point where raising a child in the home in the first few years of life will no longer be generally considered "mere mothering." I honestly cannot think of any task more exciting and more valuable that any of us do in our daily work than the task of providing an early education for one's own child under three years of age. The parent who takes the responsibility for structuring the experiences of the first three years of his child's life is at the same time taking on an important responsibility for helping to mold that child and helping to give that child's natural tendencies the best possible opportunities to flower. What could be more important and rewarding than this? Should this idea become more widely accepted, I think we will find several interesting and pleasant consequences. First of all, we are likely to find a more responsible public educational system, which devotes resources to preparing and assisting families for the child-rearing function. Second, we will find fewer families in conflict or dissatisfied about the woman's role. We will less frequently see a woman going back to something "more important" than child-raising as soon as possible in the child's first year of life. Finally, we are likely to find an increase in the tendency of men to find it acceptable and even desirable to assume more of the child-rearing function on a regular basis.

THE ROLE OF THE FATHER

I find people increasingly asking how well a father might do in child-rearing. On the basis of extensive research we have done on this topic over the last several years, I believe that fathers, mothers, and day-care centers are *all* capable of providing an excellent early education for children. All things being equal, I think mothers will probably do better at the task than others. But if anyone could do as good a job as a mother in providing beneficial early childhood experiences, I would guess that it would be the father. The reason I say this is because when you look closely at what it means to be a child-rearer in the child's first three years, you find that most of the factors involved do not seem to be sex linked. Designing a home that is safe and interesting for a child does not seem to require male or female genes. Nor does responding naturally to a child's overtures and providing assistance when needed. In general, as you look beyond the superficial and into the actual details of the provision of early educational opportunities, I see nothing that a mother does (except breast-feeding) that a father could not do. The reason I am inclined to think that mothers and fathers are better at child-rearing than day-care centers not only has to do with the absence of any special professionalism in day-care centers, but also with the fact that requirements with respect to social development and attachment are more adequately met in the nuclear family than they are in an institutional setting. The negativism and other stress-inducing behaviors that infants exhibit are more likely to be borne gracefully by the child's parents than by nonfamily members.

In summary, I would say fathers could probably do the job not only as well as the mother, but in some instances even better. The thing to keep in mind is the child's needs, and then on a point-by-point basis to ask whether he is getting what he requires from the person or persons involved.

WHAT HAPPENS AFTER THIRTY-SIX MONTHS OF AGE?

Sometimes when I present my views about the importance of the first three years of life I notice sad looks coming over the faces of parents. Such sadness is sometimes followed by the questions, "Is it all over after three? Is there nothing further I can do to be useful? Is there no way I can compensate for mistakes that I may have made?"

Answering these questions is rather difficult for me because *to some extent* I really believe it *is* too late after age three. But the qualifications I place on this statement are important. Children continue to develop after age three, as we all know. Indeed, I am inclined to believe people like Erik Erikson, who say that human beings continue to develop in important ways until they die.

I do believe, however, after studying human development for twenty years, that the degree of flexibility that humans have, their capacity for fundamental change in their life style, in their intellectual capacity, and so forth, declines steadily with age. This has been the theme of any number of studies of child development, and I do not know of anybody who has studied human development in any serious way over the years who disagrees with it. What the argument boils down to is the *degree of flexibility* that remains at various stages of life, and our capacities as individuals, professionals, and as a society to use that flexibility to induce changes for the better at any point in a human's life.

I think Hollywood has done us all a dirty trick. During the golden years of Hollywood—the Thirties, Forties and Fifties, when so many of us spent so much time at the movies—a particularly powerful cinematic theme was the sudden dramatic conversion or reformation of a human being. On the screen, before our very eyes, we saw adult human beings being converted from mean, vicious, small-minded people to open-minded, "I see the light and now I am going to be a perfect human being'' types, thanks to a single dramatic event. This theme also was played out in stories concerning young boys and girls who seemed to be on the wrong track, but who as a result of meeting up with someone like Spencer Tracy suddenly found ''the way.''

When a movie like *The Bad Seed* was made, in which a young child was portrayed as completely evil from the earliest days of her life, regardless of experience, audiences throughout the country were shocked. Such a point of view was inconsistent with such modern American principles as, ''Hope springs eternal,'' ''There is always room for a change,'' ''We can always aspire to the best,'' ''It is never too late.'' My feeling is that once a child reaches two years of age, his primary social orientation has been established, and from then on it becomes increasingly difficult to alter this significantly. For example, if a child has been taught that the world revolves exclusively around him; that if he simply insists on having his way, he will find resistance crumbling; then I feel that he will be predisposed to operate in a self-centered fashion in all of his subsequent interpersonal relationships. This does not mean that a three-year-old spoiled child cannot be changed. However, it does mean that it probably will not be easy to change him. Nowhere in child-development research have we demonstrated a strong capacity to alter early personality patterns, or early social attitudes.

Nevertheless, in spite of the lack of demonstrated ability to make fundamental personality changes after the early years, I strongly advocate that we all keep trying. It seems to me that each person responsible for influencing the growth and development of a young human has no choice but to continue to do the best he can to induce the most beneficial course of development for every child in his or her care. What it all boils down to is that there *is* capacity for change, including dramatic improvement, after the child is three years of age. However, it is often very difficult to bring about desired changes, and more often than not, remediation will not be achieved. We must therefore pay much greater attention to the prevention of difficulties, to the prevention of the loss of capacity and potential from birth, rather than continue the way we have been going.

As noted earlier, in our research on the first six years of life we found that children doing remarkably well at three years of age had achieved a good start in regard to the major distinguishing elements of competence of the outstanding six-year-old. What we found between the ages of three and six years was a process of refinement of those abilities rather than the emergence of new abilities. The description of the special attributes of the well-developed three-year-old in this book applies as well to the well-developed six-year-old. The difference is one of degree, not quality. The well-developed six-year-old has significantly greater language abilities than the well-developed three-year-old. Likewise his capacities in the area of thinking ability, complex fantasy activity, executive skills, and in the other dimensions cited, are going to be considerably greater on an absolute level than the same abilities in the three-year-old. Again, we could not find other kinds of distinguishing abilities emerging between three and six.

Another aspect of the three-to-six-year age range that has been mentioned earlier but deserves reemphasis here is the growth of interest in peer activities during this period. I mentioned that true social interest in peers seemed to begin at about two years of age. That interest grows steadily from two right through to six years of age. In fact, it appears that interest in peers continues to grow until, by the time children enter adolescence, you frequently find that what peers think about a child becomes considerably more important than what parents think. This seems to be a developmental fact that accompanies the shifting of interest away from the nuclear family during the long-term process wherein a human being goes from total dependency to as much independence as any of us ever achieve.

There are equally dramatic developments in the area of mental ability after three years of age. Again, I would refer you to the work of Piaget, who claims that one particularly important plateau is reached somewhere between six and eight years of age, as children leave egocentric modes of thought and move over toward what he calls "socialized thought." As a child comes to value his peers, he becomes very much interested in being understood when he speaks to them. By seven or eight years of age this need to be understood causes him to start thinking about how to frame his ideas so that another person can deal with them. In contrast, the three-year-old does not actually go through that preparatory step. He is likely to assume that because his parents seem to be able to read his mind, just about anybody he speaks to will be able to understand him.

In Piaget's system a later plateau occurs in early adolescence when children achieve an adult style of thought and become mature, reasonable individuals. It is interesting to note that Rousseau advised several centuries ago that the best thing we could do about early education was to guard *against* it until children reached the age of eleven, twelve, or thirteen years and their "reason matured." Some modern educational theorists think that he was probably correct.

WHAT WILL THE FUTURE BRING?

I am quite confident that within two or three decades the public educational system will routinely be acknowledging the fundamental importance of the development of educational foundations in the first years of life. I think the results will be multiple. One will be that high schools will *require* participation in courses on early human development and child-rearing practices for both boys and girls. Maternity wards of hospitals will have mini-courses available (perhaps on videotape or film) during the three- or four-day postnatal hospital stay. We will probably see a corresponding decline in magazine articles on child-rearing problems, as public responsibility for the provision of guidance on those topics is increasingly assumed. Correspondingly, books on the private market on the topic of child-rearing will become fewer.

Families will continue to be the primary agents for the early education of their own children. Instead of going it virtually alone, however, as they do today, they will hopefully become more adequately prepared and assisted each year for this very important task. This raises the question of who will bear the professional responsibility for preparing and assisting families as the first educational delivery system. At the moment, as we have seen, there are very few people employed specifically to train parents to be educators. We have occasional opportunities to do this kind of work in new experimental programs, but we do not have broad institutional support for such a specialty. We have public-health nurses, homemakers, and so forth, but they have a variety of duties other than assisting parents as educators. Some leading pediatricians I have known may very well move strongly into the area of professional responsibility for this particular task. There are signs afoot that a few progressive pediatric training programs are moving increasingly into the field of early childhood education. Medicine may or may not be the best way to go. My personal feeling once again is that *the*

public educational system ought to take on the job as part of its responsibility to provide education for young people.

The pediatric profession, however, has something going for it that the educational system does not in terms of educating parents. Pediatricians have access to families when children are very young. The school system does not; besides which, in our society the family is traditionally considered to be a private domain. The fact that the physician has access to the home may give him a head start with respect to this particular function.

We see an increasing need today for the allocation of responsibility among parent-educators, because in our experiences in experimental programs, we have noted a remarkable number of professionals who feel that they have an important primary claim to the terrain. People in such fields as general medicine, pediatrics, child psychiatry, child psychology, early education, social work, public-health nursing, and nursery school education all feel that they are the logical candidates to take over the job. Since they can't all do so, something has got to give.

Section III

CONCLUDING
REMARKS

NO JOB IS MORE IMPORTANT THAN RAISING
A CHILD IN THE FIRST THREE YEARS OF LIFE

I have devoted my whole professional career to pursuing the question of how competent people get that way. On the basis of years of research, I am totally convinced that the first priority with respect to helping each child to reach his maximum level of competence is to do the best possible job in structuring his experience and opportunities during the first three years of life. Now, if I am totally convinced of that concept then it becomes painfully obvious that to me, at least, any other kind of job, be it formal or informal, working as an engineer somewhere, working as the president of a bank, working as a career professional in designing, or in the arts, cannot really compete (in humanistic terms) with the job of helping a child make the most of his potential for a rich life. Therefore I do not think any job is more important in humanistic terms than the one this book describes.

NO JOB PROVIDES DEEPER SATISFACTION

It is possible that you have gained the impression that child-rearing in the first three years of a child's life is nothing but one problem after another. It is indeed true that child-rearing involves a lot of hard work and some stress. Let me hasten to assure you, however, that our research has taught us that when the process goes well, it is hugely rewarding and not unduly burdensome.

The most difficult period for most parents is the second half of the second year of life. This is a stressful time for *all* parents and children, but is less difficult for families where the child is developing very well. We have seen modest indications that better-informed parents have less testy children and handle negativism better during Phases VI and VII than those who are unprepared. I have dealt at length with the importance of helping a child maintain a balance of interests as he goes from eight months of age on through twenty-four months. If you do manage effectively to nurture the child's natural interests in exploration of the world, and in the mastery of motor skills, you will find the task of dealing with him on a social plane during the second half of the second year of life considerably easier than it otherwise might be. When he reaches the point where he can engage in simple conversation with you, you will be rewarded by a simultaneous easing of his testiness and a remarkable rush of impressive achievements which is unique to this time in a child's life.

Also on the positive side of the balance, do not forget the pleasures surrounding the first smiles and social responsiveness of a baby, the absolutely delightful fourth month of an infant's life, the excitement of a child's first learning to walk, and so many other joyful moments. It is indeed worth the effort.

THE AVERAGE FAMILY HAS ENOUGH RESOURCES TO DO A FINE JOB

One of the most comforting and exciting findings of our research has been the notion that at least for the first three years of a child's life most families have adequate resources to rear him well. We have seen families from all levels of society, with many kinds of cultural backgrounds, doing every bit as good a job as the most generously endowed families. We have seen low-income families with as many as six closely spaced children, where each of the children turned out to be beautifully developed not only at age three, but on into the elementary school years as well. We have concluded that you do not need much in the way of formal education to be an effective and outstanding child-rearer. Some of our most impressive child-rearers have had no more than a high-school education. You certainly do not need a high family income. Nothing that I have recommended in this book costs a significant amount of money. Many of the materials are items that one would ordinarily have anyway. You do not even need remarkable intelligence.

What you do need to do a good child-rearing job is a strong feeling of love for the child, a great deal of patience and stamina, and some degree of knowledge. You should know something about the details of all the different major developmental processes in children, and have an idea how to help a child by your direct and indirect actions, which affect the kind of experience he has during these crucial years.

The science of human development is still at a very primitive level. With time, however, more and better information will become available to help parents do the best possible child-rearing job. I urge you, if you continue to have babies, to keep your eyes open for any new findings that may evolve, and I wish you good luck.

RECOMMENDED READINGS

INTRODUCTION

This section deals with what I believe to be the most useful writings currently available on the development of very young children. Obviously the list is not complete, since there are undoubtedly writings of excellence that I do not know about. On the other hand, many popular writings are missing from the list because I cannot endorse them.

As noted earlier, few books of the huge numbers written contain extensive, reliable facts about the rapid development of the first years of life because comparatively few people have sought and discovered such information. Gesell, Hunt and Piaget are among that exclusive group who have made major contributions. Work that is more limited in scope but still highly valuable has been produced on this topic by M. Ainsworth, Thomas *et al.,* and Wolff, among others.

While detailed information about infants and toddlers has been scarce, reliable ideas about how to rear a child have been even scarcer. Notice I said *reliable* ideas; there has been no shortage of opinions and writings on the topic.

IDEAS ABOUT CHILD-REARING PRACTICES (1900–1975)

For an introduction to the recent history of ideas about children I suggest the following works:

Spock, Benjamin. *The Common Sense Book of Baby and Child Care.* New York: Duell, Sloan, and Pearce, 1945.

No single published work has influenced more families in this country in the rearing of their children during the last two decades. Dr. Spock's forte is the physical welfare of the baby, but he has a good deal of useful advice on management issues as well.

Gesell, A. *How a Baby Grows: A Story in Pictures*. New York: Harper, 1945.

Gesell, A., and F.L. Ilg. *Feeding Behavior of Infants: A Pediatric Approach to the Mental Hygiene of Early Life*. Philadelphia: Lippincott, 1937.

Gesell, A., et al. *The First Five Years of Life. A Guide to the Study of the Preschool Child*. New York: Harper, 1940.

Gesell, A., and F.L. Ilg. *Infant and Child in the Culture of Today: The Guidance of Development*. New York: Harper, 1943.

Dr. Spock succeeded Dr. Gesell; both were pediatricians. Gesell's work may strike you as somewhat archaic. It is mostly, after all, more than thirty years old. Gesell provided information of remarkable usefulness in the diagnosis of developmental difficulties in preschool children. He was not very much impressed by the power of early experiences to influence development. His views emphasized the role of maturation and genetics. As such, his recommendations for child-rearing only occasionally resemble mine.

Freud, Sigmund. Three essays on the theory of sexuality (1905), *Standard Edition of Complete Psychological Works of Sigmund Freud*, Vol. 7, 1901–1905. London: Hogarth Press & Institute of Psychoanalysis, 1957.

Freud's ideas about the motives behind the behavior of young children (and their parents) have had enormous influence. Although very few modern child-development theorists endorse his views about the primacy of sexual and aggressive drives, you would be surprised at their vitality in the fields of psychiatry and pediatrics. There is a very substantial lag between research and practice, such that ideas that have declined in acceptance at the research level may still determine practice twenty years after their peak! Freud was a gifted writer as well as a brilliant theoretician.

Hunt, J. McVicker, *Intelligence and Experience*. New York: The Ronald Press Company, 1961.

Hunt, along with John Flavell of the University of Minnesota, played a leading role in spreading the ideas of Piaget in this country. This book is a beautifully written and scholastically powerful treatment of the heredity-environment controversy as it relates to the development of intelligence. Pay particular attention to the first few chapters, which describe the evolution of thinking about the role of experience in the development of intelligence in young children. Few child-development researchers have devoted themselves as conscientiously and as effectively to the study of this problem as J. McVicker Hunt.

GENERAL DEVELOPMENT

Additional readings of value in the area of the overall development of a young child are as follows:

Gesell, A., and Catherine S. Amatruda. *Developmental Diagnosis Normal and Abnormal Child Development*. New York: Paul B. Hoeber, Inc., 1960.

This particular book, one of several by Gesell, is meant to accompany the Gesell developmental schedules which the pediatrician can use in his office to assess the child's overall developmental status. While you will find the language a bit out of date, and some of the general discussions of only modest interest, the basic information about how the very young child will behave in the Gesell test situations at various points throughout the first years of life is still essentially correct and being used in several standard tests of early development.

Stone, J., and J. Church. *Childhood and Adolescence: A Psychology of the Growing Person*. New York: Random House, 1964.

This particular book is and has been perhaps the most readable introductory textbook in child-development courses in colleges. The authors are very practiced and knowledgeable, and present a humanistic view of early child development. Other texts may be more powerful from a technical standpoint, but no other text gives a better general appraisal of development of the young child.

Wolff, P. "Observations on newborn infants." *Psychosomatic Medicine,* 1959, Vol. 21, pp. 110–18.

Peter Wolff was one of the modern pioneers in the practice of direct, long-term observations of the young infant in his natural circumstances. The information in this very brief article about the daily experiences of the newborn baby is both accurate and, as far as I know, unique.

Pratt, K. "The neonate," *Manual of Child Psychology* 2nd ed., ed. L. Carmichael. New York: John Wiley & Sons, Inc., 1954.

This particular chapter by Pratt has been for years a standard reference work. In it you will find several thousand bits of information about the child less than thirty days of age. A word of caution, however. The writing is highly technical.

MANAGEMENT OF THE YOUNG CHILD

Spock, Benjamin. *The Common Sense Book of Baby and Child Care*. New York: Duell, Sloan, and Pearce, 1945.

Again, Spock's recommendations about how to cope with feeding and sleeping problems and other typical issues in child-rearing have been more widely read and followed than any other single work over the last several decades in this country. This book would not have been so popular if it were not such good, solid material. Spock performed an extremely valuable service to the young families of this country. The topic of management is a classic case of a topic that bridges two fields: medicine and educational psychology. Nowadays most pediatricians find themselves not only concerned with the physical welfare of the young baby, but also with the mother's desire to raise that baby well. Although, strictly speaking, whether the child eats or sleeps well is not an educational topic per se, to understand how to cope with such behavioral problems requires knowledge not only of the child's physical makeup and health, but also about the way his mind operates, the way he learns, what kind of discipline will work with him, etc.

Infant Care. Children's Bureau Publication No. 8, 1963, reprinted 1967. U. S. Department of Health, Education, and Welfare. Superintendent of Documents, U. S. Government Printing Office, Washington, D. C. 20402.

Infant Care has for the better part of this century been distributed broadly to the families in this country. It is apparently the single most popular document that the U. S. Government Printing Office has ever made available to the public. The fee for it has always been nominal (under one dollar), and within its pages you will find a distillation of the conventional wisdom of each decade as it concerns the management of the infant. There have been historical analyses of the contents of the ideas of *Infant Care* which show that its recommendations to parents have shifted with whatever ideas were prevalent in child-development research at any point in time. Furthermore, there are topics within *Infant Care* wherein the directions to parents have taken a 180-degree turn in the space of only a few years. This vacillation on fundamental issues in child-rearing is a reflection of the immaturity of the knowledge base in the field.

THE DEVELOPMENT OF INTELLIGENCE

Piaget, J., *The Origins of Intelligence in Children*, 2nd ed. New York: International Universities Press, 1952.

Piaget, J., *The Child's Conception of the World*. Patterson, N.Y.: Littlefield, Adams & Co., 1963.

Piaget, J., *The Language and Thought of the Child*. New York: The World Publishing Company, 1963.

Without question, Piaget has been head and shoulders above the rest of the field with respect to new knowledge about how the intelligence of man develops. These three writings of his are classics.

The first has to do with the first years of life and is extremely difficult reading. I would advise you to read translations of this book by Hunt (see below). The extremely courageous, however, may find Piaget's own version a worthwhile challenge.

The second and third books deal with the mentality of the slightly older child, ranging in age from three years up to twelve. Although they were originally written many years ago, many of the ideas they contain are remarkably fresh. If you want a firsthand look at genius, read these books.

Hunt, J. McVicker, *Intelligence and Experience*. New York: The Ronald Press Company, 1961.

This book has been referred to in an earlier section. Suffice it to say that several of its pages are devoted to a translation into understandable terms of Piaget's original work. Other chapters relate his work to many other forms of study of the same sorts of processes. A book well worth reading.

White, B. L., "The initial coordination of sensorimotor schemas in human infants—Piaget's ideas and the role of experience," *Studies in Cognitive Development: Essays in Honor of Jean Piaget*, J. H. Flavell and D. Elkind, eds. New York: Oxford University Press, 1969, pp. 237–56.

White, B. L., et al. *Experience and Environment: Major Influences on the Development of the Young Child*, Vol. I. Englewood Cliffs, N.J.: Prentice-Hall, Inc., 1973.

Although my own research has not focused upon the development of intelligence, it has touched upon the development of intelligence; and in its treatment of the concept of general abilities or competence, we are dealing with overlapping subjects. While I am not a particularly technical writer, these readings are more technical than typical works written for a popular audience.

THE DEVELOPMENT OF COMPETENCE

Competence includes intelligence, but is considerably broader. In general it refers to all the significant abilities that a creature has in coping with his environment. A definition of competence is, of course, presented in this book in reference to my own research. It includes intellectual, linguistic, perceptual, motor, and social skills.

White, Robert. "Motivation Reconsidered: The Concept of Competence." *Psychological Review*, Vol. 66, No. 5 (1959).

Robert White is another one of the small group of outstanding scholars in the field of child-development research. Now retired, he—like Hunt, Freud, Erikson, and several others—is not only a gifted scholar, but a superb writer as well. In this technical study he reviews all sorts of research on the topic of the drive to become competent, a fascinating semi-difficult subject that I recommend strongly.

Stone, J. L., Smith, H. T., and Murphy, L. B. *The Competent Infant—Research and Commentary*. New York: Basic Books, Inc., 1973.

This up-to-date encyclopedic work is a compilation of most of the major approaches to the study of the young infant. It contains selected readings which, when put together, provide the reader with a rather complete, fairly technical introduction to modern research on the very young baby.

PERSONALITY DEVELOPMENT

The development of personality in young children is no longer a particularly popular topic with child-development researchers. While the importance of the topic is still broadly acknowledged, the fact that it is considerably more difficult to study in a scientifically respectable way has discouraged people from pursuing the topic. Nevertheless, some of the most exciting and interesting reading about the young child is contained in works on this subject.

Murphy, Lois. *Personality in Young Children,* Vol. II. New York: Basic Books, Inc., 1956.

Lois Murphy, working with four colleagues from related disciplines, studied the growth of personality in a group of nursery school children at Sarah Lawrence College some twenty years ago. This entire book is devoted to the description of the ups and downs of the one nicely put-together child from the time he was two and one-half until he was five and one-half years of age. The scene is usually his nursery school class, and the result is a rich documentation of normal personality development.

Thomas, A., et al. *Behavior and Individuality in Early Childhood.* New York: New York University Press, 1964.

The introductory passages of this small, well-written volume add to one's understanding of the history of research in personality development in particular. The remainder of the book is an attempt to show how competent researchers investigate the individuality of the child, beginning with his very first days of life. It is essentially a treatment of the topic of temperamental differences in young children. It is somewhat technical, moderately difficult reading.

Erikson, E. *Childhood and Society.* New York: W. W. Norton & Co., 1950.

In Erikson we come to a man who has had enormous influence in the last two decades or so on the thinking in child-development fields having to do with the motivation and personality of the young child. Erikson is a psychoanalyst, teacher, writer, and artist. He is, by anyone's definition, a virtuoso; and if for no other reason, you should read this book because of the beautiful writing style of the author. Beyond his gift with words, however, Erikson weaves fascinating theories of the relationships among early child-rearing practices and the growth of personality and character in the young child. He was heavily influenced by Freud, but went considerably beyond Freud's early orientation to include many other factors, giving due respect to the complexity of the human personality. A rich book, a classic, and well worth reading.

THE MOTHER-CHILD RELATIONSHIP

Few topics have been of more lasting interest than that of the growth of the relationship between the mother and her young child. It has been of particular interest to people in the areas of child psychology and psychiatry, but just about any subject area within child-development research must recognize the central fact of the mother-child relationship.

Ainsworth, Mary D. Salter, "Object relations, dependency, and attachment. A theoretical review of the infant-mother relationship." *Child Development*, Vol. 40 (September 1969).

Ainsworth, Mary D. Salter, and Silvia M. Bell. "Attachment, exploration, and separation: illustrated by the behavior of one-year-olds in a strange situation." *Child Development*, Vol. 41, No. 1 (March 1970).

Ainsworth, Mary D. Salter, et al. "Individual differences in the development of some attachment behaviors." *Merrill-Palmer Quarterly of Behavior and Development*, Vol. 18, No. 2 (1972).

Ainsworth, along with several other researchers in child development, has invested heavily in the study of the process known as the attachment of infant to mother and vice versa. This study is concentrated on the first two years of the infant's life, and is especially interesting in the light of the study of similar processes in other animal species (see below). The reports are technical in nature, but Ainsworth writes well and you will find this reading worthwhile.

Many others have studied and written on this topic. They are too numerous to list. Ainsworth's work is among the very best.

ISSUES IN EARLY EDUCATION

The effects of nursery school experience are part of the larger story of early education. This topic is an extremely broad one, but the following readings are of particular value.

Montessori, Maria. *The Absorbent Mind*. New York: Holt, Rinehart, and Winston, 1967.

While Maria Montessori did not provide the last word to all topics in early education, she did have an interesting and an original view of the growth and development of the young child. This well-written book is well worth your time.

Swift, Joan W. "Effects of early group experience: The nursery school and day nursery." *Child Development Research*, M. L. Hoffman and L. W. Hoffman. New York: Russell Sage Foundation, 1964.

There is a huge amount of controversy over the pros and cons of nursery school experience for the two-and-one-half- to five-year-old child. As far as I can see, there is no terribly important educational reason to send an average or above-average child to any nursery school. But many will argue that point. For some solid, unbiased information on the topic, read the review chapter by Swift. It is the only one I know of that has attempted to track down the research on the various effects of nursery school experience on the young child.

Ulich, R. *Three Thousand Years of Educational Wisdom*. Cambridge, Mass.: Harvard University Press, 1961.

Robert Ulich has been one of the few great thinkers in the modern history of Western education. This beautiful book, containing original writings on the subject of education, does not often talk specifically to topics in early education, but at times it does. Pay particular attention to the writings of Plato, Pestalozzi, Froebel, Comenius, and others who do refer to what is going on in the development of a young child. This is a very rich book. It should be in the library of everyone who reads and thinks at all about the human condition.

OTHER ANIMALS AS THEY DEVELOP

I have always believed firmly that the study of other animal creatures helps us understand our own condition.

Lorenz, K. *King Solomon's Ring*. New York: Thomas Y. Crowell, 1952.

This is an absolutely delightful book by a leading ethologist who will introduce you to the fascinating study of growth and development in the young of other animal species. If, as a result of reading this book, you become interested in pursuing the topic of ethology, Lorenz will point the way to you.

RECOMMENDED FILMS

Joseph Stone of Vassar College has produced more first-rate film material on the young child than any other single person on the United States scene. His films are available through any of the major film-lending services, several of which are listed below. In particular you should, if you can, get a chance to look at his new films on the Israeli kibbutz. Also highly recommended to help you understand the growth of the mind from Piaget's point of view are six films by J. McVicker Hunt and Ina Uzgiris.

JOSEPH STONE—VASSAR COLLEGE—FILMS

1. *Rearing Kibbutz Babies*
2. *Infant Development on Kibbutz*
3. *Day Care for Kibbutz Toddler*

   The above-listed films may be obtained from:

   Campus Film Distributors Corporation
   20 East 46th Street
   New York, New York 10017

J. MCVICKER HUNT AND INA UZGIRIS—FILMS
ORDINAL SCALES OF INFANT DEVELOPMENT

1. *Object Permanence*
2. *Development of Means*
3. *Imitation: Gestral and Vocal*
4. *Operational Causality*
5. *Object Relations in Space*
6. *Development of Schemas*

   The above-listed films may be obtained from:
      Visual Aids Service
      Division of University Extension
      University of Illinois
      Champaign, Illinois 61820

   Other major distributors of films on early childhood are:

      EDC Film Library
      Educational Development Center
      55 Chapel Street
      Newton, Massachusetts 02160

      McGraw-Hill Films/Contemporary Films
      1221 Avenue of the Americas
      New York, New York 10020

      Indiana University Audio-Visual Center
      Bloomington, Indiana 47401

      Davidson Films (especially Piaget films)
      3701 Buchanan Street
      San Francisco, California 94123

INDEX

277